AT LENINGRAD'S GATES

AT LENINGRAD'S GATES

The Story
of a Soldier with
Army Group North

By WILLIAM LUBBECK
with DAVID HURT

Pen & Sword
MILITARY

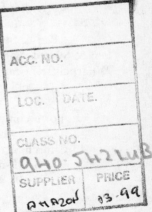

First published in Great Britain in 2007 by
Pen & Sword Military
An imprint of
Pen & Sword Books Ltd
47 Church Street
Barnsley
South Yorkshire
S70 2AS

ISBN 978 1 84415 617 7

A CIP catalogue record for this book is
available from the British Library

Pen & Sword Books Ltd incorporates the Imprints of
Pen & Sword Aviation, Pen & Sword Maritime, Pen & Sword Military,
Wharncliffe Local History, Pen & Sword Select, Pen & Sword Military
Classics and Leo Cooper.

For a complete list of Pen & Sword titles please contact
PEN & SWORD BOOKS LIMITED
47 Church Street, Barnsley, South Yorkshire, S70 2AS, England
E-mail: enquiries@pen-and-sword.co.uk
Website: www.pen-and-sword.co.uk

CONTENTS

MAPS

PREFACE

IN TELLING MY STORY, I do not wish to impress anyone or present myself as a hero. Like millions of other troops on the frontline of the Second World War, I was just a soldier who obeyed orders and carried out my duties. The heroes were those comrades who never returned home and were often left unburied in far-off fields.

God had other plans for me and spared my life. This testament of my experience is a memorial to the service and sacrifice of those soldiers who did not come back.

This book is also dedicated to Anneliese, who served as a Red Cross nurse in German field hospitals attending wounded troops during the final two years of the war. On a more personal level, words cannot express my eternal gratitude for the hope that her love gave me during my long years in combat and for the many happy decades of marriage that we enjoyed after the war.

During a trip to Germany in the summer of 2003, my daughter discovered my wartime correspondence with Anneliese. Reading through these letters brought forth bittersweet emotions, but helped to give me a kind of closure. I also feel a sense of relief in being able to share my experiences of the war with my family and a broader audience.

It is my hope that this account will help to increase public understanding of the Second World War, especially of the brutal nature of the fighting on the Eastern Front. In particular, Americans often misunderstand the motivations of German troops who fought in World War II. Most of the common soldiers were not supporters of Hitler and the Nazi regime, but simply patriotic Germans who sought to serve their country.

I am deeply indebted to the people of the United States for accepting my family and me as their fellow citizens and for allowing us to realize the American dream. It is my hope that this story may help the citizens of my adopted country to gain a more complete appreciation of the diverse experience of American immigrants.

WILLIAM LUBBECK
July 2006

INTRODUCTION

READING THE FIRSTHAND account of a soldier who marched into Russia with Napoleon's army in 1812 personalized that distant conflict for me in a way that a general history could not. By the end of that memoir, Jakob Walter's *The Diary of a Napoleonic Foot Soldier*, I had become convinced that a more recent veteran of warfare in Russia, William Lubbeck, should narrate an account of his own remarkable experiences as a German soldier during the Second World War.

While from today's vantage point we often perceive the past as following an inevitable course to the present, Lubbeck lived through the unfolding history of that struggle, uncertain of his own fate or of the larger outcome. His modesty made it difficult to persuade him to share his exceptional story, but he ultimately concluded that the testimony of a surviving German soldier would serve to honor the memory of his fallen comrades. In addition, a memoir could help a modern audience to develop a wider perspective on an increasingly remote war.

The writing process involved countless hours of recorded interviews as well as even longer periods transcribing the tapes. Memories do not occur in chronological order, so as the story gradually revealed itself it was necessary to flesh out ever-more details and fill in the gaps. In this task, Lubbeck's recently discovered wartime correspondence with his late wife Anneliese proved invaluable in helping him to recall events as well as recapture his personal feelings at different stages of the war. A divisional history written by Kurt von Zydowitz, *Die Geschichte de 58.Infanterie Division 1939–1945* (Podzan, 1952), was also invaluable in reminding Lubbeck of the larger chronology.

After many years living in the United States, Lubbeck generally related measurements in non-metric terms. For consistency we have kept the American usage of yards, miles, Fahrenheit, et al., throughout, at times calculating them from metric. He also often utilized American syntax in other observations, employing terms like "gung-ho" and "boot camp." With military ranks he made distinctions in German which are included here in parentheses.

Although Lubbeck has naturally acquired a greater overview on the war today than he had while serving in it, we made a conscious decision to confine this work to his personal experiences at the time rather than overviews, criticisms, or "what ifs." His actions, observations, and emotions during those tumultuous years were our sole focus.

While he had never spoken in depth about the war since his arrival in North America—in fact, he was reluctant to do so—the wealth of information that poured out as our interviews progressed impressed me greatly. The decades faded away as he recalled his prior life as a citizen and soldier for Germany, leaving the vigorous younger man in the photographs only barely concealed behind the erudite, retired U.S. engineer.

In the period before and during the Second World War, the German people's perception of events contrasted sharply with the American outlook. Allowing ourselves to see these events from a different point of view does not undermine the ultimate morality of the cause for which the United States and the Western Allies fought, but rather helps us better comprehend why educated, civilized Germans were prepared to fight and die under such a regime.

William Lubbeck's account of these years explains how the Nazi regime's early success in reviving Germany's power and prestige helped it win a broader measure of public support. Yet, he also argues that many Germans nonetheless mistrusted the Nazis and recognized a darker side to Hitler's dictatorship. This contradiction raises the critical question of why many Germans were prepared to wage war, even if they often held deep and growing doubts about their government.

Nazi propaganda played an important role in shaping German public opinion, manipulating deeply held popular convictions about the world. In the end, most Germans accepted that war was necessary to overturn the perceived injustices inflicted on their nation by the Treaty of Versailles and to eliminate the threat to European civilization posed by Stalinist Communism.

While Lubbeck approved of the rebuilding of Germany's economic and military power and believed in the justice of his country's cause, he opposed the Nazi regime's repressive character and radical extremism. Yet, despite his mistrust of Hitler and lack of faith in the Nazi ideology, he was nonetheless willing to persevere through six years of war. As with most German soldiers, his fight was inspired by a patriotic love for his country, a deep sense of commitment to duty, and a basic desire to bring himself and his comrades through the war.

Born in 1920, Wilhelm Lübbecke (as he was named at birth) grew up on his family's farm in the village of Püggen. During the 1930s, he witnessed the rise of the Nazis and their consolidation of power in Germany with mixed feelings. Like most other Germans, however, he was primarily focused on pursuing a career and enjoying life, rather than on politics.

Leaving Püggen for the city of Lüneburg in early 1938, Lubbeck began work as an apprentice electrician, which was a requirement of students planning to enter a collegiate electrical engineering program. Meeting Anneliese Berndt a year later, he began a relationship that would give him hope during the dark years of war that followed.

Drafted into the army at the outbreak of war in 1939, Lubbeck entered a heavy weapons company in the 58th Infantry Division. After first seeing battle during the German Blitzkrieg through France, he was posted to occupation duty in Belgium. In the spring of 1941, his division was transferred to Army Group North to prepare for the invasion of Russia.

Followng the commencement of Operation Barbarosa that summer, Lubbeck was assigned to serve as forward observer for his company's howitzers. After penetrating into the suburbs of Leningrad, his unit was soon pulled back to the outskirts of the city. There it joined other German forces initiating a siege of Leningrad on Hitler's orders at the start of a brutal winter.

As Soviet forces steadily grew in strength and capability over the next two years, Lubbeck fought in a series of increasingly desperate battles at the Volkhov River, along the corridor to the Demyansk pocket, at Novgorod, and near Lake Ladoga.

Soon after receiving the Iron Cross First Class, in late 1943 Lubbeck entered an officer training program in Germany. Following his return to the front in the late spring of 1944, he took command of his old company as it battled through a harrowing year-long retreat back through the Baltic region and into East Prussia.

Upon his release from a POW camp after the war, Lubbeck struggled to survive in Germany's calamitous post-war economic conditions. With little food to eat, he and his new wife were ultimately forced to risk crossing the Iron Curtain in order to reach his family's farm in the Soviet Zone. After six difficult years, they finally made the decision to leave Germany.

Emigrating from their homeland with almost nothing, he and his family spent the next decades building a new life, first in Canada and then the United States. His triumph over adversity and integration into a new society as an American immigrant is an extraordinary tale in itself, and provides him with a unique perspective from which to relate his experiences as a German soldier.

Every effort has been made to recount the events in this memoir accurately in the hope that it can contribute to the historical record. Beyond adding significant new insights into the experiences of German soldiers in the frontlines of the Second World War, William Lubbeck's account reveals how a man's character, deep sense of discipline, and love for a woman and his family shaped the course of his life and allowed him to survive and prosper in the face of great adversity during and after the war.

It is a privilege to share his compelling story with a wider audience.

DAVID HURT
July 2006

AT LENINGRAD'S GATES

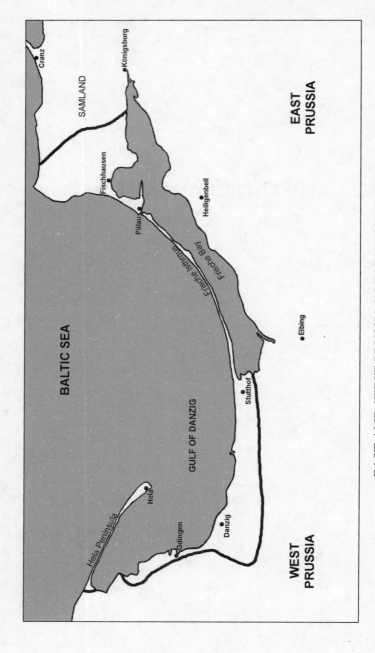

EAST AND WEST PRUSSIA IN EARLY APRIL 1945

Heavy lines indicate the front encircling the remaining German-held territory between the
Samland and the Hela Peninsula.

PROLOGUE

APRIL–MAY 1945

LAST ORDERS: APRIL 16–18, 1945

It was the end.

It was the end for my company.

It was the end for the 58th Infantry Division.

It was perhaps the end for Germany and for me.

In the four years since the invasion of Russia, April 16, 1945 was for me the worst day of the war. In the past hours, the heavy weapons company under my command had simply ceased to exist.

The disaster at the key road junction of Fischhausen was not a battle, but rather the catastrophic climax to the unrelenting Soviet barrage that had pursued our retreat westward during the previous weeks. Finally, trapped in a congested mass with other German units trying to move down the single main road through this East Prussian town, there was no longer any way to move forward.

Concentrating on this chokepoint, the artillery of four Soviet armies combined with several hundred aircraft to let loose a devastating assault. Everyone who failed to escape into one of the side streets was annihilated in a cataclysm of Russian rockets, shells, and bombs. A strafing run by a Soviet fighter plane on the western outskirts of Fischhausen left my face perforated with small bullet fragments and my eyes almost blinded by dirt and blood, but I realized that I had been fortunate simply to survive the onslaught.

Of the roughly 100 remaining troops from my company who had entered Fischhausen, it was clear that most had been killed in the

1

attack. The death of so many of my men was emotionally wrenching, even if the loss of soldiers had become tragically commonplace during the course of the war.

What was most shocking to me was the ongoing collapse of military order that had begun even before we reached Fischhausen. Until this point, even as the military circumstances had grown more calamitous, the *Wehrmacht* (German armed forces) had successfully maintained its discipline and unit cohesion. Now, everything was in utter disarray.

In our catastrophic condition, it seemed impossible that only three and a half years earlier these same Russians had appeared to be on the verge of collapse as we stood at the gates of Leningrad. Yet I had seen the tide of war steadily turn as the Soviets recovered, joined by the Western Allies, to force Germany onto the strategic defensive in the years that followed.

When I returned to the Eastern Front from officer training in May of 1944, the Wehrmacht had already retreated from most of the conquered Soviet territory. Army Group North, one of the three large German Army groups in the East, had pulled back from Leningrad into Estonia. Weeks later, Army Group Center to the south of us was nearly destroyed by a gigantic Soviet attack. In the months that followed, we withdrew ever further west back into the territory of the German Reich.

Since late January of 1945, I had led the steadily thinning ranks of my heavy weapons company in continuous combat against the inexorable torrent of Soviet forces pushing into East Prussia. Overwhelmed by the Red Army's enormous advantage in men and equipment, it was clear that our situation was worsening by the day. Nonetheless, we battled on. What choice did we have? Faced with enemy troops to our front and the Baltic Sea to our rear, there was little hope of ever getting back to central Germany. Like cornered animals, we were simply fighting for our lives.

Promoted from first lieutenant (*Oberleutnant*) to captain (*Hauptmann*) in late March, I struggled to maintain discipline and morale among the troops under my command. The men in my company attempted to retain their usual confident spirit, but there was little secret what the future held for us. In these circumstances, falling to a Russian bullet on the battlefield seemed far better than the hellish conditions that faced a German POW in the Soviet Union.

As an officer, I felt a special dread of capture by the Red Army. If not killed in combat, I expected to be confronted with a choice between surrender and suicide. I planned to save one last bullet for myself, though it was uncertain whether I would be able to summon the courage to use it. Just two months short of my twenty-fifth birthday, I did not wish to die. So far, I had succeeded in escaping death and eluding this terrible dilemma.

With Fischhausen now reduced to smoking rubble and the Red Army only a couple of miles away, I wandered west from town along with other surviving German troops heading along the main road into the pinewoods.

At the limits of physical fatigue and psychological stress, my body moved forward almost robotically. My mind was numb, but I still felt a deep responsibility to my men. My purpose now was to locate any others who might have evaded the slaughter and taken refuge in one of the abandoned homes or many empty ammunition bunkers that filled the forest.

Sand and blood from the earlier attack still clouding my vision, I stumbled along beside the road, barely able to see where I was going or what was around me. Every twenty yards or so, the whistle of another incoming artillery shell forced me to throw myself against the ground. Getting back to my feet, I staggered forward again, constantly trying to blink my eyes clear in order to be able to identify the next position where I might seek cover.

Perhaps a mile from Fischhausen, a group of ten soldiers from my company appeared on the north side of the road, huddled just outside the entrance to one of the immense 60-by-100-foot earth-camouflaged bunkers. Among them was Senior Sergeant (*Hauptfeldwebel*) Jüchter, the head of the *Tross* (rear area); a couple of other sergeants (*Feldwebels*); two lance corporals (*Obergefreiten*); and several privates (*Schützen*).

"Where are the rest?" I asked in a somber voice. One of the men quietly replied, "We were attacked with bombs, rockets, and artillery fire. We lost our horses. We lost our equipment. We lost everything. It is all ruined. We are the only ones left." Anyone else who may have survived the assault had disappeared in the ensuing confusion or had simply fled west.

There was little further conversation. The events of the preceding hours and weeks had left us traumatized and exhausted. With the end in sight, a bleak mood filled the bunker. The men only wanted basic information and direction. They looked to me to provide it, but I knew no more than they did. For the first time in the war, I was on my own with no orders where to go and no idea what to expect.

In urgent need of new orders, I told my men that I would seek to locate the commander of our 154th Infantry Regiment, Lieutenant Colonel (*Oberstleutnant*) Ebeling as soon as my vision cleared. By the time one of the men had finished wiping my eyes and removing bullet splinters from my face an hour later, I could see well enough to commence a search.

Ordering my men to remain at the bunker, I set out into the woods on the narrow neck of land farther west. Shells continued to rain down intermittently, but did little to hamper my reconnoitering of the area. Fifteen minutes later, I came upon a small camouflaged bunker about 25 yards south of the main road. When I stepped inside, I anticipated nothing but another vacant chamber.

To my astonishment, the bunker instead held half a dozen senior German generals, easily identifiable by the red stripes that ran down the side of their pants. Left momentarily speechless, I reflexively came to attention and saluted. Gathered around a table studying maps, they failed to show any surprise at my abrupt appearance and simply returned my salute.

Just as I was about to request new orders, the sudden drone of planes outside ended the awkward moment. As the generals scrambled under the table inside, I ducked back outside the entrance. From the south, a formation of about a dozen American-made B-25 bombers marked with Soviet red stars had already begun to dive toward our area. Still 3,000 feet up, a steady stream of small black objects began tumbling out from beneath the aircraft. There were only seconds to take cover before their bombs commenced plastering the ground where I stood.

Sprinting twenty feet from the bunker, I leapt into a long, six-foot-deep trench. If you seek shelter in a bunker that takes a hit and collapses, you are doomed. If you can take cover in a foxhole or a trench, however, a shell or bomb must land almost directly on your position to cause death or serious injury. You might suffer a concussion if a shell or bomb impacts nearby, but you will live.

Crouching down in the trench, I kept my head just below the surface to avoid the risk of being buried. With my hands cupped loosely over my ears, I opened my mouth. This allowed the air pressure inside my head to match that of the atmosphere. If an explosion occurred nearby, it would prevent my eardrums from blowing out. Combat teaches a soldier many tricks of survival, if you live long enough to learn the lessons.

At the same moment that I gained cover, the Russian bombs began detonating around my position in rapid succession, almost like a salvo of giant rockets. A succession of deafening blasts shook the earth and convulsed the air with indescribable violence. In that instant, I wondered whether my luck had finally run out and it might be the end for me. Strangely, perhaps, I experienced no sense of terror. Shelling, rocketing, and bombing had become such a routine part of my existence in the preceding years that I had almost grown accustomed to them.

As the bombs pulverized my surroundings, there was nothing for me to do but wait it out. My mind became a numb void as an animal instinct to survive took over. Even with my mouth opened to equalize the pressure, an explosion perhaps six feet away generated such concussive force that it nearly blew my eardrum out.

When the minute-long rain of bombs finally ceased, I knew that I was fortunate to have survived once again. With my ears ringing and my mind dazed, I unsteadily climbed out of the trench. Despite minor wounds, lack of sleep, and inadequate food during the preceding weeks of combat, I was still in fair shape physically. My psychological state was more battered, but I had to try to remain clear-headed. As an officer, it was my duty to lead and take care of my men.

Though the generals' bunker was still intact, I decided that they had greater concerns than providing orders to a company commander. Renewing my search for my regimental commander, I headed back in a northerly direction and recrossed the main road.

Perhaps ten minutes later, I unexpectedly found Lt. Col. Ebeling attempting to establish a new defensive line a quarter of a mile away.

Relieved, I could now finally find out what was going on and obtain new orders.

In a short conversation, he informed me that the high command was sending us back to Germany. All the surviving officers from our 58th Infantry Division were to return there to serve as the nucleus for a new division that the army planned to create in Hamburg. Meanwhile, the few remaining enlisted men in our division would be transferred to the still intact 32nd Infantry Division, which would remain behind as a rearguard to slow the Red Army's advance.

After explaining the directive, Ebeling wrote out and signed the order in my small *Soldbuch* (military record book). Since the officers of our division would be traveling on their own to increase the likelihood that some would reach Germany, these written orders would prevent the SS (*Schutzstaffeln*) from punishing me as a deserter if I was stopped. A stroke of the pen had opened the door for me to escape death or capture by the Russians.

Grateful for the chance to escape the mounting chaos, it was nonetheless apparent that accomplishing such a journey would be almost impossible. Already, the Red Army had cut off the overland route back to Germany farther west beyond the Frische Isthmus, a long, narrow strip of sand that ran along the coast of the Baltic Sea. At the same time, ships attempting to reach Germany over the Baltic faced great risk of Soviet attack.

When I reached my remaining soldiers waiting at the bunker, I pulled aside Senior Sgt. Jüchter and explained that I had been directed to return to Germany with one soldier from my company. As my second in command, Jüchter was the natural choice to assist me in building a new unit, but I felt it was important to allow him to make his own decision rather than issue an order. "Will you go with me?" I inquired. With a simple "*Jawohl*" he assented.

While our own prospects for reaching central Germany appeared doubtful, Jüchter and I would at least be given a chance to try. Aware that such information would only compound their sense of hopelessness, I did not divulge my own orders as I informed the other men of their imminent reassignment to the 32nd Division.

With almost all of my company lost, it was anguishing for me to leave these few men behind. In the two days that remained at the ammunition bunker, I sought to oversee the successful transfer of these surviving troops in my company to their new unit. Meanwhile, Jüchter attempted to use his connections with the rear echelon of our regiment to obtain medals that several of them were due.

Two days after the disaster at Fischhausen, I was able to present an Iron Cross First Class and several Iron Crosses Second Class, but it simply proved impossible for me to oversee their reassignment in the prevailing chaos. In the end, I had to leave my men to report to the 32nd Division on their own, like lost sheep in a storm.

Unless they were killed in the final days of the war, they almost certainly became Soviet prisoners of war. If they were strong and lucky, they perhaps endured the ensuing three or four years of captivity in Russia to return home to Germany. Even now, sixty years later, the thought of their suffering and the uncertainty of their fate deeply torments me.

A DESPERATE JOURNEY: April 18–May 8, 1945

Under sporadic fire from Soviet artillery, Jüchter and I left the bunker late in the afternoon of April 18 and set out down the main road toward the city of Pillau, located about six miles away. If we were able to reach the harbor there, we hoped to cross over the short span of water that separated Pillau from the northernmost spit of the Frische Isthmus.

Approaching the city as dusk fell perhaps three hours later, a gruesome scene greeted us. Along the road, a dozen or so bodies of German soldiers hung down from the branches of tall trees. Jüchter and I remained silent, but it was apparent that this was the grisly handiwork of the SS. Whether the men were deserters or simply soldiers who had been separated from their units or in shell shock would have made no difference to them.

Most German troops with whom I had fought perceived the Waffen SS (the military formations of the Schutzstaffeln) to be, in essence, part of the Wehrmacht, but disdained the regular SS, which was seen as a thuggish Nazi political militia. With the Nazi regime facing its end, it was not surprising that the SS would string up any of those they judged to be traitors as a warning to others. Witnessing their crude "justice," I hated them.

As we made our way through Pillau in the lingering twilight, the intensity of the shelling grew heavier as the Russians concentrated their fire on the sector's one remaining major target. Whenever there was a momentary lull, Jüchter and I left our cover and raced to the next ruined building, always remaining alert for the next incoming rounds so as to avoid being caught out in the open.

When we arrived at the inlet on the west side of town a few hours later, there was already a growing throng of hundreds of troops and civilian refugees gathered at the dock. Despite the chaos, one or two ferries continued to carry passengers and a few vehicles across the 200 yards of water that separated Pillau from the start of the Frische Isthmus. There was nothing for us to do but wait our turn under continuing intermittent artillery fire.

It was dark a half hour later when Jüchter and I squeezed onto a ferry with perhaps 100 soldiers, refugees, and a variety of trucks and other military equipment. As soon as the boat docked on the far shore ten minutes later, we joined a couple of dozen other soldiers cramming onto one of the trucks just ferried across the channel.

As shells still occasionally dropped around us, our truck joined the impromptu convoy departing westward down the Frische Isthmus. The column proceeded slowly through the darkness, driving without headlights in order to avoid attracting the attention of any Russian aircraft that might be lurking above

A few hours into the trip, we passed a group of burning buildings. Since there was no artillery fire or bombing in the area, this seemed very odd to me. Turning to the soldier seated next to me on the truck, I asked what had been there. "Oh, they are probably burning the KZ," he responded.

My unfamiliarity with the word led him to explain that a "KZ" was a *Konzentration Lager* (concentration camp) for enemies of the Nazi regime. As incredible as it may seem, it was only at this moment at the end of the war that I became aware of the existence and function of concentration camps.

The revelation left me bewildered, though I still did not connect such camps to a Nazi policy of genocide. My ignorance of the system of concentration camps during the war matched that of most other

Germans. Actual photos of the camps were not seen by any public, German or Allied, until after the war.

In his fascinating memoir *Europa, Europa* (John Wiley & Sons, 1997), Solomon Perel, a boy who kept his Jewish identity secret throughout his years at a Hitler Youth school in Germany, related a similar astonishment when he first learned about the Nazi death camps after hostilities had ended.

The ability of Hitler's regime to keep this massive atrocity a secret from the population demonstrates their effectiveness in controlling information that would have jeopardized their support. Like most Germans, I felt bitterly betrayed when I eventually learned that Nazi leaders had directed the execution of millions of Jews, Gypsies, and other prisoners in these camps. That was not the cause for which I had fought and for which so many of my comrades had sacrificed their lives.

Just before dawn, our ad hoc convoy reached Stutthof, an assembly point for the troops who had made the 35-mile journey from Pillau. We spent the rest of the day under cover before renewing our journey northwestward by sea. Boarding a ferry that night, Jüchter and I crossed the Gulf of Danzig to Hela, a port located on the end of a long peninsula about 20 miles from Stutthof.

Disembarking at Hela, we took refuge in a bloc of three-story brick apartment buildings which had been deserted by their owners. Exhausted after months of combat and our long trek, we fell into a deep slumber.

While we were unaware of it at the time, the disaster at Fischhausen had occurred on the same day that the Red Army had commenced its final assault on Berlin far to the west of us. This offensive made the whole Baltic coast a relative backwater in the larger war, though Hela's geographical isolation probably also served to deter the Russians from trying to occupy it. In any case, they appeared content to keep hammering us with artillery fire from the area around Gdingen, a town and harbor about ten miles away on the Soviet-occupied mainland.

Finally out of combat, I thought almost constantly of my fiancée Anneliese, whom I had met six years earlier, a few months before being drafted into the military. Though several months had passed since we had last corresponded, my love for her remained my lone source of hope in the otherwise dark and uncertain future that lay ahead. In my heart, I felt sure that we would be together for the rest of our lives, if I could somehow evade the Russians and reach Germany.

Throughout the days that followed, we did little more than rest and try to scrounge up something to eat. One afternoon, I caught sight of Lt. Colonel Ebeling and a group of staff officers from the 154th Regiment off in the distance, but did not speak to them. Though we were all seeking to find our way back to Germany under orders, it was clear that the Wehrmacht was in the process of disintegrating. Everyone was now basically on their own.

During this period we received word of two of the worst maritime disasters in history. In back-to-back tragedies in January and February of 1945, the German liners *Wilhelm Gustloff* and *General von Steuben* had been torpedoed and sunk by the Russians while evacuating thousands of civilian refugees and wounded personnel from East Prussia back to central Germany. Despite all we had endured at the front, this news further deepened the overpowering sense of grief and despair among us.

Even if it was possible to find space on one of the few vessels departing Hela, the threat of Soviet naval attack made the prospect of reaching Germany appear more remote than ever. At the same time, most of the officers on the Hela Peninsula were not even making a serious effort to leave, regardless of their orders to return to Germany. A lingering sense of honor and a bond of solidarity among us created a kind of inertia. In spite of the general breakdown in military order, none of us wished to give the appearance of deserting our comrades by departing before they did, even if it served no purpose for us to remain where we were.

About two and a half weeks after our arrival on Hela, Jüchter was outside the apartment building one afternoon when a sudden Russian artillery barrage began hammering the area. Caught in the open, he was hit in the thigh by a piece of shrapnel. Notified by a medic of his injury, I requested that our regimental physician come to examine him.

Observing the doctor as he bandaged Jüchter's wound, I asked whether he should place a tourniquet around the sergeant's leg as a precaution to ensure that he would not lose any more blood. The physician assured me that this measure was not necessary and that his injury was not life-threatening.

Once the bandaging had been completed, the doctor directed me to take Jüchter to a field hospital that had been established in an underground concrete bunker. Together with the medics, I assisted in carrying Jüchter the 75 yards to the facility.

Inside, wounded men were lying like cordwood along the bunker's walls. Locating the doctor on duty, I informed him that I had a badly wounded soldier who needed urgent medical attention. He responded, "Yes, but take a look. We have to go in order of priority. Lay him down there and we will take care of him." Leaning down to Jüchter, I assured him, "I will be back tomorrow to see how you are doing."

On my return to the hospital bunker the following morning, I was told that Jüchter had passed away during the night. Realizing that he probably died from shock and loss of blood, it was difficult not to feel angry and bitter at the regimental doctor's decision not to apply a tourniquet that might have saved his life. Even after experiencing the loss of so many comrades, Jüchter's death seemed an especially needless sacrifice to me.

Now alone and possessing nothing other than my uniform and a couple of pistols, I contemplated my situation. Nothing had changed in my orders, but I finally felt a renewed sense of motivation to find a way off Hela.

Early the following evening, I wandered the 500 yards from the apartment building to the harbor area to find out what was happening. Unexpectedly, I stumbled onto a chance situation that changed the course of my life.

Observing about 400 fully equipped troops standing around near the dock, it was obvious the unit was preparing to depart Hela. In an instant, I made up my mind to tag along with them wherever they were destined. Conversing with the soldiers, I recognized their Silesian accents and learned that their infantry regiment had orders to sail for Germany. Oddly, no one here or elsewhere ever challenged my presence or asked to see my orders during my entire journey from Pillau. Whether this deference was due to my rank and decorations or to the general chaos of the situation, I am not sure.

When the order to depart came just after dark, I simply filed onto the deck of one of the small barges with a couple of hundred of the soldiers. A half hour later, a mile of so outside the harbor, a giant shadow loomed up in front of us. A brand new destroyer of the *Kriegsmarine* (German Navy) was readying to sail for Germany.

After climbing up a net hung down the side of the ship, we were warmly welcomed by the crew and directed where to go. While the enlisted personnel bedded down in the cool night air on the deck, I was escorted to one of the cabins below.

Despite the recent torpedoing of other German ships sailing west, I finally felt a flicker of optimism about my chances of survival as I lay in my bunk. What would happen now?

Early the following morning, a sailor came to my bunk and woke me. In a somber voice, he announced, "*Herr Oberleutnant, der Krieg ist vorbei.*" ("Lieutenant, the war is finished.")

The date was May 9, 1945.

Looking back, my lucky escape from Hela that night probably saved me from making a choice between going into captivity in Russia or taking my own life. Yet at that moment when I learned of the surrender, my mood was neither one of joy nor sadness. Instead, I felt only numb disorientation at the loss of all that I had known, and deep uncertainty about what lay ahead for me and for Germany.

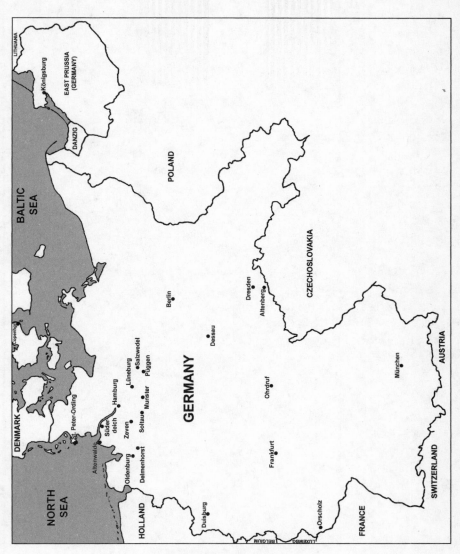

GERMANY IN 1937

CHAPTER I

A VILLAGE UPBRINGING

JUST FIVE YEARS AFTER the Second World War ended for me on that destroyer, the ominous specter of a new war with Russia haunted my thoughts and dreams.

I knew what war meant. Relentless heat and dust in summer. Bone-chilling cold in winter. Bottomless mud in fall and spring. Insatiable mosquitoes and incessant lice. Sleep deprivation and physical exhaustion. Bullets whistling through the air. Shells and bombs shaking the earth. Stench from rotting corpses. Constant fear of capture or death. The agony of losing comrades. Numbing brutality. Painful separation from my loved ones.

As the tensions between the Soviet Union and the West increased during the late 1940s, war again darkened the horizon. Having barely survived my years of combat in Russia, a return to soldiering and the battlefield weighed heavily on my mind. As a still young veteran who had served as a junior officer in the Wehrmacht, it was almost certain that West Germany's *Bundeswehr* would call me back to duty if another war broke out, but I wanted no part of it.

Confronted with the prospect of a new military conflict in Europe and the still grim economic conditions in post-war Germany, my wife and I debated whether to leave behind our families and Fatherland to seek a better and more secure future abroad. The decision to emigrate from Germany was one of the most difficult and momentous choices of my life. In retrospect, it was the turning point when I put Germany and war behind me to begin a new life, first in Canada and ultimately in the United States.

Yet, as I grow older, the past increasingly draws me back. They say that the older you get, the more you remember what happened long ago. Perhaps that is true. Even after more than a half-century, memories of my childhood in Germany, the years of soldiering in the Second World War, the struggle to survive in post-war Germany, and my first years as an immigrant remain vividly and indelibly etched on my mind.

My generation was brought up differently than are young Germans today. The family was at the center of German society and worked together with the schools, churches, and the government to reinforce the social order and conservative values. In Germany, families and schools taught my generation a respect for our fellow men and for authority that is absent today.

This respect for others was perhaps best manifested in the basic courtesy that we were taught. If a man was riding a full bus or train and a woman or an elderly person boarded, he gave up his seat. If a man came into a house, a church, or a school wearing a hat or cap, he removed it. When a gentleman met a lady, he lifted his hat from his head and made a slight bow to her. He always escorted a lady on his right arm and opened the door to allow her to enter first. Such practices may appear quaint today, but they were the reflection of deeper values of society in Germany at that time.

The society at large accepted and respected authority because we grew up with it, particularly in the more conservative rural areas away from the big cities. There were strict rules for social behavior and official permits for everything from marriage to a change of residence. Public protests were uncommon and were generally small affairs in comparison to the frequency and scale of those today.

When demonstrations did occur in the 1930s, they were limited to the large cities and organized by a political party like the Nazis or the Communists. Most German citizens would never have considered going into the streets to march and chant for any cause. The amount of protesting and demonstrating in modern Germany would be unimaginable to my generation.

Long before the Nazis came to power, Germany's military had internalized a culture of respect for order and authority that was rooted in every social institution: the family, the schools, churches, the law, and everything else. When training for the army, our instructors drilled discipline and obedience into us. We obeyed the commands of our officers without question, regardless of the casualties we might suffer.

The German people at home, in turn, had long given their respect and patriotic support to the military, much like the esteem that Americans today feel for the U.S. armed services. During the war, the speeches and rallies, propaganda posters and films, collection drives for precious metals to make weapons and munitions, the hardships, and even the Allied bombing reinforced the sense of unity between the German population at home and the German troops fighting abroad. This was the social fabric that made Germany so strong during the Second World War.

FAMILY HERITAGE

I grew up in a farm family.

Although my maternal grandfather, Gottlieb Matthies, originally trained as a schoolmaster and taught in a one-room schoolhouse, his life changed when he met my grandmother, Luise Schulz. Luise's parents owned a farm of about 200 to 250 acres that had belonged to her family since the 1700s. When my grandfather and grandmother married in 1889, he stopped teaching to run the farm because Luise's father was ready to retire and there was no male heir in her family to inherit the property.

My mother, Margarete Matthies, was born to them in 1896. She, with her older brother and younger sister, grew up on this farm in the small village of Püggen, typical of the small towns and villages that dot Europe's landscape. Located among the rolling hills of the Altmark agricultural region, midway between Hanover and Berlin in north central Germany, the village's roughly 200 residents lived between a pinewood forest to the north and meadows to the south.

As in other German farm villages, the homes and other buildings in Püggen were clustered in a central location surrounded by the farmland. The closest train stop, stores, and policeman were located in larger neighboring villages, the nearest being a couple of miles away.

Born in 1892, my father grew up as the second son of the

Lübbecke family with one older brother and seven sisters. They lived on a large farm of about a thousand acres dating from the 1700s. It was located in the village of Hagen, which is now part of the city of Lüneburg. Because the law of primogeniture at that time dictated that the oldest son received all the family's property when the father passed away, my father eventually left Hagen to train as a manager on several different large farms in northern Germany.

During the Great War of 1914 to 1918, later called the First World War, my father was drafted into a cavalry unit, as was customary for members of the landed gentry. He joined the 2. Hannoversches Dragoner Regiment Nr. 16, based in Lüneburg. Meanwhile, as part of the national effort to support the army at the front, my mother helped ready Christmas packages to send to troops. Upon receipt of a parcel prepared by my mother, my father wrote a letter back, initiating a correspondence that would eventually lead to their marriage.

In late 1917, my father suffered a foot wound that led to his discharge from the military. Though the injury forced him to wear a special shoe for the rest of his life, he soon recovered enough to return to work, taking up a position managing a large farm of a couple of thousand acres in Dromfeld, located near Göttingen in central Germany. My father also recommended that his employer hire my mother to run the household, which of course gave him an opportunity to get to know her better as well.

While my parents' situation was somewhat unique, it was then a common practice for young German females who grew up on smaller farms to leave home to work at a larger farm for a couple of years. Beyond improving the skills necessary to run a household of their own, it also gave young women a chance to meet eligible males outside of their community.

Arriving to work at the farm in Dromfeld, my mother met my father for the first time in person. While their relationship was a natural partnership, they also fell in love. Within about six months, they became engaged.

Following their marriage in October 1919, they came to live on the Schulz/Matthies farm in Püggen. Because my mother's elder brother had died from an illness while serving as a soldier in Russia during the Great War, she was in line to inherit the farm as the oldest living heir. With my father's experience as a professional farm manager, my grandfather immediately allowed him to begin running the farm.

Because my father was raised on a sizeable farm and then managed even larger ones, he found it somewhat difficult to adjust to running the much smaller farm in Püggen. Although it was common for small farm owners in Germany to perform the hands-on labor alongside the hired help, he was not accustomed to doing this type of manual work, despite being a physically large man.

Adapting to this new role was a challenge for him, but he was a good organizer and had the freedom to run the farm as he saw fit without interference. Usually, he and my grandfather agreed on decisions relating to the farm and maintained a good relationship. In his dealings with the neighbors, my father sought to help out whenever he could, though he could be a difficult man to get along with and preferred to operate independently whenever possible.

Because my birth on June 17, 1920 came just eight and a half months after my parents married, my father's family kidded him lightheartedly about my early arrival. As their first child, I received the same name as my father, Wilhelm Lübbecke. Following my birth, my parents had a son, Joachim, and a daughter, Elisabeth, but they both died at a young age from illness.

My twin brothers Otto and Hans were born five years after me, followed by my brother Hermann in 1928. My sister Marlene was born in 1930, almost exactly ten years after me. With the birth of my sister Christa in 1934, my parents did not plan to have any further children.

It was therefore a surprise when my mother became pregnant with my youngest sister, Margarete, in 1937. I felt embarrassed and angry. I was seventeen years old and already dating. Even after my parents made me her godfather, it was hard for me to accept that my mother could still be having children.

In our family, my six siblings and I were closer to our mother, who was very loving and affectionate with all of us. Unlike my father, she possessed a deep faith in God and set aside a daily devotional time for Bible-reading and prayer. Her outgoing personality made her the friend of everyone in the village where we grew up. In every task she pursued, my mother was determined and diligent to ensure that it was properly done. For every task she accomplished, she was humble and uncomplaining about her labors. While she was a nurturing parent and played the largest role in shaping our values, both of our parents taught us to stand on our own feet and take care of ourselves.

WORKING THE FARM

Fond memories of my family's life in Püggen fill my mind, but life on a farm was not easy. Chores frequently occupied my time after school. During busy periods on the farm, my days off school often revolved around work, broken by a series of meals from six in the morning until eight in the evening.

Lacking trucks, tractors, or indeed any form of automotive vehicle, we did everything with manpower and our eight horses. During normal operations, we had two or three hired employees to assist us in the fields and in taking care of our livestock. In the fall, my father would hire more help or obtain assistance from our neighbors in order to provide the five to ten additional workers needed to harvest our crops of wheat, barley, rye, potatoes, and sugar beets.

While we had to dig the sugar beets out of the ground by hand and swing scythes to harvest the barley, rye, and wheat around the edges of our fields, we employed the forerunner of the combine to harvest most of the crop. Pulled along by horses, the combine cut the grain and spit out bundles. Following along behind it, we stacked about 15 or 20 bundles into upright piles about every 20 feet or so.

Feeding the fifteen or so hungry people gathered around our dining room table at mealtimes during the harvest also meant a lot of work inside the kitchen. Everything we cooked came straight from our fields or gardens. About twice a month the house was filled with the smell of bread baking in our clay-brick oven. After heating the large wood-fired oven for about half a day, my mother would shove in a dozen big lumps of dough, usually made from rye. Despite weighing about six to eight pounds each, these loaves never lasted very long with so many hungry workers around the farm.

Although most of our livestock were raised to be sold, some were retained for our own use. To this end, my family butchered a portion of our cattle once a year and several of our 100 to 200 pigs three or four times a year. Due to the lack of refrigeration, we had to preserve the majority of the meat by making it into sausage and bacon or by curing it.

In the meadows surrounding our village, we grazed our 15 to 20 cows. Some of our cow pastures had fences, but in other unfenced fields the cattle required monitoring to prevent them from wandering onto a neighbor's property. When I reached the age of ten, my father began tasking me with the boring but simple job of keeping an eye on them. Though I took no pleasure in watching the cows, it was better than the monthly cleaning of the manure from their barns.

On one occasion, just after harvesting one of these unfenced pastures, we let the cows out to graze and I took up my post at the edge of the field. Lying back on a cushion of two-foot-high grass under a cool breeze, it was easy for me to pass the time staring up at the drifting clouds. This would last until five o'clock, when a three-engine Junkers passenger aircraft appeared up in the sky on its regularly scheduled flight, signaling the end of my day.

On this particular afternoon, my daydreaming in the grass turned into napping. As I snoozed, the unattended cows crossed into our neighbor's pasture, a serious offense in a farming community. When my father learned of my negligence, he scolded me severely, "How could you let that happen? Now I must go talk to the neighbor." Being a ten-year-old was no excuse.

In addition to our gardens, fields, and meadows, my family also possessed a couple of large apple orchards. Following school or during school vacations, I would climb up in the trees to pick apples. Munching the fruit and singing songs as I worked, life seemed pretty good to me. Only later did I realize the constant stress my parents endured in trying to operate our farm as a successful business.

CHURCH AND SCHOOL

While many Germans were Catholic, our family lived in a Lutheran region of the country. In my youth, religion was, however, more of an obligation than a source of spiritual fulfillment for me. Although my faith and involvement in church were not nearly as significant in my youth as they became later, they still played a more important role in my life than they did in the lives of most Germans.

My father's family was not very religious, but my mother and her parents were involved in the Lutheran Church and possessed a strong Christian faith that shaped our spiritual upbringing. Although infrequently reading or studying the Bible when we were growing up, my siblings and I did receive a religious education at home and in our confirmation classes at church. We learned to follow the Bible's teachings to tell the truth, and to work hard. We were taught to always consider the needs of those around us and remember that we have an obligation to them.

Because the local Lutheran pastor served several other villages at the same time, he only held services in Püggen every second Sunday. On these Sunday mornings, my family dressed in our best clothes and walked over to the small fieldstone church in Püggen. Seated in our family's pew, we joined thirty or forty other people from six or seven local families in the community for an hour-long worship service. On special Sundays we would sometimes attend church in the nearby village of Rohrberg.

After the church service, our family would sit down at the dinner table for a formal family lunch, our largest meal of the week. We would refrain from eating until my mother sat down and recited the prayer, "Thank the Lord for He is good and His mercy endures forever." Similarly, we waited to leave the table until she gave another prayer or otherwise dismissed us.

Over food, we would talk about the farm gossip in Püggen or politics, but there was not much banter unless it was of a very socially acceptable type. When the meal ended, my father would sometimes hitch up a couple of horses to our family's open-air buggy. Our family would then pile into it for a drive around the fields or the nearby pine forest. Sundays were relaxing and enjoyable for me, but I never looked forward to the next five days of the week once I started my schooling.

At age six, I began my education in Püggen's one-room schoolhouse, located on the first floor of a two-story building right across from our farm in the center of the village. Our teacher, *Herr* (Mr.) Künne, lived in the rooms next to and above the classroom with his family and taught perhaps 30 to 40 local children.

When Herr Künne entered the classroom, we would all immediately stand at attention behind our desks until he said, "Good morning boys and girls. Please sit down." Because the pupils in the large classroom ranged from first to eighth graders, he would then have to give separate lessons to each grade, though everyone would, of course, hear it all.

In running his class, Herr Künne maintained strict discipline and none of us ever dared to challenge him in any way. While he was always demanding, his dictations proved especially difficult. Depending on the number of errors a student made in copying his dictation, he or she might receive a spanking with a switch in front of the entire class or have to remain after school to complete additional assignments.

Although maintaining only average grades in all subjects, I was generally able to avoid Herr Künne's punishments. When school let out, I would return to our house to do my homework. Afterward, my time was spent on farm chores or playing with some of the other children in the village.

Early on, I became friends with several of the boys my age in Püggen: Otto Werneke, Fritz Dampke, and Otto Tepelman. Among my peers, I tended to be a more reserved and private person, like my father. For me, friendship was less about camaraderie and more about exercising leadership and cooperating with others to accomplish some purpose.

Upon finishing fourth grade in 1930, I left the village school in Püggen and spent the next eight years attending a larger and better school in the town of Beetzendorf, located about six miles from our village. Like many upper level schools at the time, this school required the payment of a small tuition, which helped support a dedicated and professional staff.

Around 7:30 every morning, I would set out on my bicycle on the thirty-minute trip to school, even if it was raining or snowing. This journey was often miserable in the cold and snow of winter, since I was dressed in the short pants that most of us wore year-round. A pair of knee-high stockings provided my calves with a little warmth, but my knees were often red and numb by the time I reached the school.

While we remained together with the same group of male and female students throughout the day, our teachers would circulate among the school's classrooms to provide us with an hour or so of instruction in history, German literature, science, mathematics, English, and French.

The school offered more engaging give-and-take discussions between the instructors and students, but my academic struggles persisted. A couple of times, my parents had to read me the riot act when I received a note from the school informing them that I was not doing well in my classes. Such letters bothered me deeply because of my parents' disappointment, but my performance never greatly improved.

It was rare for children from Püggen to attend the school in Beetzendorf. Children were only required to attend school through the eighth grade and most either apprenticed to learn a trade or began working full-time on a farm or in some other employment after that. As part of an extended family that included teachers, doctors, and lawyers, my parents perhaps placed a higher value on education than most other families in our farming community. This commitment was also demonstrated by my father's willingness to pay my tuition in the midst of the Depression.

When outside the school buildings during recreation periods or after class, the boys would wear caps with colored bands identifying their class year. While discipline was strictly enforced inside the school building, there were occasional full-scale brawls right behind it. Typically, these slugfests resulted from disputes among boys of different class years or different towns around Beetzendorf. In one instance when another student began calling me names, I engaged in one of these fistfights, but I generally tried to avoid such crude behavior.

On most days, I rode my bike straight home, where I would work on my homework assignments and help out around the farm. Despite the many hours spent completing my farm chores and schoolwork, I generally enjoyed a carefree youth and often found time to pursue other interests and activities.

GROWING UP

Probably more curious and adventurous than most other kids, I always wanted to explore my surroundings and learn what was going on around me. At the same time, my father and mother were especially strict parents and disciplined me sternly if I misbehaved. While they accepted my independent spirit, they also taught me responsibility and respect for authority.

One summer afternoon when I was about ten years old, I was playing soccer with some other local kids in a sports field just behind our farm. Feeling the urgent call of nature, I opted not to take the time to run back to our family's outhouse and instead headed into a near-by field of rye about five feet tall.

Unfortunately, a neighbor saw me and informed my father that his son had trampled another farmer's field, an almost sacrilegious act. When I returned home that evening, my father gave me a forceful lecture on respecting a neighbor's crops. Though I tried to explain the urgency of the moment, my father dismissed my pleas and reinforced his point with a severe spanking with a wooden switch.

About this same time, I joined a group of other boys from Püggen who wanted to play a prank on an elderly man in his seventies who regularly walked down the sandy road that ran between our farm and the pastures to the south. There was some debate over what we should do, but everyone eventually agreed on my scheme of outfitting myself as a ghost in order to scare him.

While the boys remained behind in the woods to watch, I went out to the road covered by a white bedsheet as our victim approached. Though hardly able to see anything in the darkness through the sheet, I knew he was coming closer to me so I began making what I thought were creepy noises.

Much to my surprise, my supernatural appearance did not produce the desired alarm. Instead of cowering in fear, the old man began whacking me repeatedly over the head with his cane. With my plan gone awry, I attempted to make a run for it, but could only manage to stumble away blindly. Alas, the identity of the culprits behind this fiasco was obvious in a small village like Püggen. On reaching home that night, my father made me pay a visit to the gentleman and apologize.

Being athletic, I enjoyed playing a number of different sports when growing up, especially soccer. In the winters we played ice hockey on a frozen pond located about a half-mile from the school in Beetzendorf as part of the school's physical education class. Often lacking enough players to have a game, one of the teachers would occasionally join us. To express our gratitude, we took every opportunity to knock him onto the ice. Those games provided a rare opportunity to ignore the normal social rules that demanded respect for those in authority.

Equestrian sports were not a hobby of mine, but I often rode on horseback and developed into a competent rider. Most nights, I would take the horses down to our pasture on the south side of our property, and then in the mornings lead them up to the farm where we would put them to work. Additionally, my father gave me the responsibility of taking our mares to visit a nearby stud farm about four or five times a year.

When I was about 15 years old, I began participating in our region's annual equestrian competition. Riding our horses bareback, we would maneuver a long spear in an attempt to snag a six-inch diameter ring hung about 15 feet above the ground. I never won the contest, but the riding skills I developed later proved very beneficial in the army.

Having an independent nature, I was content to do things by myself and spent many hours reading history, especially about the recent battles of the Great War. While fascinated by the stories of the fighting at places like Verdun and the Dardanelles, as well as by U-Boat operations and naval battles, I never expected to see a war myself.

Intrigued by all sorts of technical devices, I spent much of my teenage years experimenting with lights, electrical motors, and radios. I was absorbed for endless hours determining how various mechanisms operated and conducting my own hands-on experimentation in our family's barn.

When my family needed a light to help illuminate the central area among the barns so that we could unload our wagons at night, I volunteered for the project. Stringing a wire from the house, I installed a light on the barn and placed the switch next to my father's bed. In addition to allowing us to work outside after dark, it permitted my father to light up the area with a flip a switch if he heard any suspicious noises at night. As he himself was not technically inclined, he greatly appreciated my accomplishment.

At this time, my family had to grind our harvested rapeseed by hand in order to obtain canola oil for cooking, and I became determined to figure out something better. Finding an electric motor, I attached it to the wheel of the press. It worked like a charm. My mother was particularly grateful to have such a labor-saving device and used it for years.

Despite my successes, some of my projects did not turn out so well. Quite a few times, I was knocked off my feet when I touched the wrong wire. Gradually, through trial and error, I learned what and what not to do.

My fondest memories of our family life come from the Christmas Eves that we shared together. Wearing a big fur coat, my father would load up the whole family in our large, black horse-drawn Landauer (coach) and drive us to Rohrberg for the special evening church service and the singing of hymns.

Once we returned home, my father and mother would lock the doors to the living room. While my siblings and I impatiently waited outside in the hallway and pounded on the door, they decorated a freshly cut spruce tree with wax candles and set out our unwrapped gifts around it, as was the German custom. Finishing their preparations, they allowed us to enter the room in single file from youngest to oldest. After the excitement of Christmas Eve, we celebrated Christmas Day the following afternoon with a big dinner of goose, potatoes, and other special dishes.

Just before the Easter holiday, the residents of small rural communities in Germany would often construct large 20- or 30-foot-high bonfires from logs and other flammable materials on a hill near their village. On the Saturday night before Easter, the bonfires are lit. Growing up in Püggen, we would watch as the horizon was illuminated with the bright glow from 10 or 15 fires burning in the neighboring villages. It was an unforgettable spectacle.

The following morning, my siblings and I awoke to Easter baskets stuffed with treats and boiled eggs before attending a special worship service at our church. Later that day, my parents held an Easter egg hunt in the garden for us. Afterward, my father would come out to the yard with a boiled egg hidden under his jacket.

Squatting down, he would loosen his jacket and let the egg drop down to the ground under him. My young sisters would squeal with delight at the presence of a real Easter Bunny. Though my father was generally a serious man, he also possessed a sense of humor and enjoyed teasing us in a good-natured way, especially my sisters.

Weddings were always major celebrations in Püggen. Everyone in town would ride flower-festooned horses or drive decorated carriages in a large procession over to the farm of the bride's family to pick her up for the trip to our small church. Following the marriage ceremony, it was customary for the bride and groom to jointly saw a log into halves, which would serve as the legs for a baby cradle. According to the tradition, this assured the couple a family with many children.

While such happy occasions with our families and community did not cease to take place, life became much more difficult, however, during the Great Depression.

CHAPTER 2

UNDER THE NAZI DICTATORSHIP

1928–1936

THE GREAT DEPRESSION: 1928–1932

In 1929, a financial disaster struck the world's economy that sent international investment and trade spiraling downward. In Germany, where business had already fallen into a recession in 1928, the international collapse accelerated a precipitous economic decline, which led to steadily rising levels of unemployment.

During the years of the Great Depression, my family fared better than many other Germans, but the early 1930s were still difficult years for us. Being a child, I never appreciated the severity of the problem and life seemed to go on pretty much normally for me. I still had enough to eat, slept with a roof over my head, and attended school. The economic hardship was more pronounced in the cities than in farming communities, though my parents experienced daily stress as they struggled to pay our bills and keep the farm on a sound financial footing.

When my family could not pay our creditors on time, officers from the local court would come to our home. These visits were a humiliating experience, particularly for my father. My siblings and I were not allowed in the room as the officers affixed *Kuckucks* (government repossession stickers) on two or three pieces of our best furniture like wardrobes and desks.

Eventually, my father would manage to sell enough livestock or agricultural produce to permit us to pay off our 300 to 1,000 Marks of debt and eliminate the *Kuckuck*. However, any improvement was temporary. My father's fine oak desk received a *Kuckuck* two or three times as we went in and out of debt.

Even in these difficult circumstances, the six farms in Püggen managed to continue operating and providing work for the local laborers. While many farmers around Germany had to sell off part or all of their land because they could not pay their bills or meet their mortgages, my family fortunately avoided having to resort to such desperate measures.

Still, my father sometimes had to stretch out payment for fertilizers, new farm equipment, and repairs to worn out farm machinery, and had to compensate our hired labor with production from our farm rather than cash. Our farm provided us with adequate food, but there was little spare money, even for basic items like new clothes or the replacement of the soles on our shoes.

Aunt Hedwig, a distant relative who lived with us, would stitch labels from various apparel manufacturers into the clothes she sewed for my siblings and me. It was a very thoughtful effort to fool us into thinking that the clothes were purchased from a store, even if we saw through the deception. We probably would have liked to have more and newer outfits than the refurbished ones we ordinarily wore, but realized that our family could not afford such items.

Though it was hard to find the money for such necessities, my father still occasionally treated himself to small luxuries like a mug of beer or the cigars that he loved. On one occasion, he sent me to purchase a stein of beer for him at Püggen's pub just down the street from our house. Taking the opportunity to taste beer for the first time, I started sipping from his mug on the five-minute walk back home. By the time it reached my father's hands, a half an inch or more was somehow missing from the top. Growing angry with me, he snapped, "You spilled it again Wilhelm!" Even children never completely escape the stress when times are hard for a family.

Coming when Germany was less than a decade from the economic struggles during and after the Great War, the Depression years tended to reinforce the nation's conservative social values and increase popular discontent with the post-war state of affairs. Conversations about the recent war itself were frequent and generated strong emotions.

Like most other citizens, I believed that the Great War arose from the refusal of the existing powers—Great Britain, France, and Russia—to accommodate Germany's rising economic and military strength and to accept our nation's rightful place as a leading state in the world. Despite the loss of many sons and fathers in the conflict, there was a sense of pride that Germany had defeated Russia and successfully resisted the combined military forces of much of the rest of the world for more than four years of war.

Though Germany agreed to an armistice in late 1918, most Germans did not accept that the nation had truly been defeated, since the German Army still existed as a coherent military force and occupied part of France as well as wide territories in the East. Instead many, if not most, Germans believed it was the revolutionary actions of left-wing Communists and socialists on the home front that had undermined the army's morale and ultimately compelled the nation to seek a negotiated settlement.

Discussions of the Great War inevitably led to bitter denunciations of the unexpectedly harsh Treaty of Versailles that the Allies subsequently forced on Germany in 1919. Unjustly holding Germany guilty for starting the war, the Treaty inflicted harsh financial reparations, required the surrender of German territory and colonial possessions, and imposed a 100,000-man limit on the German military. Unsurprisingly, many Germans felt a lingering sense of grievance toward France and Great Britain for the country's difficult conditions.

With my interest in military history, I often spent time talking with local veterans in Püggen and neighboring villages. They invited me along to the meetings of the *Stahlhelm* (Steel Helmet), a large right-wing paramilitary organization comprised of former soldiers who served in the Great War. Wearing their old uniforms and bearing their military rifles, these veterans assembled together a couple of times a year for large outdoor gatherings in various places across Germany.

Beyond reminiscing about the war, delivering patriotic speeches, eating bratwurst, drinking beer, and leading the crowd in traditional German songs, the group also offered weapons exhibitions to the crowds. More importantly to me, they also gave boys my age a chance to shoot their Mauser rifles on firing ranges. It was a lot of fun, even if the rifle's recoil would leave my shoulder sore for days.

Although possessing limited knowledge of political matters at that age, I agreed with what I understood of the patriotic nationalism of the *Stahlhelm* veterans. Their hostility toward the limits placed on the strength of the *Reichswehr* (pre-war German armed forces) and other unjust aspects of the Versailles Treaty seemed justified. Although many local *Stahlhelm* members were hostile to the extreme chauvinism and racial nationalism of the National Socialist German Workers (Nazi) Party, the national *Stahlhelm* organization did at times cooperate with other nationalist groups, including the Nazis.

While the Nazis shared common opposition to Germany's postwar political order and certain nationalistic views with groups like the *Stahlhelm*, they would not tolerate any competing groups. After coming to power, they would absorb the *Stahlhelm* into the Nazi SA, or *Sturmabteilungen*, their brown-uniformed party paramilitary organization.

HITLER IN POWER: 1933–1935

Among farm owners in our community, there was strong support for the ultraconservative German National People's Party. My parents backed it and my grandfather sometimes attended its local party meetings. In contrast, they viewed the Nazi Party as a fringe group filled with crude and dangerous extremists who were only marginally better than the Communist radicals. At the same time, my parents did not consider national politics very important to their lives and were primarily concerned with local issues.

Despite widespread discontent with the political and economic conditions of the early 1930s, I believe most Germans respected the existing government led by President Paul von Hindenburg, a hero of the Great War. They were not looking to eliminate the post-war republic instituted at Weimar in 1919.

Even if there may not have been broad support for a return to the prewar political system, many Germans did feel a certain nostalgia for the better times the nation enjoyed under the old Kaiser (Emperor). Many times, we sang the popular drinking tune, "*Wir wollen unsern Kaiser Wilhelm wieder-haben!*" ("We want to see our Emperor Wilhelm back!") Yet, the more the economic crisis deepened, the more the mainstream political parties lost out to extremist organizations like the Nazi and Communist parties.

Various political parties visited even small communities like ours to pass out leaflets and plaster their campaign posters, but the Nazi Party's SA was by far the most visible. The Nazis were also the most effective in using party propaganda and the media to spread their nationalist and demagogic message. Fanning popular resentment over the Versailles Treaty, the Great Depression, and the ineffectiveness of Germany's existing political institutions, their leader, Adolf Hitler, pledged to restore Germany to greatness and face down all its enemies at home and abroad. His promises to lift the nation out of crisis were particularly successful in winning him support among less educated, working class laborers.

Yet, uneasy as many educated Germans felt about the Nazis, their left-wing counterparts, the Communists, appeared even worse. Many viewed the Nazi Party as the strongest alternative to the Communist Party, fearing that the Communists might impose the same repressive political and economic system that existed in the Soviet Union. Even though my family strongly disliked the Nazis as a party, we did favor their opposition to Communism and Versailles and their calls for Germany to restore its economic and military power.

In the election of November 1932, the Nazis actually lost seats in the *Reichstag* (German parliament), but they did receive more votes than any other party. As a result, after political maneuvering, President Hindenburg named Hitler to be the new chancellor. Few Germans even remotely imagined the future consequences of placing Hitler and the Nazis in charge of Germany.

Upon gaining control of the government, Hitler soon began to mobilize the six million unemployed for projects like the building of the Autobahn (highway) system. From the perspective of an unemployed man without the means to support his family, it was natural to support a government that brought work and good wages.

Furthermore, the Nazis introduced other programs designed to win popular support for the party and its policies. For example, the regime offered workers who joined the government's official labor union the chance to take discounted vacation cruises abroad, while rewarding highly performing workers with completely free cruises. Because of the program's success, the government's union paid for the construction of purpose-built cruise ships like the *Wilhelm Gustloff* to meet the demand. The Nazis' program to provide families living in large cities with the opportunity to send their children to specially built camps in the countryside was also highly popular.

On March 16, 1935, Hitler unilaterally scrapped the Treaty of Versailles and ordered Germany's rearmament. In addition to creating the Luftwaffe (German air force), the Nazi government also commenced the rebuilding of the Wehrmacht, which previously had been limited to 100,000 troops under the Treaty of Versailles. The rising economy and renewal of Germany's military power helped build popular support for the Nazis and give Germans a growing sense of national confidence.

My family supported these measures and benefited from the greatly improved business climate that permitted us to sell more of our farm products at a better price. Yet, whatever agreement we may have had with specific policies, we still remained opposed to the Nazi Party. Perhaps what most affected our lives was the gradual but continual increase in the dictatorial character of the government as it inexorably transformed Germany into a totalitarian state.

When a fire at the Reichstag in February 1933 was blamed on the Communists, we supported a crackdown against them. Like most Germans, we were pleased that the government seemed to be restoring a sense of social discipline and political order to society. However, Hitler used this incident to claim emergency powers and eliminate all open political opposition. Within a short period of time, the Nazis began issuing more and more orders about what we must do, and imposing more and more restrictions on what we were permitted.

Although my parents and my grandfather were not politically inclined, they perhaps possessed a more independent mindset and more questioning attitude than many other Germans. They strongly opposed the huge expansion of government control over our lives and felt a deep sense of mistrust for the regime as well as unease about the future.

Though the Nazis came to power when I was only twelve years old, I began to follow politics at this time very closely and develop my own opinions on the new regime. It seemed to me that the overall situation in Germany was improving under the Nazis, but I also possessed mixed feelings about Hitler and doubts about where he was leading the country.

In 1934, a guest Lutheran pastor visited our church in Püggen. Sitting in our pew, we were shocked when he began to preach Nazi ideology from the pulpit, his loud voice booming through our little chapel. Pounding on the lectern, his sermon proclaimed that God had blessed Germany by bringing Hitler and the Nazis to us. Claiming that everything that the Nazis were doing was good for Germany, he told us that we must follow them. My family shook our heads in stunned disbelief at the government's sacrilegious misuse of religion in an attempt to justify its own authority.

NAZI RULE

The sense of political repression may have been more pronounced in the larger cities, but it would be an exaggeration to say that there was a climate of fear in our rural community. Although the Nazis increasingly restricted the freedom to express dissenting views in public, we still openly discussed politics inside our families and among close friends. Still, I grew increasingly cautious about sharing my opinions if I was uncertain of someone else's political views, even if I knew them fairly well.

It was understood that we risked denunciation to the police or the party if we expressed anti-Nazi views around the wrong people. Once the authorities identified you as holding anti-Nazi sentiments, they would make it difficult for you to keep your job or operate your business. They would isolate you within your community. If you openly opposed the regime and resisted these lesser pressures, you would almost certainly face arrest and imprisonment. Under a dictatorship, intimidation and fear are enough to force most people to keep their mouths shut.

Only a small group of top Nazi leaders dominated government policymaking, but the Nazi Party began to recruit many more people into its ranks as the regime increased its control over German society. Probably half of the new members joined for pragmatic reasons like maintaining their job or gaining advancement, while the other half joined out of ideological conviction. Of course, many people sought membership in the Nazi Party for a combination of reasons.

In our extended family, one of my uncles in the nearby village of Hohendolsleben became a Nazi Party official. He wanted to improve his situation as a farmer, but also believed in the Nazi ideology. My parents were very careful to avoid any discussion of politics when our families spent time together, but strongly disagreed with his views. Their son later volunteered for the SS and was killed at the age of 18 during the first week of fighting in France.

Although the higher echelons of the party included a number of educated people who believed in the Nazi ideology, the Nazis relied primarily on supporters among the less educated working class to fill its ranks. My family and most other farm owners in Püggen found it very difficult to accept the authority of these kinds of people when they became Nazi officials.

After putting on a Nazi uniform, a former hired laborer who was once a nice fellow quietly doing his job would suddenly start acting like a petty tyrant. While exercising great caution in expressing our political opinions around such people, we frequently grumbled about this phenomenon among ourselves. "This son of a gun was shoveling manure, but now he acts like a big shot. You have to watch out for him."

If a farmer or businessman applied to the local government for some type of required permit, his request first had to obtain the written approval of the local Nazi Party organization before the government would consider it. If the farmer in question was not a member of the Party or at least friendly to it, Nazi officials would frequently make it difficult to acquire the necessary document. A direct appeal to the Party might resolve the problem, but would leave the citizen indebted and humiliated.

My family never publicly expressed our disapproval of the regime, but our unfavorable attitude was recognized by the local authorities. In response, they would sometimes burden our family with certain undesirable tasks. When one of the newly minted local Nazi Party officials demanded that my grandfather perform some unreasonable order, he simply refused to obey. Believing that he could intimidate this elderly man into submitting to his authority, the party official came to our farm a couple of days later and confronted my grandfather in front of the *Altenteil* (my grandparents' home).

Instead of yielding, my grandfather grew angry. Grabbing a shovel, he threatened to chop the man's head off unless he got off the property and stopped harassing him. If this Nazi had not backed down, I feel certain my grandfather would have tried to kill him. The Nazis rarely tolerated such resistance, but perhaps because of his age my grandfather suffered no punishment for his bold act of defiance.

Some years later on his eightieth birthday, my grandfather received a gift from the local company that purchased our family's grain. Anticipating that the wooden box contained several bottles of wine, he reacted with disgust when it instead held a framed photograph of Hitler. Of all my family, his view of the Nazis was perhaps the most unrelentingly negative.

Before Hitler came to power, what I least comprehended was the depth of Nazi animosity toward Germany's Jewish population. Because I viewed a Jewish person as simply being a German of a different religion and had never experienced problems with one, the Nazis' hostility seemed irrational to me, as it probably did to most Germans.

While there were no Jewish families residing in Püggen, my family had long maintained a friendly commercial relationship with a Jewish businessman from Berlin. Until the mid-1930s, he regularly showed up at our farm with a truck to buy the apples from our orchards. The only other Jewish person I knew about in my youth was a German veteran of the Great War who had been wounded in battle and left with a metal plate in his head.

Beginning in 1933, the Nazi Minister of Propaganda, Josef Göbbels, unleashed a long and intense media campaign that attempted to dehumanize and vilify the Jewish population. A more educated man, Göbbels oratory was the equal of Hitler's and highly effective.

In various ways, he and the Nazis sought to blame the Jews for exploiting Germans who were facing financial hardship in the Great Depression. More generally, they also alleged that the Jews conspired in one way or another to bring about most of Germany's and the world's other problems. Because most people tend to believe what they read and hear, the Nazi dictatorship's monopoly over the media gave it a powerful ability to manipulate German opinion.

The relentless accusations gradually convinced large numbers of Germans to see the Jews as a threat to society. While not personally developing anti-Semitic feelings, I probably did grow more indifferent to what happened to Jewish people. As a result of the Nazi propaganda, many Germans like myself would react with apathy to the increasingly ruthless measures taken against the Jewish population in the years to come.

CHAPTER 3

PRELUDE TO WAR

1936–1939

ON MARCH 7, 1936, WE LEARNED from the radio that Hitler was ordering the army to march into the German Rhineland, a territory next to France, which the Treaty of Versailles had demilitarized. The commentator told us what Hitler was saying and described the deployment of German troops into the region. While the action only represented a reassertion of full sovereign control over German territory, there was a sense of pride among Germans at what was seen as a rectification of a wrong done to our country. Encountering no foreign resistance, the operation increased Hitler's public support.

When we went to the cinema in the mid-1930s, we frequently watched the large Nazi Party rallies and parades on the newsreels that ran before the start of the feature film. My parents even encountered a display of Nazi pageantry firsthand when they attended the 1936 Olympic games in Berlin. My family and many others considered these spectacles simply another form of propaganda. Nonetheless, we perhaps naively thought that relations with our foreign neighbors would improve if they witnessed Germany's renewed national strength.

Most people continued to feel a sense of bitterness toward France and Britain for the isolation and humiliation of Germany by the most civilized and developed group of countries of which Germany was naturally a part. We also felt threatened by what we saw as a barbaric and backward Communist regime in Russia. While Germany's security justified an increase in the size of its military beyond the restrictive levels permitted under the Treaty of Versailles, Hitler would ultimately make Germany threatening to its neighbors rather than respected by them.

As the Wehrmacht expanded in size and increased the tempo of its training, we began to see more military activity. On September 21, 1936, the German Army conducted its largest military maneuvers since the Great War, an exercise in which my cousin Heinrich participated. In this operation, trucks were used to transfer a whole division from the Rhine River in the west to the Oder River in eastern Germany in a single night. Heinrich later told me that the division's shortage of vehicles had required it to confiscate all the civilian trucks it could find in order to pull the mission off.

As a 16-year-old, I was naturally excited by the impressive military display. Standing alone outside in front of our farm, I watched for hours as the long convoy of vehicles hauling infantry and artillery rumbled through our village along the main highway. Even as my desire to experience soldiering firsthand grew, the Nazi regime was leading Germany inexorably into another war.

By this time, too, females were beginning to dominate my thoughts. The year before, I had taken my first train trip alone to visit relatives in Nordhausen, where I met my second cousin, Ruth. Two years later, she made a return visit to our family in Püggen. Our relationship developed into my first romance, though we never did more than exchange a few innocent kisses. As a token of my affection for her, I would leave a chocolate candy on her pillow in the guestroom at night.

After turning sixteen, I asked my parents to pay for weekly dance lessons with a group of other students in Beetzendorf. Since there was almost no opportunity for us to socialize at school, these dance classes were one of the few places that boys my age could meet girls outside our immediate community. Indeed, it was better to see girls who lived elsewhere in order to facilitate the secrecy that surrounded relationships at that time.

While learning to dance the waltz, the polka, and other popular steps, I met a pretty girl named Hilde, who lived in the nearby village of Audorf. Because dating was not socially permissible, we had to keep the relationship concealed from her parents. Although my parents knew that I dated, they trusted me to behave appropriately and never questioned me about whom I was seeing.

Hilde and I arranged each of our three or four meetings like a clandestine operation. About six or seven in the evening, I would ride my bike the eight miles from Püggen to Audorf and meet her secretly at her family's farm. Hoping her parents would not discover us, we would talk and flirt with each other until about midnight inside their barn. Despite contemporary social conventions that placed kissing out of bounds, we did it anyway. Once, she even invited me into her room in the house, but I declined the offer, fearing there might be real trouble with her family.

Even as we remained alert for her father during the hours in the barn, I also had to keep an eye on my bicycle. Boys from Audorf who were rivals for her attention might try to steal it as punishment for "poaching" a female on their territory. Happily, I succeeded in eluding either fate.

About this time, my family welcomed two 17-year-old females from eastern Germany who would assist my mother and spend a year learning to run a farm household. Instead of freely choosing such training as in the past, these girls had been compelled to undergo this instruction. They were only the latest trainees to stay with my family in what was now a steady cycle of involuntary female apprenticeship imposed by the Nazi regime.

Since there were only three or four girls their age in Püggen, our trainees naturally drew the interest of the four or five boys in our community. My parents had given these girls rooms on the second floor of the south side of our house, but the local boys mistakenly thought they were staying on the north side.

On several nights, the boys stood under those windows and whistled, attempting to draw the attention of the girls they believed to be upstairs. Much to their misfortune, Aunt Hedwig's room was located close to that side and the commotion outside annoyed her. When she had finally had enough, she opened the window and dumped her chamber pot on the unsuspecting boys below. They never returned.

While there was no romantic interest between me and our female trainees, we occasionally kidded around together and played tricks on each other. Having further developed my technical knowledge of electrical equipment by this time, I hatched a rather devious scheme.

One evening as we were eating supper and listening to music on the radio, I excused myself from the table and left the dining room just before the regularly scheduled news program was to begin. In another room I had rigged up a microphone made from a spare radio and wired it into the speakers of my family's radio. Cutting off the regular broadcast, I switched on the microphone. Mimicking the normal announcer I intoned, "The government has decided that all young women who have been assigned to work on farms will have to serve another six months."

Hearing what they thought was an official broadcast stating government policy, both girls immediately broke into tears. Returning to the dining room, I informed everyone that it had only been a prank, but no one believed it had been me on the radio. When I finally convinced them, my family members thought it was hilarious, but neither of the girls found my deception amusing.

As they consolidated power, the Nazis took control of existing German social, cultural, and educational groups and established new organizations such as the *Hitlerjugend* (Hitler Youth). No one was forced to participate in such groups, but the regime created an environment that strongly encouraged people to become involved in some type of Nazi organization, while suggesting unspoken consequences for those who declined. Despite my desire to have nothing to do with the Nazis, I thought it would be unwise to risk completely avoiding any involvement with the Party.

In mid-1937, some friends of mine suggested that I join the NSKK or *Nationalsozialistische Kraftfahrkorps* (National Socialist Motor Vehicle Corps). The NSKK was separate from the Hitlerjugend, but operated under the control of the Nazi Party. It seemed to me that if I failed to voluntarily join the NSKK, the Nazis might pressure me to join the Hitlerjugend. Compared to the latter, the NSKK seemed to offer a relatively minimal connection with the Party. Besides feeling it was politically expedient to join, I also liked the idea of working on and riding motorcycles.

Wearing our NSKK uniforms, between six to fifteen of us would gather for a couple of hours at night every two weeks in various members' homes in our villages. During the half-year or so that I was part of the club, there were only two occasions when we rode motorcycles, much to my disappointment.

However, once a month I did get the chance to speak for an hour or so on current issues, something about which most of these farm boys knew little. Using newspapers and the radio for information, I led discussions of national and international politics with other members of our group. Despite being unable to speak freely or to discuss politically sensitive topics, I nonetheless enjoyed the opportunity to develop my leadership skills.

LEARNING A TRADE: January–August 1938

Nearing completion of my eight years of schooling in Beetzendorf in the summer of 1937, I was ready to take my life in my hands and determine my own destiny. I had grown up watching my parents labor long hours on our farm but struggle to pay our bills. This experience and my own lack of interest in agricultural work led me to decide that I wanted to pursue a different profession, even though it meant one of my younger siblings would inherit the farm instead of me.

With a natural ability to take things apart and figure out how they worked, I informed my parents of my decision to leave the farm and pursue a career as an electrical engineer. While my declaration was probably somewhat of a surprise to them, they both supported my desire to pursue a career outside farming. Since they had seven children, they were probably also relieved to have one less mouth to feed.

Shortly after I told them of my intentions, my father and I traveled the 10 miles to Salzwedel, the largest town in the area, where we met with an educational expert to evaluate my potential as an engineer. Although only an average student in school, the results of my engineering aptitude test were excellent.

Engineering colleges, however, mandated two years of "hands-on" experience as a prerequisite for all students intending to pursue three years of academic coursework in the *Diplom Engineer-Fach* program—an engineering degree program with a more practical, rather than theoretical, orientation. Taking a train to the town of Lüneburg close to the village where my father grew up, my father helped me find a large electrician's shop where I could fulfill my two-year requirement working as a "voluntary"—which meant unpaid—apprentice electrician.

When I arrived in Lüneburg to start my apprenticeship with the

Johann Brockelt Company in January 1938, the head of the shop provided me with some basic instruction and immediately put me to work. Trained to disassemble, repair, and reassemble electrical motors as well as to install electrical wiring, I was soon performing all the basic tasks of the electrician's trade.

Arriving at 7:30 in the morning, I worked until 4:30 each afternoon. My schedule included a half-day on Saturdays to make up for the one day a week that I attended electrical engineering classes at a special school in the city. Now pursuing a career of my own choosing, my academic performance greatly improved.

A major part of my work as an apprentice involved installing electrical wiring in newly constructed military barracks, unaware that I would soon be housed in such structures. One particularly cold winter day, I was up on a ladder installing lights on the ceiling of a large windowless room inside a barracks. To keep warm, I shut the door and lit a coal-filled drum below me on the floor.

Suddenly, I was struck by a tremendous headache and sensation of dizziness. Barely able to remain conscious, I climbed shakily down the ladder and stumbled out of the building. Only later did I learn that the culprit was carbon monoxide gas generated by the burning coal. It could have easily killed me if I had not managed to get out of the room and obtain fresh air when I did. Whatever such occupational hazards, my work as an apprentice electrician proved both interesting and useful to my career.

Though enjoying the freedom of being on my own, Lüneburg did not particularly impress me. Located on the Ilmenau River, it was a river port and rail junction with about 40,000 inhabitants. Its infantry regiment, cavalry regiment, two battalions of artillery, and two Luftwaffe squadrons gave it the feeling of a military town.

Despite the daily five-mile commute into town on my bike, I preferred to be living out in the countryside on my Uncle Heinrich's farm. Located in the village of Hagen just outside of town, I occupied a room in the same house where my father had grown up.

Before my arrival, my father had arranged for my food and lodging during my apprenticeship. He would also provide me with pocket money and pay for my weekday lunches at the boarding house of an elderly woman in Lüneburg, while Uncle Heinrich would allow me to live in their large farmhouse as well as share their family suppers and weekend meals free of charge. This agreement served as a sort of compensation for the fact that my father had inherited nothing, whereas my uncle had received the family farm as the firstborn son.

My only complaint with my new accommodations was an uncomfortable bed that left my back aching in the morning. Examining the mattress, I discovered that one of the spiral springs was coming up through it. Approaching the matter like an engineer, I unscrewed the offending spring, pleased that I had resolved the problem so easily.

When I informed my uncle of my success in repairing the bed, he went through the roof, "You ruined the mattress!" Arriving home after work the next day, I found the mattress replaced with a sack of straw that would serve as my bed throughout my time in Lüneburg.

In spite of a quite formal relationship with my Uncle Heinrich and Aunt Dora, my time in Hagen was generally pleasant and quickly brought me closer to people of my own age who lived there. In addition to my cousins Hartwig and Irma, there were two or three girls in residence there who were learning how to run a household under my aunt's direction. Our group also included Bodo Voss, a distant relative who was learning to farm from Uncle Heinrich.

In the evenings after we had been dismissed from the dinner table by my aunt, the six or seven of us who made up our group enjoyed kidding around together out in the expansive ornamental garden behind the house. On one occasion, I thought that I could brashly slip a light-hearted kiss on the neck of one of these female trainees. Before I knew it, her hand swept through the air, etching all five of her fingers into my cheek. To this day, my cousins still tease me about that slap.

Our group sometimes went into Lüneburg see a movie, have ice cream, or celebrate a special occasion. Five or six times I went into town with just Hartwig or Bodo to go dancing and meet local girls. Of course, I also occasionally did things separately from the group as well.

When returning to the farm late at night alone, I sometimes would find that the front door had been locked. Lacking a key, I would whistle to my cousin Irma upstairs and she would come down to let me inside.

Coming back late one night toward the end of the summer of 1938, my whistle produced no response. Taking an alternative route through the connecting cow barn, I entered the house by way of the attic. Reaching Irma's room, I knocked on her door to inquire why she had failed to come downstairs. Receiving no answer, I opened the door and found her lying still in her bed.

When I spoke to her, she made no reply and failed to stir. At that moment, I saw the pistol laying next to her hand and the blood on her pillow. In a state of shock, I woke her older brother Heinrich who was home on leave from the army and told him that there was something gravely wrong with Irma.

Only a couple of weeks before I found her body, she had casually asked our opinion regarding the best way for someone to commit suicide. Never dreaming that such a beautiful girl might take her own life, I offhandedly suggested a pistol. Though no one ever offered me any explanation for her suicide, I can only speculate that she had been raped or had become pregnant. It is my belief that she simply could not stand the shame and put a pistol in her mouth.

Her tragic death was something that I never forgot, even with all the deaths and grief that followed in the years to come.

ROMANCE IN THE LAST MONTHS OF PEACE
September 1938–August 1939

In September 1938, I closely followed news of Hitler's meetings with British Prime Minister Chamberlain and French Premier Daladier in Munich, at which the leaders agreed to the transfer of Czechoslovakia's German-speaking Sudetenland territory to Germany. I thought that this was a sensible development. Like the *Anschluss* (political unification) with Austria the previous March, this diplomatic triumph had broad popular backing and bolstered national pride, though the approval was balanced by concern that Hitler might eventually push neighboring countries too far.

Despite becoming conscious of the possibility that I might be called to duty, the peaceful resolution of the Munich conference, which amicably corrected a division of our people after Versailles, led me and most Germans to believe that war was less likely.

On the night of Wednesday, November 9, the Nazis' uneducated, brown-shirted SA thugs attacked Jewish businesses and assaulted Jewish people in the streets all over Germany. The events of what was called *Kristallnacht* (Night of Broken Glass) dominated the news, with the state-controlled media justifying the rampage as a popular retribution for alleged "Jewish crimes."

On my way into Lüneburg on that Thursday morning, a few SA men and a small crowd were gathered in front of a shop on the central street. The shattered glass of a large display window littering the pavement identified the store as a Jewish business, something of which I had not even been aware until that moment. By that time, the propaganda had helped induce a lack of popular sympathy for the suffering of Jews, but most Germans felt that this type of public violence went too far and experienced a sense of apprehension about what the Nazis might do next.

Disturbed by this radical escalation, I began to ask myself questions. What caused the Nazis to act so brutally? What was happening to Germany? Though concerned, I was afraid to speak out and hoped that the situation would somehow improve. While the Nazi measures against the Jews did indeed become much less visible to the German public in the years that followed, they grew unimaginably worse in secret.

Reflecting back on that time, there was widespread dislike of the crude officials and extremist tendencies of the Nazi Party. Most Germans felt uneasy about the future and were not content to be living under a dictatorship that abolished their freedoms. Even many citizens who had previously supported the Nazis probably recognized the regime was growing too radical both in its domestic and foreign policy. Whatever the extent of their opposition, individuals remained deeply fearful of the consequences if they openly expressed their dissent.

At the same time, many of the Nazi government's policies had broad support. Germans credited Hitler with bringing a measure of social order and an economic recovery that achieved nearly full employment. Perhaps more importantly, they felt a tremendous sense of patriotic pride in the revocation of the injustices of the Versailles Treaty and the revival of Germany's national power. It was perhaps these conflicting sentiments that allowed the Nazi regime to maintain its control.

The atmosphere in Hagen, meanwhile, became more tense and cheerless following Irma's death. Even though I continued to enjoy the time spent with my cousins and the trainees, my relationship with my uncle and aunt grew more distant. Spending less time in Hagen, I began to make more of an effort to get out and meet girls.

As the weather was warming up in the spring of 1939, Bodo and I decided to bicycle into town from Hagen to attend the regular Saturday evening dance at a hotel in the center of Lüneburg. As was the custom at such events, males wearing coats and ties collected on one side of the large, chandeliered ballroom, while girls in formal dresses sat on the benches that lined the opposite wall.

The band was already playing as Bodo and I took our seats. About half an hour later, a beautiful girl across the floor from us caught my eye. Hastening to the other side of the room, I quickly reached the table where she was sitting with a female friend. Bowing my head to her, I requested the favor of a dance.

We danced well together and enjoyed three or four more waltzes and foxtrots before the evening was over. When it ended, she agreed to allow me to escort her the few blocks to her residence, located above the flower shop where she worked. Entering the darkened store, we sat down on a bench. Over the next hour or so, we gradually slid closer to each other and mixed a little kissing into the conversation. Though neither of us probably imagined it, that night would begin a courtship that would last throughout the coming war.

A year younger than me, Anneliese Berndt was a 5'6" beauty with brown hair and brown eyes. Her looks were matched by a natural grace and an innocent simplicity that was highly alluring. While friendly and outgoing in public, she turned out to be more quiet and serious in an intimate moment. Her reserved nature regarding her private thoughts and her past only made her more enchanting to me. Indeed, it is difficult for me to imagine a girl at that age who could have been more captivating.

Anneliese had grown up in a middle-class family in the Hamburg suburb of Wandsbek. Her father owned four acres of land on which he operated six or eight large greenhouses growing flowers to sell in local florist shops. Following the divorce of her parents when she was about eight years old, her mother was subsequently hospitalized with a long illness, leaving her unable to care for both girls. Consequently, her younger sister Friedel remained with her mother while Anneliese lived at the flower nursery with her father. As joint owners of the nursery, his two sisters, together with one of their husbands and two daughters, also lived with the Berndts.

Sadly, these relatives relegated Anneliese to the role of unwanted stepdaughter. While her father was a kind man, his gentle nature made it difficult for him to assert his authority in their home to ensure that she was treated fairly. Despite his affection, she lacked adequate love and support from her mother during a difficult transition in her life. This psychological isolation in her childhood would negatively affect her for the rest of her life.

After completing the tenth grade, Anneliese sought to escape this loveless environment by leaving Hamburg in October of 1937 to pursue a three-year apprenticeship at a florist shop in Lüneburg. Not surprisingly, she was reticent to share her childhood experiences and only gradually revealed some of the details of her past to me.

My relationship with Anneliese was not initially serious, but I increasingly enjoyed our long conversations and banter as we came to know each other better. Because of our work schedules, we were only able to get together for a movie or a walk around Lüneburg about once a week. Arriving outside the florist shop, I would alert her to my presence with a special whistle. In response, she would come outside or open her window. Although seldom able to afford to buy us dinner, I would occasionally take her to eat at a restaurant in the main park close to town.

On one of our long strolls through the park, we experienced a close call when my Aunt and Uncle Stork from Lüneburg suddenly appeared off in the distance up the trail. Spotting them, I quickly pulled Anneliese into the bushes beside the path just before they caught sight of us. Hiding from relatives might seem an overreaction, but people at the time viewed an unmarried man and woman alone together as improper. Had they seen us, it would have been a highly embarrassing situation.

While Anneliese never met my Aunt and Uncle Stork, I made occasional visits to their large home for meals. When they adopted my ten-year-old brother Hermann in April 1939, I initially approved of the arrangement as beneficial to everyone. My mother had been hesitant about the adoption, but grandfather Lübbecke strongly encouraged it as a means to assist my parents financially and provide his daughter's childless marriage with a son.

By the summer of 1939, any optimism that the Munich agreement had achieved a lasting stability in Europe had faded as the international situation again grew tense. In spite of the increasing likelihood of war, I had no hesitation about fulfilling the two years of military duty required of all males reaching 18 years of age. Still, if service had not been compulsory, I would probably not have volunteered at that time. Even with my long-held desire to experience life as a soldier, I was simply not interested in a professional career in the army.

Rather than waiting to be conscripted, I decided to volunteer with the intention of entering the military in January 1940 after completing my two-year apprenticeship as an electrician. This would allow me to perform my required two years of military service before beginning my college engineering program.

In early May, I took a train to the army recruiting center in the nearby town of Winsen to volunteer, or rather to complete the necessary paperwork to commence my military service at the start of the next year. Despite my interest in reading about naval combat during the Great War, I possessed no love for the sea or interest in being a sailor. Nor was I interested in serving as a pilot. Long before reaching military age, I determined that I wanted to serve as a soldier in the German Army when I performed my military service.

With my strong interest in mechanical and electrical machinery, my ambition was to join one of the new *Panzer* (armor) units. While feeling my technical skills could be useful as part of a tank crew, I was also simply drawn to the exciting and prestigious reputation of the armored branch. After receiving a short physical exam and quickly completing the necessary paperwork, an officer informed me I would begin training with a Panzer division in Berlin that January as I had requested.

At that time, all German males were obligated to serve six months in the RAD, or *Reichsarbeitsdienst* (National Work Service) before their two years of military duty. The RAD operated along military lines, except that its members carried spades rather than weapons. It provided the state with a free labor force and helped prepare young men for military service. Perhaps because I had volunteered for the army, I was never drafted into the RAD. Of course, the imminence of war may also have played a role.

Several times since arriving in Lüneburg, I had joined the crowds that gathered to watch the local cavalry regiment's band stage one of its three annual parades. As the slow-moving procession of 30 or 40 magnificent horses mounted by soldiers in dress uniforms promenaded down the town's narrow streets that summer, the thunderous din of the brass instruments and great kettle drums reverberating off the high walls of the houses seemed to echo the martial mood of the times. Europe was on the edge of another war and would not see peace again for six terrible years.

CHAPTER 4

TRAINING FOR COMBAT

AUGUST 1939–MAY 1940

BY THE LATE SUMMER OF 1939, an intensive Nazi media campaign was stridently demanding that Germany be granted a land corridor through Poland that would link East Prussia to the rest of the country. Because the hated Treaty of Versailles had imposed this separation of German territory, there was widespread public support for what was seen as Germany's just territorial claim. The anti-Polish mood was further heightened by repeated accusations of Poland's severe mistreatment of its ethnic German population.

On August 23, 1939, the Treaty of Nonaggression between Germany and the Union of Soviet Socialist Republics was signed in Moscow. While the bitter ideological hostility between the Nazi and Communist regimes made the agreement paradoxical, this diplomatic move seemed to ensure peace with Russia if military hostilities broke out between Germany and Poland. Since Great Britain and France were not expected to go to war over Poland, a wider European conflict now appeared less likely.

When I arrived back at the house in Hagen from a trip to Lüneburg on the morning of Sunday August 27, Aunt Dora handed me a special delivery telegram that had just arrived. It was an order from the Wehrmacht directing me to report the next day to the barracks in Lüneburg for a short period of military training. Until that moment, I still believed that I had another four months to complete my apprenticeship before I would be called to military service. Now it was clear that my plans might have to change.

Despite this uncertainty, I was immediately swept up in a wave of eager anticipation that one feels at the start of an adventure. In my excitement, I did not know whether to call my parents or pack my belongings. When I reached my parents by phone, their reaction was more subdued. Naturally, my mother was particularly concerned. She made plans to come visit me that first week, though I saw little of her since boot camp was already underway.

This unexpected induction into the army left me feeling something between a volunteer and a draftee. My earlier plans to enter a Panzer unit in Berlin where the army had assigned me would not work out. Instead, the army had conscripted me into the newly established 58th Infantry Division.

Pursuing a meticulously designed plan of expansion, the Wehrmacht created new divisions using a nucleus of troops from existing active-duty divisions. The already existing 20th, 22nd, and 30th Infantry Divisions based in northern Germany each provided a cadre of troops to train the freshly inducted recruits for the 58th Infantry Division's regiments. These divisions also provided the 58th Division with a veteran core of personnel comprising about 20 percent of its final troop strength.

In accordance with this plan, most of the Lüneburg-based 47th Infantry Regiment of the 22nd Infantry Division departed for the French border to deter any potential military action from the west. Only a cadre of experienced officers and sergeants from the regiment remained behind to instruct raw recruits who would bring the new 58th Infantry Division to full strength.

For the duration of our basic training, the army temporarily called up Great War veterans to fill out the ranks of the 58th Infantry Division in order to strengthen the German defenses on the French border. Once our instruction was completed, we would replace these older reservists at the front. At this time, I still believed that my preliminary training period would only last a short time.

When I arrived early that Monday morning at the former base of the 47th Infantry Regiment in the western part of Lüneburg, my initial excitement had somewhat cooled, though I did not share the sense of anxiety that most of the other conscripts seemed to feel. I thought to myself, "This is it. I am going to be a soldier now and have to do my best." From the start, my competitive nature compelled me to prove myself and seek to become the top soldier in my unit. My aim was to obtain recognition in order to ultimately earn a leadership role.

On reaching the barracks, all recruits were directed to the armory where we were issued a uniform, helmet, and boots. Because no one wore their hair long at that time, there was not a routine shaving of the recruits' heads. Following a lesson in how to salute properly, the drill instructors broke us into training companies.

Eight conscripts shared a room sparsely furnished with four bunk beds and a table. Having worked inside similar buildings during my apprenticeship as an electrician, I was already intimately familiar with the solid three-story brick and concrete structures typical of German barracks. Though they contained relative luxuries like indoor plumbing for community toilets and showers, recruits were in no way treated indulgently. Very strict maintenance regulations ensured that the buildings remained immaculate at all times. If the sergeant conducting an inspection spotted even some minor violation, it would mean extra duty for the guilty conscripts.

At seven o'clock the next morning, we headed out to an open area in the pinewoods behind the barracks where the instructors placed our new company in line according to height. At this point, each recruit was officially inducted into the army and received the rank of private (*Schütze*). During the remainder of the week that followed, our drill instructors concentrated on teaching us how to march in close order and to goose step as we began our transformation from civilians into soldiers.

That Friday morning, September 1, 1939, we woke to hear the radio solemnly announcing that Germany was at war with Poland. Among the conscripts around me, there was immediate recognition that we would not be released back into civilian life any time soon. Though we would not be involved in the immediate campaign, my mother understood clearly what the news meant, telling my family, "Now Wilhelm must also go to war."

Few Germans doubted the government's allegation that the Poles had started the war by staging a cross-border raid against a German radio station, and no one I knew questioned the basic justice of the war, even privately. Like most other citizens, I believed Germany had legitimate grievances and had launched the invasion of Poland following the exhaustion of diplomatic efforts. In retrospect, however, it is clear to me that Hitler sought war and simply exploited these issues to accomplish his aim. For him, the attack represented the next step in an aggressive plan of military conquest designed to impose Germany as the dominant power in Europe.

The day after the start of the war, our induction ceremony was held in the drilling area behind the barracks. Standing at attention at the end of the event, we raised our right arms and swore the oath of loyalty for Wehrmacht soldiers:

> I swear by God this sacred oath: I will render unconditional obedience to Adolf Hitler, the Führer of the German Reich and people, Supreme Commander of the Armed Forces, and will be ready as a brave soldier to risk my life at any time for this oath.

In the days that followed, my fellow recruits and I generally tried to follow the progress of the war in Poland and regularly discussed the unfolding events among ourselves. While we had anticipated a short conflict, most of us nonetheless felt disappointed to have missed out on it when the war ended a few weeks later. Perhaps naively, we did not expect to have another chance to engage in combat, even though Britain and France had unexpectedly declared war on Germany in early September. None of our officers led us to believe differently.

TRAINING IN LÜNEBURG
September 4, 1939–January 9, 1940

Once we had learned how to march that first week, our company commenced its field training, which took place every day, regardless of rain or snow. It was about evenly divided between physical exercise to build our stamina and instruction in the use of weapons and other equipment. More basically, it was about learning unquestioning obedience to orders.

On most mornings, we would wake before dawn for a shower and breakfast. After strapping on our 25-pound backpacks, we formed up for the three or four mile hike out to the firing range in Wendisch-

Evern. At the start of the march, the second lieutenant (*Leutnant*) or sergeant in charge would shout, "*Ein Lied*" (A song), and then call out a title. Singing these marching tunes with enthusiasm, we set out down the road.

Reaching the site that first day, we immediately commenced drilling in an area of sandy terrain of low hills and pines. After an introduction to the bolt-action Karabiner 98K Mauser rifle that would serve as our primary weapon, our first days were spent at target practice. Both in daylight and darkness, we practiced how to disassemble and properly clean the rifle, a task that was essential to perform a couple of times a week in order to prevent jamming. In addition to working with the Mauser, our instructors soon taught us to handle and maintain a variety of other weapons as well.

All members of our training company received a cursory introduction to larger weapons like the 75-millimeter howitzer. This allowed us to have a basic level of familiarity with such weapons if we needed to operate them in an emergency. Our brief instruction in how to calculate the coordinates of an enemy target and direct the fire of the heavy guns was especially interesting to me and would prove invaluable later.

Even more elemental to soldiering, our veteran drill instructors passed along essential combat survival skills. In particular, the lesson that a good infantryman should dig a foxhole and get below ground whenever possible would save my life many times.

Though usually returning from the firing range before dark, we occasionally engaged in training at night. The return march back to the barracks was sometimes converted into a race among the hundred or so men of my training company. Jogging most of the way, I regularly completed the three or four miles before the others. Perhaps because I usually led the way in these races, the lieutenant in charge of our drilling assigned me the job of leading his horse to the stable, whereas the other soldiers had to clean the barracks or perform a similar less desirable task.

While a portion of the troops in the company acquired more extensive instruction with mortars and the 75-millimeter short-barreled howitzer, I was assigned early on to our company's communications platoon. With my civilian background as an electrician it was natural for me to join this unit. It also made sense to have the fastest members of our company in the communications platoon since they might be called on to serve as runners to deliver messages on foot, if communication links had not yet been established or had been destroyed.

After the first couple of weeks, I spent the majority of time drilling with this communications unit. Our instructors gave us specialized training in the operation and repair of radios, field telephones, telegraphs, and other equipment. Most of our time, however, was spent practicing the stringing and maintaining of communication lines. On the battlefield, these lines would be used to deliver targeting information from the forward observer's position back to gun batteries and company headquarters, as well as from the company headquarters back to the regimental command.

On many mornings that fall, the platoon practiced running a line the entire distance from the barracks to the firing range. Each of us carried a large reel on our backs with a portion of line that would be linked to the end of the preceding length of wire and then spooled out. As the line was released, those following would use long poles to hook it over limbs up in the trees where it would be less vulnerable to shellfire in a combat situation.

Since my grandparents' villa was located near our training area in Wendisch-Evern, I chanced stopping off there a couple of times on the way back to our barracks in Lüneburg. Despite the risk of punishment if I was caught, a cup of coffee with my grandmother provided a great momentary escape from our routine.

About once or twice a week after our return from the firing range, the lieutenant overseeing our drilling would announce, "It's five o'clock now. In fifteen minutes, you will be outside in formation in a clean uniform." After changing into a fresh uniform, we would wearily head out to the drilling area in the pinewoods behind the barracks. In general, my efforts to prove myself and gain top marks proved successful, but I struggled with one particular facet of training: tree climbing.

Even with a sergeant loudly badgering us, "Get up in the tree you monkeys!" I usually only succeeded in ascending about 10 feet. If I avoided sliding backward from that point, I would just hang there like an old sack. Fortunately, I performed better when the drill instructors required us to build entrenchments or to crawl on our hands and knees under barbed wire without becoming entangled as a sergeant yelled at us to keep our butts down.

A short time after the commencement of our training I befriended a couple of other conscripts, Willi Schütte and Willi Sauke, who would remain my closest comrades in the coming years. In particular, I came to know Willi Schütte with whom I frequently played cards. He was a nice guy who came from the small town of Blekede. Standing only about 5'8," he was squarely built and strong. Schütte was generally quiet, but also, like me, a bit of a prankster. He was eventually assigned to serve with one of our gun crews.

Our meals from the mess were decent and filling, but we never knew for sure what we were eating or drinking. Every morning, someone in each platoon in the barracks had to go pick up a big pot of coffee from the mess hall. If a conscript committed some violation of the regulations, his platoon leader would delegate him to deliver the coffee for the week.

After fulfilling this duty for a couple of weeks one of the men in our platoon was finally informed that his punishment was complete and he would no longer have to retrieve the coffee pot. He replied with satisfaction, "Good, then I do not have to piss in the coffee anymore." While the other troops found this prank amusing, our platoon wondered what we had been drinking.

In another instance, one first lieutenant in our regiment brought his horse up the stairs into the barracks. Though he may have been half-drunk at the time, I have no doubt that this officer was demonstrating to us that his aristocratic Prussian background entitled him to flaunt the regulations with impunity. Later, we would encounter a far different type of Prussian officer in our first company commander.

As recruits, we were only permitted a couple of hours out of the barracks on Sunday evenings. Occasionally, I visited Aunt and Uncle Stork to see my brother Hermann and have supper, but most of my free time was spent with Anneliese. Just as before the war, we would sometimes go dancing or see a movie. More often, we would go for a walk or just sit on a bench and talk. Of course, kissing was not unknown in these few moments together, but she was always much more concerned than me that we might be seen.

Taking Anneliese back to her residence at the florist shop one Sunday night after a stroll, I became so engrossed in our conversation that I lost track of the time. The distant blaring of a bugle from across town alerted me that only minutes remained before our ten o'clock deadline to report to the barracks. With a quick kiss goodnight, I took off in a mad dash. Covering the mile as fast as my legs could move, I passed the sentry post minutes later, completely exhausted, but just on time.

On another occasion following a leave from duty spent with my family in Püggen, I missed the train on which I had planned to return from Salzwedel to Lüneburg. Not seeing any alternative, I caught a taxi all the way back in order to reach our barracks before ten. The hour-long trip cost me a small fortune, but I knew that my failure to return on time would have resulted in stern disciplinary measures. Our training staff would tolerate a late arrival due to a missed train no sooner than they would excuse any other infraction.

The officers and sergeants imposed a rigorous regimen during our basic training, but I found deep satisfaction in the discipline, camaraderie, adventure, and ascetic routine of soldiering. At the end of boot camp on January 9, 1940, my sense of accomplishment and pride was great, especially given the recognition I received as one of the top cadets.

ORGANIZING FOR BATTLE
January 9, 1940–May 9, 1940

Immediately after our initial training concluded, the army shipped us 90 miles west by train to Delmenhorst, home base of the 58th Infantry Division's 154th Regiment. On our arrival, we joined additional troops of the 154th Infantry Regiment who had also just completed their training under the guidance of other cadres drawn from the 22nd Infantry Division.

Since the size of different military subunits varies among armies, it is perhaps worthwhile to outline briefly the composition and relative strengths of the infantry components in the German Army in 1940. A squad consisting of 10 soldiers was the smallest operational unit, and a platoon of four squads was the primary subunit of a company. A regular infantry company contained about 180 men, though specialized companies could be significantly larger. Each battalion contained four companies, while each regiment included three battalions and two specialized companies.

An infantry division was made up of roughly three infantry regiments, an artillery regiment, a battalion with anti-tank weapons, a reconnaissance battalion, a headquarters unit, and support troops, possessing a total strength of approximately 17,000 men. Above the divisional level, the corps, army, and army groups varied greatly in size and composition.

Once the regimental organization in Delmenhorst was completed on February 5, the new 154th Infantry Regiment made the roughly 250-mile journey south to the large training area at Ohrdruf in the hilly wooded region of Thüringen. On our arrival, our regiment united with the newly trained soldiers of the 209th and 220th Infantry Regiments and the artiller regiment, bringing together for the first time all the elements of the 58th Infantry Division.

Over the next two weeks, our regiments were organized into companies. Assigned to the communications platoon of the 13th Infantry Company of the 154th Infantry Regiment, I would be part of the largest of the regiment's 14 companies, which had a full strength of about 300 troops. In our communications platoon, there were about 25 men, all of whom had trained together in Lüneburg. Subtracting the soldiers in our platoon who drove the wagons carrying our communications gear and took care of the horses, there were about 15 of us whose primary assignment was to set up communications links and, if necessary, to serve as runners.

The 13th Company's two short-barreled 150-millimeter howitzers and six short-barreled 75-millimeter howitzers would be positioned half a mile to a mile behind the front and provide the regiment with an independent light artillery capability in support of the regimental infantry in its frontline actions. In contrast, the division's artillery regiment had long-range guns that would be deployed a number of miles back behind the frontlines and generally conduct fire missions against the enemy's more distant rear areas.

While the regiment's 13th company deployed howitzers and its

14th company operated anti-tank weapons, the other 12 companies making up the three battalions in our regiment were regular infantry troops, possessing only small arms, machine guns, and small-caliber mortars. While these 12 regular infantry companies primarily reported to their respective battalion level commanders, the 13th and 14th companies operated independently and reported directly to the regimental commander because of their unique missions.

As our new regiments organized, the Wehrmacht demobilized the Great War veterans who had been temporarily called up to fill out the ranks of the 58th Infantry Division on the French border during our training period. The demobilization of veterans also released the leadership cadre from the old active-duty army to join our company, though these members of the regular army only comprised perhaps 20 percent of our total strength.

Soon after our company had taken shape in Ohrdruf, an officer named Robert Miles Reincke introduced himself and the other new senior platoon leaders to us. A veteran of the Great War in his fifties, he was referred to as *Rittmeister* (cavalry captain) for his earlier service in the army's equestrian arm. In fact, Reincke's horsemanship was so exceptional that he had served as the Kapitän of Germany's polo team in the 1936 Berlin Olympics.

Though a highly experienced officer, he had been working as a businessman in Hamburg when he was called back to duty. As was customary for those in the Prussian officer class, he maintained an aloof distance and businesslike attitude toward subordinates, but his commanding presence only magnified our respect. Our confidence in his ability to lead our company would prove fully justified.

Under Reincke, there were two first lieutenants, but the non-commissioned officers played an equally essential role in running the company. As the highest ranking non-commissioned officer, Senior Sgt. Jüchter was the most important because he served as quartermaster, overseeing the distribution of food and ammunition supplies from the *Tross* (rear area). Highly proficient in his work, he was referred to as "the mother of the company."

In Ohrdruf, our communications platoon was placed under the command of Staff Sergeant (*Oberfeldwebel*) Ehlert who had come over with the cadre of career officers and non-commissioned officers

(NCOs) who had been serving on the French border. An easy-going, well-educated man in his mid-twenties, he would remain my immediate superior throughout the next three and a half years. Ehlert always maintained a certain distance from us and was reserved by nature, but was a good soldier and a highly competent NCO who served as our primary role model.

Following our arrival in Ohrdruf, the army forbade us to reveal our location in letters to our families and girlfriends back home. Since such restrictions appeared to be unnecessarily secretive to me, I would sometimes enclose a photograph that would "incidentally" include a public sign identifying the name of the village or city near which we were stationed in order to get around the censors.

In addition to exchanging letters with my family, I also corresponded with Anneliese back in Lüneburg, though our relationship still remained less than serious. She never expressed any particular fear about my fate as we prepared for war, though at that time I myself was not really concerned about what might happen in combat. In the vigor of youth, you naturally feel indestructible and tend to view war as a chance for adventure. If we had been older and wiser, our fears about the future would have been far greater.

During our training in Lüneburg, we had developed our basic soldiering skills and received specific instruction in some type of specialized function, such as communications. At Ohrdruf, we now engaged in advanced military exercises designed to teach us how to fight and defeat the enemy in battle. Repeatedly, the officers drilled us in basic offensive and defensive infantry tactics. Starting with our heavy weapons company, we gradually learned to operate in larger and larger formations. Eventually, the entire division joined together in field maneuvers.

Despite the cold and snow in Thüringen, we trained continuously and soon began engaging in simulated full-scale battles. Our officers made an effort to approximate actual combat conditions as closely as possible. In addition to maneuvers, the division also continued with the other aspects of our training and worked on improving our marksmanship.

Knowing that we were preparing for combat, there was no lack of motivation on our part as we drilled intensively from early in the morning until dark. There was little time for anything other than military exercises and sleeping in the homes or tents where we had been billeted. Occasionally, we also trained at night.

In winter cold, none of us looked forward to our turn on regular sentry duty. However, it was a privilege to be assigned as an honor guard for *Heldengedenktag* (Heroes Memorial Day), commemorating the millions of German soldiers lost during the Great War.

It fell on March 10 1940, which turned out to be an icy Sunday. During my 45-minute shift posted in front of the war monument in Ohrdruf, local kids approached and tried to make me laugh. It was easy to ignore them, but almost impossible to keep my body from freezing while remaining rigidly at attention. Only later would I learn what it meant to be truly cold.

Four days afterward, the division boarded trains for a roughly 275-mile trip through the night to an area south of the city of Trier in the bend of the Saar River near the town of Orscholz. Moving into positions just opposite the northern corner of France's Maginot Line defenses along the Franco-German border, we were deployed as part of the XXIII Corps of the 16th Army in Army Group A.

While our infantry company obtained living space in the elaborate frontline bunkers of Germany's West Wall defenses, other troops were housed in local villages or in tents. Soon afterward, a number of promotions were issued, following the observation of our performance at Lüneburg and Ohrdruf. Receiving the rank of private first class (*Gefreiter*), I felt like my efforts to prove myself in our training had been rewarded, even if the greater test of combat had not yet arrived.

The politics of war were rarely discussed at the front, but most Germans I knew accepted the necessity and justice of our struggle against France and Great Britain. They had declared war on Germany in reaction to the invasion of Poland. As we saw it, they were attempting to defend the unjust settlement of the Treaty of Versailles. They would not accept a new political settlement unless Germany imposed it on them with military force.

Already, there were sporadic border skirmishes with French troops in our sector of the front as well as occasional clashes between the Luftwaffe and enemy aircraft. If ordered to fight a full-scale war, we were confident in our ability to conduct operations rapidly and efficiently. Rather than another long stalemate in the trenches like Germany had endured in France during the Great War, everyone expected that a new campaign in the west would be rapid, following the model of the recently conducted war against Poland.

As the weather grew warmer that spring, the mood among the troops around me was one of anxious anticipation. Though motivated by love of country and possessing a sense of pride in our company, regiment, and division, we would quickly learn that the most basic priorities in combat were simply to obey orders and look out for ourselves and our comrades.

THE 58TH INFANTRY DIVISION'S ADVANCE IN MAY–JUNE 1940

Chapter 5

WAR IN THE WEST

May 1940–April 1941

WE BEGAN THE WAR AS SPECTATORS early on a bright May 10th morning. In the sky high above our bunkers, German pilots engaged their French and British opponents, putting on an aerial display that we observed with fascination. The chatter of their machine guns resonated to us on the ground as the planes chased and dodged each other in a relentless duel for position.

When an aircraft spun down from the sky in flames there was applause for the victor of the dogfight, as if we were at a sporting event, despite our inability to discern whether the loser had been the enemy. Within a short time, five or six planes came down, some as close as three or four miles from us. Only then did word reach us that some of the burning wrecks were German, quickly sobering our mood.

After moving up to the frontier with France, the 58th Division directed a small force to cross the Moselle River just south of Luxemburg. The detachment's subsequent frontal assault against the fortifications of the Maginot Line may have accomplished some larger strategic purpose, but it did so only at the cost of heavy casualties among the engaged units. On May 18, our division was relieved by other German forces and moved back to the rear.

This operation reflects the contrast between our approach to military objectives in France and the conduct of our future operations. In France, we simply followed orders as we had been trained. If commanded to seize a position by a certain time, we typically would attack the objective in a head-on manner, suffering heavy casualties in the process.

Later in the war, our officers generally would not carry out operations until first determining the most efficient tactical approach and the type of support necessary to minimize infantry casualties. These types of deliberations occurred to some extent in France, but the old Prussian attitude of "Do it" prevailed more often.

Two days after pulling back toward Orscholz, our division crossed into Luxembourg strung out in a long procession of men, horses, and vehicles. The most common type of vehicle in our company was a squad supply wagon, pulled by two horses. Hauling our personal belongings such as clothes and food, these wagons allowed us to march with only our rifles and ammunition. Despite being freed of the backpacks, water can, gas mask, and other gear that we would have carried in the field, long treks on foot were still exhausting.

To get off our feet, most of us managed to grab a temporary seat on a supply wagon or somewhere on a *Protze*. This was a combination of two separate two-wheeled carriages, one which carried ammunition and on which the gun crew rode, with the howitzer towed behind. While a *Protze* with the 75-millimeter howitzer required four horses, a *Protze* with the far heavier 150-millimeter howitzer needed a complement of six horses.

As was the privilege of every company commander, Rittmeister Reincke rode a horse that had its own designated handler, but most handlers were responsible for the care of four or five horses. This added up to a substantial amount of manpower given the number of horses involved.

In order to obtain an adequate number of horses in the period leading up to the war, the Wehrmacht requisitioned them from farms all over Germany, with some farms having to surrender up to half their stock. Because the requisition was supposedly a temporary measure that would only last for the duration of what was expected to be a short conflict, farmers received no compensation. Not surprisingly, the Wehrmacht ceased such unpopular measures as soon as it could obtain horses from conquered territories.

Our rapid march through Luxemburg's immaculate towns and villages soon took us into southern Belgium, allowing us to pass well north of the Maginot Line. Despite signs of much prior activity on the roads, we were unaware that only a few days earlier German Panzer divisions had broken through the French defenses in this same area.

These armored formations were now approaching the English Channel far to the west, completely undermining the French and British position. The French campaign had already been won in a strategic sense, but there was still another month of fighting ahead.

At the end of an 80-mile march over five days, the 209th and 220th Regiments of our division entered France on May 23, taking up a position on the frontline about 10 miles southeast of the city of Sedan. Replacing other German units, these regiments spread out in the four-mile-wide area between the French towns of Carignan and Mouzon. Meanwhile, the 154th Regiment was temporarily held behind as a reserve force on the north side of the Meuse River at Arlon in Belgium, until we could be relieved by other German forces.

Once our regiment reached the front, I learned how bitter the initial fighting had been. Advancing into action, our division had confronted ferocious resistance from a French-Algerian division from North Africa. In what proved the 58th's toughest combat of the campaign, these Algerian troops were firing down at our infantry from concealed positions up in the trees. To make progress, our infantry had to deploy snipers and spray machine-gun fire into the trees. In some cases, they even used flamethrowers to burn the Algerians out.

During these types of battles, the front often became fluid, intermingling our troops with the enemy's forces. In such circumstances, a regiment's heavy gun company could not safely employ the fire support of its howitzers. Instead, the infantry would have to rely on the division's long-range artillery to hammer the French rear areas in order to prevent enemy reinforcements from reaching the front.

By May 25 our regiment had marched the 45 miles from Arlon, reaching the division's new frontline in the French town of Beaumont-en-Argonne. That afternoon, I received orders from Staff Sergeant Ehlert to carry a message on foot to one of our units posted on the front. My objective was the small village of Pouilly-sur-Meuse, situated in a valley on the banks of the Meuse River about three miles to the west of Beaumont-en-Argonne.

There was no hesitation or deliberation on my part; an order was simply obeyed without question. Generally more gung-ho than most of the other members of my platoon, I was anxious to prove myself in combat, though my enthusiasm was tempered by a certain apprehension since I did not know what to expect.

The road to the village ran down a hill bereft of any tree cover, leaving me fully exposed to enemy observation and artillery fire. As I proceeded forward down the slope, there was no one else in sight. Spotting my movement, French artillery almost immediately opened up. Hearing the first round streaking toward the hill, I lunged into a drainage ditch beside the road just before the shell exploded about 100 yards ahead of me.

Later, I would learn how to interpret the sound of a shell's whistle through the air to determine its proximity and actual threat. In Russia, I would have said, "One hundred yards away, let them shoot." In my first encounter with enemy shellfire, however, everything sounded dangerously close.

Shells continued to impact to the right and left of me, with the closest landing perhaps 50 yards away. Each time I heard the whistle of another incoming round, I would jump back down into the drainage ditch that ran beside the road. If all remained quiet for a minute, I would leap to my feet and make a crouched run until I heard the sound of the next shell. Repeating this process more than a dozen times, it took me about an hour and a half to advance perhaps a mile.

At dusk, I finally arrived at our forward position in Pouilly-sur-Meuse and delivered my message to the officer in charge. While no longer out in the open, the village afforded little protection from the French artillery, which was slamming in a merciless barrage of five or six heavy shells a minute.

That night, I took shelter in the large wine cellar of a fieldstone house, huddled with 20 or 30 soldiers from another unit. The violent shaking of the earth was almost constant as round after round crashed into Pouilly. With a steady rain of dust from the ceiling in the pitch-black darkness, it was hard not to ponder the consequences if the house received a direct hit.

When the artillery fire ceased toward daybreak, I departed the ruined village by the previous day's route before it became fully light. With no one targeting me on my climb back up the hill toward my unit in Beaumont-en-Argonne, the return trip was far more relaxed. Happening across an unexploded 75-millimeter French artillery round that had been fired at me the previous day, I decided to retain it as a souvenir of my baptism of fire and lugged the heavy shell back under my arm.

For my performance in this mission and a series of other assignments, I would subsequently receive the Iron Cross Second Class for bravery on December 10, 1941. Yet, I already felt that I had achieved something greater. If combat can make a man out of a boy in a day, my experience on the hill and in the cellar had made me grow up fast, even if it was only a prelude to what I would endure in the coming years.

The next day, on May 27, the 209th and 220th Regiments made an assault through a wooded area in an attempt to seize the village of Inor, located another mile or so beyond Pouilly-sur-Meuse. With Inor still in French hands at the end of three days of bitter fighting, the 71st Infantry Division relieved our exhausted troops in the eastern portion of the 58th Division's sector.

Meanwhile, following the evacuation of British and French forces in the north from Dunkirk to England in late May and early June, the entire German Army was reorienting itself toward the south to attack the remaining French forces. On June 5, Germany began the "Battle of France" with a massive offensive. Four days later, our 154th Regiment staged an attack to seize control of the forest at *Bois de la Vache* (Wood of the Cow), which bounded the main road to the southeast about a mile from Beaumont-En-Argonne.

As we began our advance south, the French artillery again began to fire on us—but this time they were using gas shells. Having trained for just such an eventuality, we hurriedly yanked on our gas masks. Much to our amazement, the shells turned out to be duds. A subsequent examination of these rounds revealed that they had been manufactured by the German company Krupp in 1918 and delivered to the French as war reparations.

Our assault on the Bois de la Vache met further fierce resistance from the North African division and quickly broke down, forcing us to pull back with heavy losses. However, larger developments in the Battle of France soon forced the enemy troops to our front to join in the general French retreat to the south.

By June 11, the way was open for the renewal of our advance.

CAMPAIGNING IN FRANCE
June 11–June 25, 1940

Now the campaign in France progressed more and more rapidly. Our troops and horse-drawn vehicles were constantly on the move as the French steadily retreated before us. During the advance southward it only proved necessary for our infantry and howitzers to deploy into combat formation about three or four times.

Most of these actions turned out to be brief skirmishes lasting less than an hour. They typically began with a sudden barrage from French artillery that forced our infantry to spread out and seek cover. If our infantry encountered significant defensive positions such as entrenched enemy infantry or a French bunker, the regiment would request supporting fire from our heavy weapons company.

The 13th Company would then station our howitzers and ammunition as far forward as possible without coming under fire, generally within a half-mile of the first line. In most cases, our 75-millimeter howitzers were capable of dealing with any problems that arose and the 150-millimeter guns would not be brought into action.

Unless the resistance from the enemy appeared to require sustained support from the heavy guns, the ammunition would not even be unloaded from its carriage. Meanwhile, the horses and the *Protzen* would retreat to the *Tross* some miles further back, but remain ready to retrieve the howitzer and ammunition on short notice.

Except when this deployment was very brief, my communications platoon would string the telephone lines between the forward observer at the front and the company's gun positions, company headquarters, and regimental headquarters in the rear. We also had to maintain the integrity of these lines, which were highly vulnerable to enemy artillery fire.

Due to reports of poisoned wells, we were informed that we could not drink the local water. To quench our thirst, we began hunting for wine in the cellars of homes. At the end of a short search, several soldiers in my communications platoon "liberated" a wooden cask of wine and hauled it outside. Once the heavy barrel had been hoisted up on the rear of a still moving *Protze*, someone asked aloud, "Now how are we going to get the damned thing open?"

"I have an answer," a soldier replied, and pulling out his Luger pistol, he fired a round into the cask. With red wine now spurting out through the bullet hole onto the road, dozens of us immediately began taking turns walking behind the barrel to catch the dark stream in our mouths as we continued to march.

Upon my arrival at a church in a small town a little farther south, I heard that two French snipers perched high in the steeple had picked off a number of our troops a few hours earlier. Following the capture of the two French soldiers, many of our troops wanted retribution for the deaths they had caused among our men. As punishment, an officer in our regiment ordered that the snipers be forced to spend a couple of hours kneeling on the concrete steps in front of the church's altar before being led back to one of our prisoner of war camps.

On June 16, we entered Dun-sur-Meuse about 15 miles south of Beaumont-en-Argonne. The following day, my twentieth birthday, the 58th Infantry Division reached Verdun, a full 20 miles farther south. Up on a hill, a large cemetery from the largest and bloodiest Franco-German battlefield reminded us of the catastrophic cost our fathers had paid in the First World War. Whatever the historical parallels, there could not have been a more stark contrast with the relative ease of our advance after only a month of combat.

The next day, we accomplished another 20-mile march and entered St. Mihiel, where there were more small skirmishes. This progress was achieved despite the increasing numbers of French civilians who jammed the roads to the south as they attempted to flee ahead of our advance.

Forced to the side of the road to permit our passage, the mostly women and children refugees lingered among their horse-driven wagons and cars, crammed with their household possessions. From their despondent faces and blank stares, it was clear that their spirit was crushed. It was impossible to regard such a heartrending scene and not feel pity.

After St. Mihiel, we made our fastest advance to date, covering the 30 miles to Toul in a single day. Finding a position on a ridge overlooking the city, I looked down on Fort St. Michel where a number of French troops were making a stand. Our 150-millimeter and 75-millimeter howitzers soon arrived and went into action with the division's heavy artillery to pound these fortifications.

In these circumstances, the fire support mission for our heavy guns and the artillery was to prevent the enemy from offering effective resistance or to force them to retreat. If our infantry could move forward under our suppressing fire, it was not necessary to obliterate the target. At the end of a 20-minute barrage, our troops were able to take control of the fort as the French inside either pulled back or surrendered.

Once Toul was occupied, we halted our march. On June 22, word began to filter among us that the French government, realizing that further resistance was futile, had agreed to sign a *Waffenstillstand* (Armistice) to come into effect on June 25. Despite accomplishing in six weeks what our fathers had failed to achieve in four years of fighting, there was momentary jubilation but no real celebration. If this was war, it was a lot easier than we had imagined.

After a brief stay on the outskirts of Toul, we traveled a short distance to the neighboring Champagne region, where we gladly seized the opportunity to relax in relative luxury for a few days. Since the owners of the abandoned home in which several of us were quartered had obligingly stocked their cellar with a couple of hundred bottles of the region's dry sparkling wine, we naturally swigged down all we could handle. Indeed, there was so much of the stuff that my comrades and I even used it to brush our teeth and spray clean the floors of the rooms.

Back in Germany, the victory made Hitler and the Nazis more popular than they would ever be again. While most citizens at home probably attributed the rapid defeat of the French army to the superior quality of German officers and troops, I believed that our success resulted at least as much from the failings of the French military leadership and the lack of will to fight on the part of the French soldiers.

The national stereotyping that portrays the French as more focused on enjoying life and the Germans as more task-oriented seemed to have been borne out on the battlefield. The French troops appeared to have low morale and a higher concern for saving their own skins than for winning the war.

In contrast, the German soldiers around me were highly motivated and determined to complete the designated mission. In a tough fight, a French soldier's mentality was, "Things look bad, let's get the hell out of here." In the same situation, the German soldier would say, "Let's fight that son of a bitch and win this thing!"

Still, the 58th Infantry Division had not escaped losses. The fighting had killed 23 officers, 120 NCOs, and 533 other enlisted personnel, most of whom had served in the infantry companies that always bore the brunt of the combat. Finishing the mission that the army had assigned us, our main wish now was to return home.

Following our victory over France, most Germans believed that Great Britain would soon be forced to accede to a negotiated peace settlement. At the same time, we soldiers knew that as long as the British still confronted us, the war was not yet over. Some of us expected that an invasion of England might be necessary, but no one imagined that a year later we would be fighting in Russia.

OCCUPATION DUTY IN BELGIUM
July 4, 1940–April 24, 1941

In early July, we departed the Champagne region, heading north to occupation duty in Belgium. At one point, our route of march took us behind part of the Maginot Line, which now seemed a symbol of all that had gone wrong for France.

Covering roughly 200 miles in 10 days, the 58th Division finally arrived in the town of Tongeren, located in the Flemish region of Belgium about 15 miles north of Liege. Our posting to Tongeren proved to be very brief. At the end of July, we made a 25-mile march to the town of Verviers in the French-speaking region of Belgium.

In Verviers our regiment was billeted in rooms and entire homes requisitioned by the army in a little village on the southern outskirts of the town. Sleeping three or four to a room, we bunked down on makeshift beds on the floor. Because I spoke a little French, I was assigned to serve as our company's translator to deal with various problems that arose with the local civilians, though fortunately there were no major difficulties.

With light responsibilities in Belgium, our company commander soon began issuing leaves from duty. His selections were based on the recommendations of Senior Sgt. Jüchter, who kept track of which soldiers were due a furlough based on the length of time since their last leave. On average, a furlough lasting three weeks would be granted about once a year.

Obtaining my first leave since Lüneburg on August 10, I caught the train from Verviers, not forgetting to stow the souvenir shell from my baptism of fire in my luggage. Upon my arrival in Püggen, I received a warm welcome from my family, who treated me like I was a military hero.

Feeling more like I was on vacation than on a furlough, it was easy for me to reenter the routines of life on the farm. My brief experience in combat during the French campaign left me feeling like a man, but had changed me relatively little. In the middle of my leave, I made the 100-mile train journey to Hamburg to visit Anneliese for a few days. After over half a year apart, we decided to wait to meet her family and instead spend our short time together seeing the city.

Following my return to Verviers from Püggen on August 30, I settled into the relaxed routine of occupation duty. On a typical day, we spent about four hours drilling in order to maintain and sharpen our combat skills. The earlier training had prepared us well for the rigors of combat and we did not want to lose our edge. Our regiment also organized a couple of large-scale sporting competitions for the troops. Running in a tight 400-meter race, I hurled my body across the finish line at the last second, just barely pulling out a win over my opponents.

On weekends, there were frequent opportunities for us to take the 15- or 20-minute tram ride into the downtown area from the village where we were based. Normally, the regiment allowed us to leave about noon and required us to return to our assigned quarters by nine o'clock. While encountering occasional hostility from the Belgian population, most civilians behaved in a correct manner, or at least treated us with indifference. We felt at ease as we shopped and roamed around the city.

Perhaps surprisingly, some of the local girls were very receptive to a German soldier in uniform and would flirt with us shamelessly. They were often willing to join us for coffee or a drink at one of Vervier's sidewalk cafés or restaurants. While German troops ordinarily would enjoy the pleasure of female company for an afternoon or evening of innocent relaxation, a few of our soldiers developed more intimate relationships with Belgian women.

About this time, we received a small black, white and red cord to wear over our left shoulder, indicating that we were members of the 58th Infantry Division. Like other German divisions, the 58th's conscripts and future replacements were drawn from a specific region, in our case almost exclusively from northern Germany and the region of Nidersachsen. Reflecting the importance of horse farms in the traditions and economy of the region, the 58th Division introduced two horse heads facing in opposite directions as our divisional insignia, which we sewed on the left shoulder of our uniforms. This common regional background enhanced our sense of unit pride and camaraderie.

A couple of months after our arrival in Belgium, we received a lecture from our company commander, Rittmeister Reincke. Since he had English relatives, he may somehow have learned that the British were anticipating a cross-Channel invasion and wanted to prepare us psychologically. As we stood at attention, he warned us, "Boys, what you have seen in France is nothing. In the coming fight, you will be happy to dig yourself into a foxhole as fast as you can. It will be a lot tougher than what you experienced so far."

As a combat veteran of the First World War, Reincke knew from firsthand experience how much worse war could be. We were sorry to lose this respected officer soon afterward when he was promoted to take over the 2nd Battalion of the 154th Regiment. He was replaced by First Lt. Von Kempski, who had previously commanded one of our company's platoons.

During our time in Verviers, we tried to keep up with the news, but found it difficult to closely follow the course of the Battle of Britain that was then being fought by the Luftwaffe against the Royal Air Force. Though we knew nothing about it at the time, our divisional staff scouted out training areas in Holland, preparing for a possible move to the area for an invasion of Britain. Selected elements of our division actually conducted specialized training on boats in Antwerp and Rotterdam, but our heavy weapons company did nothing in particular to prepare for an amphibious operation.

There was broad recognition that any such assault from the sea would be costly, yet most of the men around me favored making the invasion, believing that it was the only way to bring a true end to the war. We were unaware that plans for "Operation Sea Lion" called for the German 9th and 16th Armies to seize a stretch of coast in southeast England.

As part of the 16th Army, the 58th Division was slated to arrive in the third echelon of forces, landing in the area between Folkestone and New Romney about 70 miles southeast of the center of London. When we finally realized in April of 1941 that an invasion would not occur, some of us felt a sense of disappointment, wondering how Germany could ever achieve a final peace if Britain remained undefeated.

That fall, I met two sisters who were relatives of the Belgian family with whom I was billeted. They would try to speak German with me and I would practice my French with them. On perhaps 10 occasions, they invited me to visit their family's home in town for a couple hours to exchange language lessons.

During these meetings we cracked jokes and laughed a lot, but it was harmless flirting rather than anything romantic. For me, it was simply a pleasant way to pass the time as well as to improve my French. Sometimes, it was easy to forget the recent fighting, but I never forgot that I was an enemy soldier in an occupying army.

Upon completing her three-year florist apprenticeship with honors at the end of September, Anneliese, meanwhile, had left Lüneburg and returned to Hamburg where she had found work at a flower shop in the main station. We agreed to see each other there on my way back to Verviers from Püggen at the end of my second furlough, which lasted from November 17 to December 12.

When the train reached the Hamburg station about noon that day, I headed over to the shop where Anneliese was working. Taking off her apron, she joined me for a stroll through the station and into the adjoining neighborhood. Reaching a quiet spot at the north side of the station, I presented her with an expensive bottle of perfume that I had purchased in Verviers. As she embraced me in thanks, the bottle slipped from her hand and shattered, filling the whole area with a powerful aroma. It did not seem like a promising omen.

Anneliese and I were still involved, but had never agreed to pursue an exclusive relationship. In fact, there was a very pretty girl from the

Ruhr city of Duisburg who I had encountered fleetingly back in 1937 when she had been visiting her relatives in Püggen. Three years after this initial meeting, I decided to renew our acquaintance and somehow obtained her address.

After we had exchanged a couple of letters, the girl agreed to allow me to come visit her in the Ruhr on my way back to Belgium, unaware that I would be coming from my brief visit with Anneliese in Hamburg. Our subsequent evening together in Duisburg inclined the girl to favor a more serious relationship, though it made me realize that my attraction was only to her looks.

Less than a month later, I joined in a drinking session with Schütte, my comrade from boot camp, and a few other enlisted men in our quarters in Verviers. Growing increasingly inebriated, we began to complain about our difficulties with our girlfriends back home. When the suggestion was made that we should write letters dumping them, we all swore to one another we would do just that.

This drunken promise gave me the final push to break off my close relationship with Anneliese, something that I had already been considering. Composing my thoughts in a letter on January 10, I told her that I was not ready for the serious commitment that she sought. We were too young to get married, especially when it was uncertain whether I would even survive the war.

While there had been no further correspondence with the girl in Duisburg in the weeks since my visit, I still felt compelled to inform Anneliese that I had met someone else. Without going into detail, I said that the relationship was not serious, but that I did not wish to go behind her back and cheat on her. Even if I had no intention of seeing the girl in Duisburg again, it just seemed to me that Anneliese and I should both feel free to see whom we desired. Concluding my thoughts, I conveyed my sincere wish for us to remain friends and keep in touch. Much later, I learned that she cried for days when she received the letter.

Late in 1940, meanwhile, each regiment of our division had been ordered to surrender one of its three battalions to serve as an experienced nucleus for new divisions. Similar to the earlier pattern, the loss of these battalions was made up by freshly trained recruits. Clearly, the army was still undergoing an expansion in size, though none of us were aware of the ultimate purpose.

That spring, our division traveled 25 miles to the east for a week or two of intensive training at a sprawling facility beside the Belgian town of Elsenborn, just across the border from Germany. In bone-chilling rain, we carried out battalion-sized military maneuvers in close coordination with Panzers and the Luftwaffe. While we in the communications platoon repeatedly practiced stringing telephone and telegraph lines from the front to the rear, our company's gun crews drilled on the howitzers with live ammunition. By the end of the exercises, our skills were honed to a fine edge.

On April 21, 1941, our *Vorkommando* (advance team) left for the east. Two days later, our division was issued 24-hours notice to prepare to leave Belgium. Even if some of the staff had been involved in advanced planning for our transfer, organizing a move was a time-consuming task due to the number of horses and volume of equipment. The lack of more advance notice was inconvenient to planners, but was intended to keep our relocation as secret as possible.

Late in the afternoon of April 24, most of our division's troops were ready to leave, though some elements would join us later. Boarding our trains in Verviers, we still lacked any information about our destination. Not even our company commander knew where we were headed. During our journey across Germany, everyone around me was wondering out loud, "Where the heck are we going?" "What will happen next?"

A funny thing about military life is the prevalence and power of rumors. The atmosphere was charged with excitement and anticipation as various theories raced around the train about our mission. Conjecture focused on a destination somewhere up north. Some predicted, "We are headed to Finland." With equal confidence, other troops maintained, "We are going to Sweden." Both rumors proved wrong.

CHAPTER 6

BLITZKRIEG INTO RUSSIA

APRIL–JULY 1941

PRELUDE TO INVASION
April 24–June 22, 1941

Traveling east-northeast into Germany, our train passed through the hometowns of many of the troops in Hamburg and Lubeck without stopping. During the 30-hour trip, only brief halts were made to change the locomotives before the journey continued. After traveling roughly 625 miles from Verviers, we finally disembarked at the city of Elbing in East Prussia.

From there, our division immediately set out on the first of two night marches. When dawn broke, we halted in the woods beside the road for a meal of cold rations. Hidden from any air surveillance by the trees above us, we rested on our canvas bedrolls in the warmth of the day before returning to the march as darkness fell.

On reaching Heiligenbeil about 25 miles northeast of Elbing at the end of April, we took up our quarters in barracks. During the next six weeks, our training exercises intensified, which only increased speculation regarding our mission.

The majority of those around me continued to anticipate that we were going to be part of a military operation somewhere in Scandinavia. Most of us found it very difficult to imagine that Germany would attack Russia. The Russo-German Nonaggression Pact signed in August 1939 probably influenced our mindset, but it was also simply the scale of the Soviet Union that tended to make the prospect of invasion difficult to conceive.

By this time, war news had grown to be routine and received scant attention. The Afrika Korps' arrival in North Africa to assist the Italians in early 1941 as well as Germany's occupation of Yugoslavia and Greece later that spring elicited only limited interest among those around me. Though I personally attempted to follow the German air assault on Crete at the end of May, such distant developments seemed to be of little direct consequence to us.

On June 8, our division departed on a further series of night marches to another undisclosed destination. The journey ended three days later at Labiau, about 50 miles northeast of Heiligenbeil. Billeted at a concealed site in the woods, we continued to prepare for an unspecified large operation, but now did so covertly.

Positioned so close to Soviet-controlled territory in Lithuania, there was increasing suspicion that Russia might be the target after all, though a degree of uncertainty still prevailed. Isolated in the woods, we failed to see the massing of infantry, Panzers, and artillery around us that would be necessary for a major operation. With the port of Memel nearby, it also still appeared possible that we might receive orders to embark on ship for a voyage across the Baltic Sea for some type of mission in support of Germany's ally, Finland. As far as the timing of any potential operation, we remained completely in the dark.

Just after my twenty-first birthday, on June 17, orders came down to us that the invasion of Russia was at hand. Almost immediately after receiving the directive to prepare for the attack, we set out from Labiau on a long but rapid march to another forested bivouac area in the northeastern corner of East Prussia at Heydekrug, a little north of Tilsit. This would place us less than 10 miles from Russian-controlled territory in Lithuania, which the Soviet Red Army had occupied just a year earlier.

Perhaps surprisingly, there was no real discussion or debate over this momentous news among the troops around me. Instead, there was almost a sense of relief that our weeks of waiting and uncertainty were over. We now had our orders and we immediately focused on preparing for war.

It is also true that, as young men, we possessed little tendency to ponder matters deeply. That may indeed be an essential quality for a soldier. If you ordered a company of middle-aged soldiers into combat, you would probably have a problem getting them to fight without convincing them of the necessity of their action. It was not that we soldiers were unconcerned about what was going to happen, but we were conditioned to obey orders as soldiers in a fighting unit.

Though most of the men around me had little or no interest in politics, it was nonetheless apparent to all of us at the time that war between Germany and Russia would be of great historical significance. When German troops and the public back home learned of the invasion of the USSR, most reacted with a deep sense of uncertainty, very different from the mood prevailing at the start of the campaign in the West. The questions that circulated reflected these concerns. "Why is this attack occurring before we have defeated the British?" "Are we going to repeat the experience of Napoleon?" "What will happen next?"

Few Germans doubted our ultimate triumph, but many wondered about the duration of the struggle and the price of final victory. Almost no one questioned the morality of a crusade to destroy Soviet Bolshevism, but there were some like me who shared practical misgivings. Germany's forces were already engaged all over Europe and it appeared to me that Hitler risked overextending our manpower and resources by undertaking such a colossal campaign in the East.

For the large majority of Germans, the war was never about the Nazi dream of conquering *Lebensraum* (living space) in the East for colonization by "the Aryan master race." Like most other German soldiers, I was fighting for my Fatherland out of a sense of patriotic duty and the belief that Soviet Communism posed a grave threat to all of Europe and Western civilization. If we did not destroy the Communist menace, it would destroy us.

In eliminating this danger to Germany and Europe, we would also be liberating the Soviet peoples from their oppressive Communist masters. Though Nazi propaganda presented the Slavic population as *Untermenschen* (subhumans), none of the men around me embraced such extreme racial views. For us, the Slavs were not a biologically inferior race of human beings; they were simply the ignorant inhabitants of an uncivilized and backward country.

At the start of the invasion, Germany possessed a large army of veteran troops who maintained supreme confidence in their ability to overcome any enemy. In the wake of our string of earlier victories in Poland, the West, and the Balkans, we could not have been more assured of ourselves. A few lines from a letter I wrote to Anneliese later that summer expressed the personal optimism that I had come to feel: "It's tough here and we fight, but we fight for a reason and I am confident we are going to win. I am positive about that."

MARCH TO THE EAST: June 22–July 5, 1941

On Sunday, June 22, 1941, the pre-dawn silence was shattered by the roar of guns, as three million German troops commenced "Operatoin Barbarossa," the invasion of Russia along an 1,800-mile front from the Baltic Sea to the Black Sea. The tremendous cascade of thunderous booms echoed around us as German artillery delivered a short but intense hurricane of shells against the Russian lines, producing flashes of light all across the eastern horizon.

As dawn broke, the dim sky above us was filled by waves of Luftwaffe Heinkel and Junkers bombers, Stuka dive bombers, and Messerschmitt fighters droning overhead on their way east. The appearance of this aerial strike force was quickly followed by the rumble of tank engines revving up, but the noise soon faded as the German Panzer units raced eastward. The shock of this combined Blitzkrieg (lightning war) routed the Red Army forces defending the border and sent them into a full retreat.

Late the following morning, the 58th Division received orders to advance as part of the second echelon of troops in the XXXIII Corps of the 18th Army. The 18th Army, 16th Army, and Fourth Panzer Group made up Army Group North, one of the three massive army groups—North, Center, and South—created by the Wehrmacht for the invasion.

As we crossed the frontier, no border defenses were visible, but we noticed an immediate difference in that roads were not as good, though a few were paved. The next evening, the 154th Regiment staged brief assaults against Soviet positions in the small Lithuanian towns of Pajuralis and Kvedama, located about 25 miles east of our jumping off point in Heydekrug. These short actions against what might have been border troops did not even require the support of our heavy weapons, and we were ready to press on the next morning.

Advancing about 15 miles a day, we reached Siauliai, about 60 miles northeast of Pajuralis, by June 28. Though the Panzer units were far ahead, the 58th Division's rapid progress soon placed it in the lead among the infantry divisions of Army Group North. Despite occasional traffic jams, everything was moving swiftly east, boosting our confidence. In the midst of our success, there was growing optimism that we could defeat the Soviet Union by the coming winter or the following spring.

Our march pressed on through long summer days that lasted from an early dawn until a late dusk when our officers ordered a halt, typically establishing our encampment in a field beside the road. Following a filling meal, the entire company would seek sheltered positions in which to sleep, in case of a Red Army attack. If camped in a village, we might sleep behind a home, but never inside, knowing that any structure presented a potential target for enemy artillery.

Unless posted to guard duty, I would prop my head on my steel helmet and instantly fall asleep. Anywhere from two to four hours later, someone would wake us with a kick in the rear. Within half an hour, we would eat breakfast and resume our trek.

Battling both stifling heat and thick clouds of dust, we plodded countless miles. There were few breaks from our march, except for the occasional chance to hitch a lift on one of our company's horse-drawn vehicles. After awhile, a kind of hypnosis would set in as you watched the steady rhythm of the man's boots in front of you. Utterly exhausted, I sometimes fell into a quasi-sleepwalk. Placing one foot in front of the other in my state of semi-consciousness, I somehow managed to keep pace, waking only briefly whenever I stumbled into the body ahead of me.

During our march across the open, flat country of northern Lithuania, we encountered no further enemy resistance, but could hear the perpetual din of gunfire and explosions in the distance as well as witness terrible scenes of carnage close at hand. In drainage ditches and out in the fields that lined the road, hundreds of still warm, contorted bodies lay where they had fallen. In many instances, there were ten or fifteen corpses grouped together, sometimes including uniformed women. The enemy tanks we passed were wrecked hulks, often still belching an oily black smoke.

Most of the Red Army's troops and tanks had been caught in the open by German aircraft as they attempted to retreat to the east. Exercising complete air superiority over the battlefield, the Luftwaffe made sure that no enemy unit could move safely. When a fighter aircraft let loose with its heavy-caliber machine guns, it would decimate unprotected targets over a wide area.

Such attacks were particularly devastating when our planes swept along roads crowded with Russian men and vehicles. Everything in the path of their bullets would be annihilated; even soldiers sheltering in ditches alongside the road were not safe. In these strafings, nearly everyone who was not killed outright would at least suffer wounds.

The Red Army tanks that had not been destroyed had been driven back by German armor. If our heavy weapons company encountered one, a well-aimed round from one of our 150-millimeter howitzers could incapacitate it by damaging its main gun or its treads with a high explosive round. Our heavy gun company's primary assignment, however, was to provide fire support for our infantry against Soviet infantry. We lacked the armor-piercing shells designed to penetrate the thick armor of these vehicles and would rarely engage Soviet armor except in a crisis. The division had a variety of other means to cope with enemy tanks.

On our march northeast, we covered the roughly 70 miles from the Lithuanian city of Siauliai to the Latvian capital of Riga within a week. Upon entering the city on July 5, small crowds along the streets greeted us with shouts of *"Befreier!"* (Liberator!) and presented us with flowers or chocolate in gratitude for their rescue from the Russian occupation. While some of the population remained fearful and hid in their basements, the generally positive reception we received here and throughout the Baltic states of Latvia, Lithuania, and Estonia reinforced our conviction that our cause was just.

As our column briskly proceeded down the streets of the city, it was easy for us to feel at home amidst architecture that differed little from that found in Riga's Hanseatic counterparts along the German coast. Our swift pace was not even disrupted by the Red Army's demolition of the bridge over the Düna River along our route.

Operating ahead of us, our *Pioniers* (engineers) had already constructed a pontoon bridge as a replacement. Within half a day, we had passed out of Riga and returned to the open countryside.

ENCOUNTERING THE ENEMY: July 6–July 21

Just after our company had halted at a Latvian village late the next afternoon, a group of us spotted perhaps a dozen Russians scurrying through a valley about half a mile away. Apparently, they had been caught behind our lines by the speed of our advance and were attempting to escape eastward. A number of soldiers around me immediately began pouring rifle fire on the men from our vantage point above them. A couple of the enemy troops may have been hit, but most of the group scattered into the woods behind them.

This incident represented our first encounter with the enemy since the initial skirmishes near the border, causing some of us to wonder whether the Russian campaign would ever involve much more than long marches in pursuit of a retreating foe. The following weeks, however, would provide a much clearer perspective on the struggle we faced.

On July 7, we reached the Latvian city of Rauna, located about 50 miles east of Riga. At Rauna our division encountered our first real fighting with the Red Army since crossing the frontier. Our company deployed its heavy weapons in support of our regimental infantry, but the fighting quickly ended as the Soviet troops retreated.

Since our Panzer formations had already outflanked the enemy's defenses, we were facing only rearguard forces protecting the Red Army's retreat. The coming days would see frequent episodes of this type of skirmishing, but they produced no more than short delays in our advance.

A couple of days later, our company bivouacked among the homes of a village located along the road. Aware that any village presented an inviting target for Soviet artillery, I chose to sleep in a shallow hole in the ground a short distance away.

In the middle of the night, I came awake to the sound of voices, but the barely audible fragments of conversation that reached me made it hard to determine whether the speakers were German or

Russian. Peering through the pitch blackness in that direction, my eyes could only make out the movement of shadows, though they were only perhaps ten feet away.

Straining my ears, I became increasingly certain that the speakers were not using German. While it could have been a night attack against us, my intuition told me that this was probably another small band of Red Army troops attempting to reach their own lines after becoming separated from the main body of forces. My first thought was that they had somehow succeeded in eluding our sentries, but then I realized that it was equally possible they may have been as ignorant of our presence as we were of theirs.

Unsure whether the men represented a threat to our company, I anxiously debated what to do. Firing my rifle or tossing a hand grenade might kill a few of the enemy, but my alarmed comrades would probably be mowed down by the enemy as they ran toward the noise. Weighing the risks, I concluded that it was better to remain quiet and allow the Russians to pass through our position. To my great relief, the shadowy figures moved on without incident.

Covering about 100 miles from Rauna in less than a week, our division entered the territory of Russia itself. On July 12 we reached Pskov on the southern tip of Lake Peipus, where we caught up with the Panzer divisions that were awaiting infantry support before renewing their advance toward Leningrad.

Turning north, we would now operate on the far left flank of Army Group North, with the 1st Infantry Division on our right and the eastern shore of the lake on our left. As we moved forward across the flat, lightly wooded terrain near its shores, Lake Peipus itself remained just beyond our field of vision a couple of miles distant.

In our advance northward, we began to be increasingly hindered by both the worsening roads and intensifying resistance from Soviet rearguards. Our advance was also complicated by maps showing main roads and highways that simply did not exist. Beyond problems with a lack of accuracy, there were also few maps to go around. While a company commander was lucky to obtain local maps, the ordinary foot soldier, of course, had little idea where he was or what significance a particular location held in the wider struggle.

Lacking radios, the only information we received came in twice weekly newssheets issued by the 58th Division headquarters. Excerpts of speeches by Hitler and Göbbels filled most of the space, but there would also be brief reports about battles and advances on the Eastern Front as well as news about the fighting in North Africa and the Atlantic. Despite featuring a great deal of propaganda and information that was heavily censored, these newspapers offered us at least a general sense of what was happening elsewhere.

Around this time I developed a high fever that left me feeling weak and exhausted. When the march temporarily halted, I entered a nearby abandoned home. Finding a bed, I collapsed into a deep sleep lasting six or seven hours. Feeling rejuvenated, I rejoined my company a short distance away. Since we were usually only able to catch short—and frequently interrupted—naps when we were on the march, my long slumber in a bed was a rare luxury.

Covering the 40 miles from Pskov in five days, the 58th Division reached the small city of Gdov on the northeastern shore of Lake Peipus on July 17. There was only light enemy opposition as we entered, but we now faced supply problems. The difficulty of transporting supplies from the south on the poor road network forced our division to instead ship supplies across Lake Peipus.

Still lacking adequate food, our division was able to put a Soviet flour mill back into operation, which helped to feed both German troops and the local civilian population. Because the retreating Red Army forces had contaminated the abandoned stores of grain with oil, the bread possessed an unpleasant taste that was barely hidden by the salt we mixed into it.

On July 19, our division renewed its advance northward and two days later reached the town of Niso about fifteen miles northeast of Gdov. Our mission was now to seize the corridor between Lake Peipus and the Baltic Sea in an effort to block the retreat of the remaining Red Army forces still trapped to the west in the Baltic states.

For the first time since the start of the campaign, our efforts to advance confronted stiff enemy opposition as Russian troops and heavy artillery battled fiercely to hold open the passage to the east. Though the key road junction in the Estonian city of Narva was only 15 miles north of us, it would be almost a month before we seized the city and sealed the escape route.

THE EXPERIENCE OF SOLDIERING

During the long marches into Russia, it was natural that my mind would dwell on my loved ones back home as well as my ex-girlfriend Anneliese, with whom I still maintained a monthly or bi-monthly correspondence. Since the end of our romantic involvement in January she had, however, already become engaged to marry the son of the proprietor of the florist shop where she had apprenticed in Lüneburg.

With the passage of time, I gradually came to realize that I had overreacted to Anneliese's desire for us to enter a more committed relationship. It also became clear to me that my affection for her ran much deeper than I had previously acknowledged. Her engagement to the florist's son made it improper for me to convey these feelings and pursue her openly, but I believed there was still hope that Anneliese would come back to me. I intended to see her again on my next furlough in Germany.

Separated from home, the bond of comradeship that I shared with other enlisted men in my company had grown deeper, even though I continued to feel myself to be naturally more of a leader than a comrade. For me, camaraderie in the army was distinct from friendship in civilian life.

In war, relationships form out of practical necessity among enlisted men forced together by circumstances, especially in the regular infantry. Camaraderie at the front reflects the soldier's practical need to depend on those around him for mutual support and protection, while friendship in civilian life involves a more intimate bond precisely because it is a relationship created by choice. It is also only natural that someone is much more willing to form a close relationship when death is not a daily occurrence.

Perhaps because we realized that our deaths might occur at any moment in war, losing comrades affected most of us only in the short term. Within a couple of days, the pain of a comrade's passing faded as other concerns took priority. By the end of a month, the lost comrade disappears from a soldier's immediate thoughts altogether.

A soldier must focus on fighting. If the loss of a comrade caused some stress, the deaths of enemy troops caused almost none and became routine. They were battling us and would kill us with exactly the same lack of emotion. In combat, it is simply you or the enemy.

All the troops focused on fulfilling their duty, but there may have been some difference in outlook between those who had volunteered and those who had been drafted. Volunteers were naturally more gung-ho about their tasks, while the conscripts were by nature more cautious.

My enthusiasm matched that of the volunteers, though unlike some of these soldiers, I was never reckless with my life on the battlefield. My only real fear was being killed or captured. Otherwise, I accepted the austerity and all the hardships that we faced as a normal part of the life of a soldier in war.

Throughout the war, I would estimate that the casualty ratio remained roughly constant at four or five men wounded for every man killed. At the front, our company possessed trained medics for emergency field treatment, but they would typically just patch up the wounded for further treatment by regimental doctors. If the injury or illness proved more severe, the soldier would be sent back to a divisional field hospital or returned to Germany.

Our medical care and facilities were excellent and helped return about fifty percent of the wounded to duty within a week. Illness was not a major problem, though minor ailments like diarrhea were common. Sometimes our medical problems required specialized care that was not available at the front and thus called for creative solutions.

As my wisdom teeth came in, it was extremely uncomfortable for me to bite down hard on anything. Deciding to resolve the problem on my own, I went to the regimental doctor. In reply to my request for a scalpel, he asked, "What are you going to do?" I refused to tell him, but he gave me the scalpel anyway.

Finding a mirror, I cut open the flesh covering the incoming teeth to relieve the pressure. Though the absence of anything to numb the excruciating pain almost caused me to lose consciousness, my do-it-yourself dentistry proved successful. In wartime conditions, a soldier learns to work with what he has and make the best of the situation.

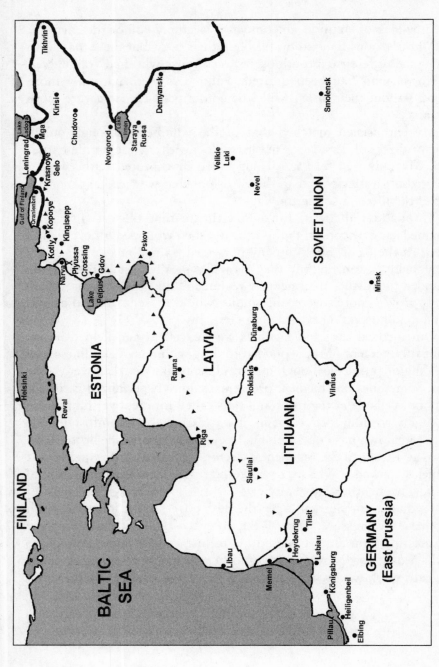

Arrows trace the route of the 58th Infantry Division's advance to Leningrad between June 22 and September 15, 1941. Heavy lines show furthest extent of the German advance into Russia during 1941.

CHAPTER 7

TO THE GATES OF LENINGRAD

JULY–SEPTEMBER 1941

FORWARD OBSERVER

Still a private first class in the 13th Company's communications platoon, I was craving a more challenging responsibility than my existing routine of establishing communication links and occasionally acting as a runner delivering messages. As always, I wanted to be in the middle of the action, even if this placed my life at greater risk.

When the company commander offered me the opportunity to serve up front directing the company's heavy guns following the promotion of the previous forward observer, or F.O. (*Vorgeschobener Beobachter* or V.B.), I enthusiastically seized the chance. In our company, forward observation was more of a task conducted on an ad hoc basis rather than an officially designated position, but the need for someone to fulfill this role was so constant that the distinction was almost meaningless. My initial assignment in this capacity was on a temporary basis, but gradually become permanent over the next half-year as I proved myself.

In my role as F.O., I would act as the eyes for our company's howitzers located about half a mile to a mile behind the front. The 13th Company's 75-millimeter howitzers had a maximum range of 5,630 yards (3.2 miles), while our 150-millimeter howitzers possessed a maximum range of 5,140 yards (2.9 miles). This meant that we could begin to bring targets under fire once they were about two and a half miles in front of us.

These howitzers were organized into four batteries with each battery operating two howitzers manned by a five-member gun crew and supported by numerous additional personnel. Three of the batteries deployed the six short-barreled 75-millimeter howitzers, and one battery deployed the two short-barreled 150-millimeter howitzers. If the forward observer called for all heavy guns in the company to deliver a barrage simultaneously, their firepower was roughly equivalent to an artillery company.

During boot camp, our instructors had familiarized us with the basic targeting procedures for the heavy guns, but since that time I had acquired invaluable additional knowledge by regularly watching and working with the previous F.O. Still, only firsthand experience working as the F.O. would allow me to gain a real feel for the position. Before long, the determination of the appropriate firing solution for a target as well as the numbers and types of rounds to employ would become second nature to me.

Nominally still a member of the communications platoon and subordinate to Staff Sergeant Ehlert, I would now usually receive my assignments directly from the company commander. As my role in the company changed, I gradually grew somewhat isolated from the other troops physically and psychologically.

My initial responsibility as forward observer was to direct our heavy guns in support of our offensive operations, eliminating enemy strong points and reducing their ability and will to resist. During intermittent fighting, the gun battery's duty officer or top sergeant would have to authorize the F.O.'s request for fire missions in support of the regiment's infantry. When combat was continuous, however, the F.O. could request fire support missions without such approval.

Once it became clear that the enemy was retreating from a position, our guns would advance as the infantry went forward. Especially during periods where there were rapid advances or retreats, enemy forces would sometimes become intermingled with our frontline. In such moments, it was not possible to distinguish between the enemy and my comrades. Though never feeling like I was really in danger of capture, I had to remain constantly vigilant and keep my newly issued MP-40 submachine gun nearby.

Combat might be described as controlled chaos, but you have to maintain a sense of calm so you can focus on your mission. The forward observer position was well-suited to my character since I found I had a knack for staying calm under enemy attack as well as an insatiable curiosity to know what was happening at the front. This is not to suggest, however, that I did not have moments of anxiety and sheer terror, especially under enemy bombardment.

If there was one thing that I learned fast, it was that you could not avoid becoming scared for the first five or ten minutes of combat. It is an instinctual animal reflex to danger. Even as an old veteran late in the war, an initial rush of fear would still run through me during the first two or three minutes under fire. Yet, after the preliminary anxiety had passed, my composure would return as my mind and training took over. From that time, I controlled my actions, not the enemy. There was a job for me to do and I was going to do it.

CROSSING THE PLYUSSA: July 21–August 17, 1941

Following a two-week pause to regroup, on August 8 the German offensive was resumed. In an effort to reach Narva and shut the corridor to the Baltic region, our 154th Regiment had pushed about ten miles north of Niso to the junction of the Plyussa and Pyata Rivers. At this point, roughly four miles south of the Estonian capital, a destroyed bridge across the Plyussa on the main road to Narva halted our advance.

Our new assault commenced early on the hot, sunny morning of August 14 with German artillery pounding the Soviet positions across the river. With enemy resistance reduced, infantry from our regiment began crossing the river on rubber rafts about 50 yards to the right of the ruined bridge.

Though lacking specific orders in my still sporadic role as F.O., I decided to tag along with a group of infantry troops heading up to the Plyussa River in order to get into the action. Just as we reached the river about nine o'clock that morning, the air around us suddenly filled with the shriek of incoming artillery fire. Reacting instantly, I darted to the left of the blown bridge, seeking cover in one of the many foxholes dug into the riverbank.

The entire area was soon inundated with a storm of shells. With some landing as close as a few feet away from my position, it was impossible even to stick my head above ground. There was nothing to do but to press myself into the bottom of the foxhole. When shelling is that heavy and that close, you simply hope the enemy gunners do not manage to land a direct hit that will turn your refuge into a grave.

A couple of hours into the barrage, a brief pause in the whistle of incoming shells allowed me to poke my head up to see how the dozen or so men around me had fared. In the foxhole just a couple of feet to the left of me, I witnessed a bizarre sight. Second Lt. Münstermann, the commander of one of our company's platoons, sat reading a book as if he were on a park bench, completely oblivious to the shelling.

It was apparent to me that he was suffering the effects of shell shock brought on by the intense barrage, but there was nothing I could do for him. To my knowledge, the German Army did not even recognize such trauma as a legitimate medical condition that would justify a soldier's removal from combat. My scrutiny of Münstermann lasted only seconds before more artillery rounds came screaming into our area, forcing me to retreat back down into my hole.

When the shelling finally slowed about five hours after it had started, Münstermann had disappeared. I decided to cross the Plyussa River in order to seek out my company and obtain new orders. Climbing out of my foxhole, I joined other soldiers who were making a crouched dash to the position about 50 yards to the right of the bridge where our troops had resumed crossing. Squeezing onto an infantry squad's raft, I headed for the opposite shore perhaps 30 yards away.

There was shooting all around us as we gained the far side. Leaving the infantry, I cautiously crept back along the riverbank toward the wrecked bridge and crossed the dirt road to the lefthand side, keeping my new MP-40 submachine gun constantly at the ready. Inaccurate beyond any distance greater than about 50 feet, the fire of the MP-40 resembled that of a shotgun more than a rifle. Though it was the standard weapon for a forward observer, I would have preferred to retain my Mauser.

Moving forward from the riverbank, I kept to the brush and trees parallel to the road on my right. Perhaps 150 yards from the river, an enemy bunker built of wooden logs appeared just ahead of me on the edge of the road. The Soviet troops inside were blazing away in the direction of German troops to my rear.

While lacking any means to communicate with our company's heavy guns, it was clear to me that our advance would be slowed until the bunker was eliminated. With the attention of the Russians focused on the road, there was a chance for me to destroy the fortification on my own, if I could get close enough to use one of the three or four grenades that I carried.

Moving out 20 yards from the road into the brush, I began working my way around to the side of the bunker. Just as I reached a position at a right angle to the structure and started crawling toward it on my belly, the gunner inside must have spied the swaying of the grass to his right.

As he swung his weapon in my direction, I flattened my body into the ground. At the same instant, the machine gun began spraying a fire that passed only a little above my head and back. Even with my body pressed against the earth, I felt one of the bullets literally rip the fabric of my uniform. Expecting to be killed any second, a wave of terror ran through me.

All of a sudden, the gunner shifted his weapon back to the road, perhaps believing me already dead. A minute passed with no further fire in my direction. Still lying on the ground, I lifted my head up. The bunker's gun portal was only 10 or 15 yards away. A quick sprint might just give me time to reach a secure location at the side of the fortification, allowing me to toss a hand grenade through the gun portal.

Yet even with my adrenalin pumping, my brain told me that I would be cut down before I could obtain a position safely out of the line of fire. Lacking any other options, I began to slide slowly backward, hoping my movement would not draw any further attention from the gunner inside.

My stealthy retreat had carried me only a short distance from the bunker when two deafening back-to-back booms resounded. Looking up, I watched with amazement as the bunker's logs rose briefly into the air before crashing back to earth in a pile of debris. It seemed almost miraculous. The mysterious source of my salvation was revealed when I saw one of our 75-millimeter howitzers deployed in the middle of the road back near the river.

Afterward, one of the gun crew explained that soldiers from my company had managed to bring the gun over the river and haul it up the road by hand immediately after the Soviet barrage had ended. Spotting the enemy bunker, the gun crew packed extra explosive charges inside the shell casings to increase the velocity of the rounds. At a range of less than 200 yards, the shots simply annihilated the target—and may have saved my life.

Later that day, I linked up with the rest of my company. With no clear frontline, it was very difficult for our heavy weapons company to provide effective support to the infantry. The Russians attempted to counterattack our bridgehead on the north bank of the Plyussa for three days before pulling back eastward toward Leningrad.

Casualties had been high for both sides. Despite the losses, however, we remained optimistic. None of us had expected that the days of easy advances would last. Now, we steeled ourselves for more bloody fighting.

VICTORY IN REACH
August 18–mid-September, 1941

The Plyussa River crossing opened the way to Narva. By the time the 58th Division reached the city on August 18 the fighting had largely ended, enabling us to move eastward down the main highway toward Kingisepp the next day. Another month of often vicious combat with the Red Army lay ahead of us before our campaign would reach its goal.

The capture of the area around Narva largely sealed the main corridor through which Red Army forces had been retreating from the Baltic states, and secured the German rear for a renewed offensive to the east. Moving close to the Baltic Sea coast, our division and the 1st Division would continue to serve as the left flank of Army Group North. Our ultimate objective was the seizure of the metropolis of Leningrad, the former Russian capital which was second only to Moscow in strategic importance.

Despite the threats to our flanks along the highway running between Narva and Kingisepp, our regiment made rapid progress and soon came to a heavily fortified line of bunkers and minefields located along the old Russo-Estonian border before the summer of 1940. With our company providing fire support, the regimental infantry quickly smashed through the barrier in a series of sharp, intense engagements.

Behind this defensive barrier lay the town of Kingisepp, located about a dozen miles due east of Narva. While the 154th Regiment approached it on the main highway from the west, other elements of the 58th Division and the 1st Division had advanced from the south and were already engaged in combat in the town. When our regiment arrived we briefly experienced our first street fighting with Red Army units, though it took place among widely spread houses rather than inside a built-up area.

Because our regimental infantry needed direct fire support in its urban combat operations, our company brought its 75-millimeter howitzers to within a few hundred yards of the front, much closer than their normal position at least half a mile in the rear. Unlike the much heavier 150-millimeter gun, the 75-millimeter howitzer could be maneuvered a short distance by its five-man gun crew, making it practical for use in urban combat conditions. Yet, even these smaller guns were relatively cumbersome and could not move nearly as swiftly as the infantry. While troops could quickly retreat or jump into a foxhole, our guns were very vulnerable out in the open.

When the gun crews could directly sight their targets, there was little or no role for either a forward observer or our communications support. Despite lacking a clear assignment, I headed up to the frontline on my own initiative. As was often the case in the middle of a battle, I was not sure where the other members of the communications platoon were. It was simply my nature to find out what was happening on the frontlines and seek to play some active part in the fight. Reaching our gun crew on the outskirts of Kingisepp, I watched as they systematically destroyed enemy strong points ahead of us.

Even with the risks to our guns in such circumstances, it was the infantry companies that always suffered the worst of the fighting, especially in house-to-house combat. With relatively limited opportunities for support from our heavy guns, they advanced through a chaos of numerous large and small engagements in which enemy attacks might come from any direction. By the time we finished eliminating the last pockets of Russian resistance on August 20, we had claimed a town in which many homes were only flattened rubble.

Following three days of desperate Soviet counterattacks at Kingisepp, our division set out on the final leg of our advance on August 23. On reaching the town of Alekseevka about six miles east of Kingisepp, we encountered more determined enemy resistance. The heavy fighting continued over the following days as the Red Army bitterly contested every mile of our push northward. By August 29, we had finally reached Kotly, roughly eight miles north of Alekseevka, while other elements of the division held Vel'kota, four miles further east.

On September 1, we captured Koporye, located about nine miles east-northeast of Vel'kota. From here it was possible to see the waters of the Gulf of Finland in the distance. Three days later we arrived at Nikol'skoye, another 12 miles further east. Another several days of severe clashes followed as we passed through a wooded region. Exiting the forest on September 6, we reached Djatlicy, located another dozen miles east of Nikol'skoye.

Though this brought us back onto a main highway, intense Soviet resistance limited our progress to about 3 miles a day over the next week. Each of the three regiments of the 58th Infantry Division were assigned different objectives. While the 220th Regiment would move directly down the main highway toward Krasnoye Selo, the 209th Regiment would capture Dudergof a couple of miles to the south, and our regiment would seize Finskoye Koyrovo and Kamen, located three or four miles to the northeast. Gaining control of this region by September 14, our division was now positioned to push into Leningrad, the center of which lay about a dozen miles north.

As we advanced in mild fall weather, the Red Army opposition ahead of us appeared to diminish, though enemy shelling continued. On one day, projectiles the size of a small car were visible overhead as they raced through the sky toward our rear with a loud "whoosh." A thunderous boom behind us would immediately be followed by the quaking of the earth under our feet, despite a distance of several miles between our location and the point of impact. A little later we learned that these massive rounds were fired from the battleship *Red October* anchored out in the Gulf of Finland.

Late in the afternoon of September 15 our company passed through Uritsk, which appeared to be just another typical Russian village of small wooden cottages. Only when we reached the shore of the Gulf of Finland did I realize our location. Just seven or eight miles away, central Leningrad's high-rises and tall smokestacks stood silhouetted against the horizon. While feeling no sense of euphoria in the midst of combat, we had every expectation that the capture of the city and victory over Russia were within reach.

As we moved up the street that ran along the Gulf, Soviet ships were still passing in and out of the harbor on the horizon, apparently oblivious to our presence. Even more oddly, an empty trolley from Leningrad passed down the street headed in the opposite direction. Later, we heard that the lead elements of our division had actually encountered the streetcar as it carried a group of Russian passengers unaware of the German arrival. Climbing aboard, the troops politely requested the civilians to exit the vehicle for their own safety as they secured the area.

During a temporary halt the following day, a group of us examined a number of abandoned Russian artillery pieces which had been positioned on high ground overlooking the Gulf. With Soviet ships continuing to cruise through the waters a couple of miles away, we decided to try our luck firing a long-barreled gun with about a 4-inch diameter muzzle that appeared to have the necessary range.

Aligning the barrel by sight in the approximate direction of our selected target, we stuck a round into the chamber and carefully yanked its lanyard. Out in the Gulf, water splashed up in the air beside a freighter without causing any damage. We never succeeded in hitting anything with the half dozen or so shells we fired, but the experience provided my one chance to claim participation in a naval battle.

Resuming the advance soon afterward, we fought our way forward into the streets of Leningrad's suburbs, past blocks of two- or three-story wooden buildings, meeting only intermittently stiff resistance from the Red Army.

After advancing a mile or two farther through the streets, we received orders to halt and pull back from the city into a more defensible position back at Uritsk. Because of our trust in our high command, we believed that they must have had a good tactical reason for such a decision. Many of us expected that this halt was a temporary measure to allow us to regroup before the resumption of our offensive with a coordinated attack. There was no indication that our effort to capture Leningrad by direct assault was at an end.

A few days later, we learned with some frustration that Hitler had ordered a siege of the city rather than an attempt to take it by storm. By this time, the Wehrmacht had completely isolated Leningrad from the remainder of the Soviet Union, except for a water route across Lake Ladoga, so it appeared that its surrender would nonetheless only be a matter of time.

While our heavy weapons company of about 300 personnel had lost perhaps 10 to 15 men over the proceeding three months, the toll of almost daily combat had been far more costly for most of our regular infantry companies. From their initial strength of about 180 troops they had typically been reduced to a force of between 50 to 75 men.

In spite of the tremendous casualties, our high morale and the much worse state of the Red Army at this time left no question in our minds that if given the chance we could have reached the center of Leningrad within days. In retrospect, it is uncertain whether we possessed adequate strength to capture the city with the available forces, but the failure to even attempt a direct assault would prove to be one of Hitler's greatest mistakes.

CHAPTER 8

WINTER AT URITSK

SETTLING INTO THE SIEGE
September–November 1941

The commencement of the siege coincided with the transfer of most of Army Group North's armored formations to the central front where they would participate in the final offensive against Moscow. Given a respite at Leningrad, the Russians regrouped their forces and began to organize counterattacks designed to break our grip on the city.

On October 8, the Red Army staged an infantry-supported tank offensive against our position at Uritsk with about 50 armored vehicles, including a number of heavily armored KV-1 and KV-2 tanks which had arrived directly from their factory inside Leningrad. Simultaneously, the enemy staged an amphibious landing about 10 miles to the west of us at Petergof.

By the time the Soviet armored assault reached our frontline, a mile or so from their starting point, German anti-tank guns and infantry had wiped out much of the attacking force. However, several of the massive vehicles successfully penetrated our defenses and advanced into Uritsk along the *Uferstrasse* (Shoreline Street) that ran between a cliff and the water's edge on the Gulf of Finland.

Operating as the F.O. in one of the frontline bunkers of our still incomplete defenses, I heard the sound of heavy fighting about a quarter of a mile away. With my habitual curiosity, I sought a position on the cliff from where I could witness the battle play out 50 yards below. Just after reaching my observation point, a battery comprised of two

German 88-millimeter Flak guns deployed on the high ground beside me. Though capable of indirect fire, the 88s were also designed to fire level, like giant rifles.

Seven KV-1s and KV-2s soon lumbered into view with troops on foot following close behind them. These larger tanks were joined by a couple of smaller Czech T-35s. Having reached a point two miles from their frontlines, the greatly diminished Soviet armored formation would advance no further.

As I watched with fascination, the crews manning the 88s quickly scored a hit on the lead tank. Unable to maneuver or to elevate their barrels high enough to hit targets on top of the cliff, the remaining Russian armor was in a helpless and hopeless position. Over the next 20 minutes, the deadly 88s proceeded to pick off one after another of the KV's and T-35's trapped on the street below.

Under continual machine-gun fire, the surviving tank crews and infantry attempted to escape back the way they had come, but found their route blocked. In an area just beyond my field of vision, our *Pioniers* had moved in behind them to detonate large explosives that destroyed the road, preventing their retreat.

In desperation, many of the enemy troops jumped into the water, but few succeeded in making it back to their lines. By the following day, the remaining Soviet forces in the Uritsk and Petergof areas were eliminated. This ill-conceived fiasco had cost the Red Army 35 tanks, 1,369 dead, and 294 prisoners.

Over time, the Russians would increasingly employ large tank formations in their operations. To meet this threat, a German division had a number of options. In the first instance, each regiment possessed an anti-tank company equipped with high velocity artillery pieces. While these companies were usually able to cope with enemy armor, the divisional artillery might also be used in extreme cases.

As the action on the *Uferstrasse* demonstrated, it was, however, the 88-millimeter anti-aircraft artillery that proved to be the most effective German anti-tank weapon of the war, even though it was typically used only in crisis situations when enemy armor came in mass or had achieved a breakthrough in our lines.

During a quiet interval soon after the tank attack, Staff Sergeant Ehlert led a small group of us from the communications platoon on an excursion to the recently captured tsarist-era palace at Petergof, near where the Red Army had just attempted their amphibious landing. At that time, the palace and the grounds around it still appeared untouched by fighting.

Inside, we strolled down the paneled wood floors through its long elegant halls, now mostly emptied of furnishings. Coming across a piano in one of the rooms, Ehlert pulled up the bench and began to play. Unaware of his talent, we were amazed as beautiful classical music began to echo around us in the chamber. As the afternoon sun streamed into the room through the large windows, it was almost possible for me to imagine the tsar playing the same piano surrounded by his family and court.

At the end of his virtuoso performance, Ehlert opened the piano and found several pages of sheet music deposited inside. After displaying his discovery, he folded a couple of sheets into the pocket of his tunic as a souvenir. Back on the frontlines a short time later, such opulence seemed much farther away than the few miles that separated us.

Having been promoted to the rank of lance corporal (*Obergefreiter*) on October 1, I was now permanently tasked to serve as our company's forward observer, which meant increased interaction with the company commander. At the beginning of November, First Lt. Von Kempski, who had earned our respect leading us since Belgium, was promoted to the divisional staff. He was replaced by Second Lt. Münstermann, who had fortunately suffered no lasting ill effects from the artillery barrage at the Plyussa.

By mid-October, a frost had already hardened the landscape and it began to snow. At about this same time, we were able to shift out of temporary shelters into our more permanent rear bunkers constructed jointly by the regular troops and our *Pioniers*. Whereas the bunkers along the front provided us with additional protection and acted as defensive strongpoints, our rear bunkers would serve as our living quarters in Uritsk.

In building our rear bunkers the *Pioniers* followed a standard method of construction. After digging out waist-deep holes between 10 to 50 square feet in size, they erected log walls and heaped part of the just excavated soil against them. Following the placement of heavy timber beams or tree trunks to serve as a roof, they then covered the top of the bunker with the remaining soil. Despite offering little protection in the event of a direct hit by the Red Army's heavy artillery, the bunkers offered us a measure of warmth from the freezing temperatures outside.

At Uritsk, my assignment as the F.O. required me to spend perhaps three-quarters of my time in one of the various bunkers located along the front or even out ahead of our infantry's frontline. In contrast with the rear bunkers, the frontline bunker was little more than a covered ditch with a slot for observation. As the snow grew deeper, we piled it into a wall that ran in front of our line of forward bunkers and trenches in order to conceal our movements from enemy observation.

If it was quiet at the front, I normally made the short trip back to my rear bunker a couple of times a day. Furnished with only a dirt floor and walls, bunks, a table, and a wood-burning stove, the rear bunkers were primitive but made a comfortable dwelling for four to six men. Because the 13th Company's howitzers were located only a quarter of a mile further back, my friends Schütte and Sauke, who were both now serving in gun crews, were able to reside with me and another comrade in the same bunker. Asserting our veteran status in the company, we posted a sign reading "The Four Old Sacks" over its entrance. Naturally, we tended to spend most of our free time with the half dozen or so other comrades we had known from the Lüneburg barracks.

Especially when there was little fighting, our bunker was a refuge for us to relax, sleep, eat hot meals, play cards, read mail, and write letters. Such a sanctuary gave us an essential escape from the stress of combat and the exhausting vigilance required at the frontline.

In November 1941, just after we had settled into our new bunkers, we began to confront bitterly freezing temperatures of minus 40 degrees Fahrenheit. This was far colder than any conditions we had ever experienced in Germany.

In the harsh months that followed, the wounded on both sides sometimes froze to death where they fell before they could be transported back behind the lines for medical care. By my estimation, the cold weather that first winter in Russia was responsible for perhaps a third of the deaths among casualties who might otherwise have survived. Of course, this type of death was even more common in mobile warfare such as that taking place on Army Group Center's front as it engaged in the Battle of Moscow far to the south of us.

The temperature dropped so low that it actually caused the grease in our weapons to freeze unless we fired them regularly or took measures to protect them from the cold. Other soldiers told me that they witnessed entire steam engines that had been frozen solid down to the grease in their wheels. The weather-related problems in the transportation network intermittently resulted in supply problems that occasionally forced the army to reduce our rations to half a loaf of bread per day. Though only providing enough for us to survive, we knew it was far more than the amount supplied to the cut-off Russian population in Leningrad.

Transportation problems and inadequate planning also led to a four- to six-week delay in the provision of warmer clothing to replace our summer uniforms. As a F.O. operating on the frontline, I needed winter camouflage and was therefore lucky to be one of the first to receive an army-issued white helmet, a white poncho, white coat, and white pants as the most extreme cold arrived.

As the snow grew to a foot in depth, it became much easier to travel by ski than on foot when I crossed the couple of hundred yards between the forward and rear bunkers. More importantly, skis allowed me to move much more swiftly across the open area that was exposed to the fire of Russian snipers.

These sharpshooters had been posted in large numbers among the multi-story buildings at the edge of Leningrad's suburbs, approximately a mile away from our front line at Uritsk. This situation reflected the Red Army's effort throughout the war to field larger numbers of better-equipped, well-trained snipers than the Wehrmacht. Our snipers considered the Soviet scoped rifles superior and preferred to use captured Russian weapons rather than the equivalent German rifle. When I once had the opportunity to test one, its precision amazed me.

The accuracy of sniper fire meant that the number of killed relative to wounded was much higher than with other weapons. Our helmets protected us pretty well from glancing bullets or shrapnel, but if a bullet hit one squarely it would easily penetrate the steel. Being six feet tall, I soon learned to keep my head down and travel quickly through any area where I might be vulnerable.

While snipers posed a great threat to us, most of our casualties at Uritsk resulted from the enemy's regular artillery barrages. The Red Army's artillery was highly accurate and equal to its German counterpart in capability.

Russian machine guns were another danger. They mostly utilized ammunition that exploded on impact, causing a lot of damage. Sometimes their machine-gun position could be a mile away, but it would feel very close when its bullets ripped up everything in the vicinity of one's position. Unlike artillery shells, you cannot interpret and react to the whistle of a machine gun's bullet. If you hear the bullet whistling past you, you are safe. If you do not hear it, you are wounded or dead.

Everyone feared frostbite and hypothermia as much as Soviet weapons. Skiing between the front and rear bunkers helped minimize my exposure to the subfreezing temperatures, but frostbite still posed a danger. Arriving back at our rear bunker one day, I realized that there was no feeling in my toes. When my boots were off, I discovered that my toes had become white and completely lacked sensation.

Though soldiers had been warned not to treat frostbite with hot water, I thought cold water would be safe to apply. Going outside, I slowly poured cold water over my feet as I massaged my toes. The pain was excruciating, but the blood gradually began to circulate again after about twenty minutes. Many less fortunate soldiers lost toes and fingers to frostbite. It was sobering for me to think that another couple of hours of exposure to the cold could have meant amputation for mine.

Returning from a long period of duty up at the front on another evening soon after the close call with frostbite, I entered the bunker to find my comrades engaged in a festive drinking party. On learning where we were stationed, one of our old comrades from another division had come to see us. Such an occasion was cause for celebration and the "old sacks" had warmly welcomed him with our stock of cognac.

By the time of my arrival an hour or two later, they had already consumed a half dozen shots. Demanding that I catch up, they ordered, "Lübbecke, we had six cognacs. You will have six cognacs and the seventh we'll drink together." By the sixth shot, I was already stone drunk. Waking late the next morning, we paid for our temporary escape from the war with aching heads.

TRENCH WARFARE: November–March 1942

When operating as a forward observer, a communications specialist would assist me since my skill with Morse code was limited. He would wire the targeting information to the gun crews located about a mile back from our bunker. When I called out, "Five more!" to indicate a correction of five meters forward or "Ten right!" to shift the aim point ten meters to the right, he would rapidly tap the instructions to the rear.

If we held a particular position for more than a day as at Uritsk, our company would typically establish a field telephone link to our bunker. These field telephone links were as secure as telegraph lines and allowed me to communicate my instructions directly to the gun crews. While also possessing radios, these were rarely employed because of their vulnerability to Russian interception.

When moving into a new position, I would carefully survey the terrain to our front against a map in order to determine the most probable path of a potential Red Army attack. After identifying a likely route of advance, I would request one of our gun crews to fire a single ranging shot at those map coordinates. About 85 percent of the time, the shell would fall where intended. If it did not, the second round would almost always confirm the range.

Following the verification of the coordinates, I would instruct the gun crew to retain that target as Position A in order to allow for a more rapid reaction from our guns if an attack was attempted. Repeating the procedure at other probable routes of advance, we would establish Position B, Position C, etc. At others times I used first names instead of letters to identify a preset target.

Once the process was complete, I could simply call back, "Position A: five rounds, two guns." Of course, when the enemy fired a single shot, we recognized that the Soviets were establishing their own network of predetermined firing coordinates. Before long, the whole area of No Man's Land between us became one large pre-targeted kill zone.

The primary responsibility of a F.O. in a static position is to remain vigilant for any changes in the enemy's frontline that might indicate an impending attack and to alert the company commander of any developments. If possible, it was also crucial to provide the gun crews with an advance warning to prepare the howitzers for action so that they could respond rapidly to any request for a fire mission.

In relatively active environments like Uritsk, it would typically take about two minutes for the gun crews to ready the guns and deliver a salvo if I was unable to alert them in advance before issuing target coordinates. Where the fighting was more intermittent, gun crews often remained in their bunkers rather than with their guns. In these circumstances, it might take up to four minutes for the crews to man their batteries and deliver the first shell. If the firing had commenced or the crews had received advanced warning, rounds would usually arrive on the target within a half minute or less of my request.

Once the enemy's attack is under way, the forward observer must simultaneously select the number and types of guns and rounds to employ and precisely orchestrate their firing so as to break up the assault swiftly and efficiently. Though it was very technical in some respects, it was as much an art as a science.

During larger battles, both sides also conducted intense but brief artillery barrages to soften up enemy positions. In contrast to the First World War, where shelling of entrenchments might last for days or weeks, artillery in battles on the Eastern Front fired smaller caliber rounds and expended many fewer shells. Normally, these bombardments lasted for perhaps 20 minutes, though they might occasionally persist for an hour. As long as this pounding continued, a soldier could remain under cover in his trench or bunker.

As soon as the barrage began to roll back toward the rear areas, it was critical to get rapidly into position to defend against the infantry assault that would immediately ensue. Larger enemy attacks put pressure on our front, but we typically pushed them back before they penetrated our lines. In some instances, the Russian assaults reached our frontlines and forced us to retreat, but we usually staged a quick counterattack with the help of reserves and regained the lost ground. Because we generally had good intelligence on Soviet dispositions at

Uritsk, the Red Army rarely achieved surprise.

Over this period of stationary warfare in front of Leningrad, the numbers of the German and Russian forces were about equal, though the enemy lacked our training, experience, and leadership. Both sides constantly engaged in numerous smaller reconnaissance missions and larger probing attacks in order to test the other's defenses as well as to gain intelligence through the capture of prisoners. As the F.O., I remained constantly alert for any Russian attempt to infiltrate small groups of men into our lines for this purpose.

If I observed Red Army troops out in the open, I would immediately inform the rear and try to place a curtain of shells in front of them in order to deter any further advance. Our heavy guns had a great advantage over machine guns in that they possessed the range to take the enemy under fire much farther back. If we had to use our machine guns in such an engagement, it meant that they had gotten too close to our lines.

When German troops staged reconnaissance and probing operations into the Soviet lines, we kept our guns on call in case our men needed covering fire as they retreated. In addition to seeking prisoners and assessing Soviet strength, such missions also helped to draw Russian artillery fire, allowing us to determine their positions. Using a network of listening devices, a special unit would triangulate their location for our artillery to target highly accurate counterbattery fire. It was a deadly game of cat and mouse.

Soon after Christmas, Schütte began to complain to me that he was bored with the monotony of his routine with the gun crew. One subfreezing night, he decided to take action and snuck alone across the snow-covered No Man's Land that separated us from the enemy. Armed only with his MP-40 submachine gun and a satchel containing a kilo of dynamite, Schütte slipped past the Soviet sentries and crept up to a Red Army bunker. As he heaved the satchel inside, he shouted to the doomed Russians, "Here's your bread!"

Fighting his own war, he pulled off this crazy feat at least a couple of times. On the second occasion, I even heard the sound of the dynamite's explosion. What had begun as an unauthorized action soon won the approval of our superiors. On my and their recommendation, Schütte was later awarded one of Germany's highest military decorations, the Gold Cross.

The critical food shortage in Leningrad that inspired Schütte's black humor also led to more serious discussions among us. There was real concern that the Russian authorities might decide to send the city's women and children across the lines to our side. It was not clear what would ensue in such a situation, but everyone agreed that mowing down a crowd of civilians with our weapons was inconceivable. My own inclination was to feed them and then send them further back, once we made certain that the enemy had not exploited such a population transfer to slip military-age males into our rear areas.

About this time, our intelligence learned that the Red Army was infiltrating dogs across the lines. These poor animals had been strapped with dynamite around their bodies and trained to run under our vehicles. When they did so, the triggering antennas on their backs would bend and detonate the explosive.

Though there were probably few dogs actually armed this way, the army directed us to shoot all dogs as a precautionary measure. Carrying out these orders was especially painful for us, but we obeyed. Over time, war hardens your heart and leads you to do brutal things that you could never have imagined yourself doing in civilian life.

In early 1942, a reporter from a German-language newspaper in Reval in Estonia came up to the frontline to do interviews with the troops. When he asked me if they could take my photograph, I willingly agreed. To my surprise, that picture eventually ended up on the front page of *The Revaler Zeitung* on April 2, 1942 above the caption, "This is the German soldier who you will find in the trenches, young, agile, and sure of victory." Though it was amusing to be featured in such heroic terms, the words accurately reflected the high morale that we felt.

At the beginning of March, Army Group North ordered our division to make urgent preparations for redeployment. A couple of nights later, we pulled out of the trenches. Our replacements were a police division composed of police officers who had volunteered for the unit and a Waffen SS division filled with troops from Nordic countries like Sweden, Norway, and Denmark.

Because many of these Scandinavians were tall men, their heads frequently poked above the snow walls in front of our trenches, making them especially easy prey for Soviet marksmen. Before we departed Uritsk, we heard they had suffered perhaps a dozen such casualties in just their first day at the frontline. Following this cruel lesson, they too would respect the Russian snipers.

By the time of our departure from Uritsk, confidence in an early victory had faded. It was already clear that the war in Russia would be a long struggle. Nonetheless, I remained utterly certain of the Soviet Union's ultimate defeat as we departed for our new mission.

BEHIND THE FRONT

Uritsk was a battle zone largely deserted of inhabitants, but it still retained a small population of about 100 Russian civilians, mostly women and children. These few residents kept their distance, but were not visibly hostile in their behavior. Curious to gain my own impression of the Russian people, I decided to pay a visit to one of these families.

Inside their small, clean home, we somehow managed to communicate in a limited fashion through gestures with our hands and feet. Yet, while the brief encounter perhaps somewhat humanized the Russians for me, their true emotions toward me and the German presence in their land appeared hidden behind a mask of inscrutability.

There was one Russian girl as well as a couple of Soviet POWs who worked in the company kitchen, located back about two miles behind the front. Not surprisingly, the girl became involved in a romantic relationship with one of the German kitchen staff. Military regulations prohibited such fraternization with the enemy, particularly out of concern that they might be spies.

Although this was the only truly romantic liaison of which I had firsthand knowledge, there were other German troops in my regiment who exploited the dire Russian food situation for sexual gratification. Putting a loaf of bread under their arm, these men would head for a certain area a couple of miles behind the front where there were hungry Russian women or girls who would willingly exchange sexual favors for food.

One tale circulated that a particularly heartless soldier had responded to a woman's request for her "payment" of a loaf by slicing off a couple of pieces for her while retaining the remainder for himself. Most German officers and troops disapproved of such behavior, but I knew of no one who was reprimanded or punished for engaging in this type of act.

What was more difficult to explain was the widespread absence of a strong urge to have sexual relations with women as would be normal among a group of young males. Naturally, the rumor mill provided an answer: our cooks were under secret orders to mix an agent into our food that chemically suppressed our sex drives. While it might make sense for the high command to take such a radical step given the general lack of women at the front, the true explanation for our low libidos remained a mystery.

Generally, our own food supplies in Russia remained constant throughout the war, once the crisis of the first winter had passed. During heavy combat or when on the move, our company's quartermaster supplied only canned goods like tuna, sardines, herring, or sausage with canned crackers or bread which we kept in our *Brotbeutel* (food bag) on the side of our belts.

When we were engaged in stationary warfare, troops from the *Tross* would come forward at night to deliver food and mail up to the bunkers. Typically, they brought an insulated kettle of hot soup from our company field kitchen containing a generous ration of beef or pork and potatoes, or perhaps sausage for dinner.

They also left us with a small round loaf of brown bread from the large divisional bakery and butter, or occasionally cheese, to eat the following morning. Frequently, the quartermaster also provided us with chocolate. Since real coffee was rare, we ordinarily drank a fairly tasty artificial coffee which we called *Mukefuk*, made from roasted grain.

Troops rarely went hungry, but our diet quickly grew monotonous. In certain circumstances, the army provided us with additional items that helped break the routine of army food. In the winter, we received a regular ration of a couple of small bottles of vodka to help us keep warm. At Christmas and Easter, they sometimes issued a bottle of cognac that would last for three or four days. Patients recuperating in the rear from injury or illness frequently enjoyed better foods like a roast of beef or pork, a chicken, or boiled sausage.

Studio portrait taken during basic training in Lüneburg, Germany in 1939, shortly after conscription into the German Army.

Swearing the Wehrmacht loyalty oath in Lüneburg on September 2, 1939, the day after Germany's invasion of Poland.

Visiting my family in Püggen early in 1940.

Above: Pushing for a win in Verviers, Belgium, at the end of the 154th Regiment's 400-meter race in summer 1940.

Left: Practicing with a radio as part of my training with the communications platoon during fall 1939.

Below: A crater made by a shell from the Russian battleship *Red October*.

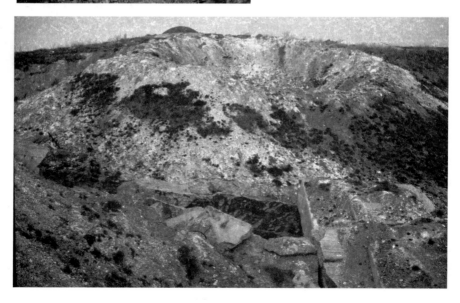

Our company's march through the Baltic region toward Leiningrad in the summer of 1941. I am pictured to the left rear of our company commander, Oberleutnant Von Kempski.

Below, left: A photograph from Uritsk used on the front page of a German-language newspaper in Reval, Latvia, dated April 2, 1942. The caption reads, "This is the German soldier who you will find in the trenches: young agile, and sure of victory."

Below, right: Another photo taken in the spring of 1942.

Der deutsche Soldat, wie wir ihn vorn in den Gräben finden: jung, elastisch und siegesgewiss

Left, and with detail above: The "Old Sacks" bunker at Uritsk that I shared with my close comrades Willi Schütte and Willi Sauke.

A crossroads in the late fall of 1941 with a sign pointing to Petersburg (Leningrad).

Below, left: Skiing between the front and my bunker in the rear at Uritsk during the winter of 1941–42. Below, right: Taken at Uritsk after my promotion to *Obergefreiter* (corporal) and my receipt of the Iron Cross Second Class.

Standing between two comrades outside of our bunker at Oranienbaum in the summer of 1942.

Below: My comrades and I celebrate Christmas 1942 in our bunker near Demyansk.

A studio shot taken while on leave from the East in 1942.

Below: Dressed in a padded winter uniform, I am at the entrance to a bunker near Demyansk, Russia, early in 1943.

A respite from the fighting as we find a piano and also discover the hidden talents of some of our comrades.

Anneliese's nursing identifica-
tion card, dated May 1, 1943.

Below: Sitting on a fortification behind a 105-millimeter
mortar in the Lake Ladoga
area durig the summer of
1943.

On leave in Germany during
the spring of 1943, my future
wife Anneliese and I relax
together on a park bench.

Little did I suspect that her
home city of Hamburg would
be devastated months later,
putting her in as much danger
as a frontline soldier.

Above: Operating as a forward observer in 1942, I am carryig my MP-40 submachine gun and wearing a pair of binoculars.

Right: Sitting along the shore of Lake Ilmen outside of Novgorod in the fall of 1942.

Striking a rather proud pose after receiving the Iron Cross First Class.

Above: A 105mm artillery piece pulls through a Russian town already devastated by fire.

Left: A comrade at Demyansk displays his scoped rifle during the winter of 1942–43.

One of our 75mm howitzers in action on the open steppe.

A field command post on the Ladoga front in 1943.

A mortar platoon of my heavy weapons company. The so-called "spit and polish" of the Wehrmacht was not always evident on the frontline.

One of my heavy weapons company's 75-millimeter light infantry howitzers in the Lake Ladoga area during the summer of 1943.

Our company on the move sometime during 1943.

Standing next to my bunker near Narva, Estonia in 1944 as a newly-minted *Leutnant*.

Below: Petting my horse Thea during a peaceful moment in the Düna region of Lativa in the late summer of 1944.

Below: Awarding decorations to several men in my company during our retreat through Latvia in 1944.

A studio portrait taken while on leave in early 1944.

Below: One of our 105mm pieces during the retreat through the Baltic region.

Below: With several men at Narva, Estonia in May 1944, just after becoming company commander following my return to the Eastern Front.

Getting a haircut in the field. This was slightly less painful than the dental work, performed under similar circumstances.

One of the more important tasks for a soldier in the East: dealing with the ubiquitous lice.

Just after my marriage to Anneliese at a ceremony in Hamburg on December 22, 1945.

A studio portrait of Anneliese and I from 1946. Though it was a difficult year for all of Germany, we managed to maintain our hopes for a better future.

Above: Outside our home in
Cleveland, Ohio in 1967, Anneliese
and I are pictured with our oldest
son, Harold, our daughter, Marion,
and our youngest son, Ralph.

Right: Anneliese and I at a northern
Ohio Oktoberfest in 1980.

Below: At the Aberdeen Proving
Ground museum in Maryland in
2003, I am standing behind one of
our 75-millimeter pieces.

Even if my closest comrades and I were somehow able to acquire potatoes or meat to supplement our rations, we lacked the means to cook such items. In these instances, we would pass along the potatoes or other foods obtained outside of normal quartermaster channels to our company cooks to prepare.

On a few rare occasions, we were lucky enough to find something to eat that did not require any preparation. Although most Russian houses had burned down, we once discovered a barrel of sour pickled tomatoes in an abandoned home that provided us with a rare treat that lasted for several days.

Once the war became stationary, the issue of sanitation grew increasingly important, so building latrines was one of the first priorities. These *Donnerbalken* (literally, thunder-beams) were simply wooden planks on which the soldier could sit with holes dug into the ground beneath them.

In certain ways, our position in the outskirts of a city had its advantages in that some of the troops could find more satisfactory shelter. There were even toilets in a few of the three-story wooden buildings in Uritsk that offered a small measure of civilization in the midst of our primitive conditions. However, because the apartments' plumbing was comprised of narrow square wooden channels inside the walls instead of pipes flushed by water, the sound of the waste tumbling down through the structure was audible to anyone in close proximity every time someone used the toilet on one of the upper floors.

Thinking that it would be a pleasant alternative to our latrines, I once made use of the toilet on a visit to that area of the front. The next day, my groin began to itch terribly, leaving me hardly able to function. Unfortunately, the large number of people sharing the toilet had led to the sharing of multiple diseases, including lice in the groin area. Distinctive from the larger head and body lice, an infestation by these nearly invisible groin lice caused much greater irritation.

Embarrassed that my comrades would think that I had visited one of the local Russian women, I attempted to take care of the problem on my own by shaving the area, but the terrible itching persisted. Unable to bear it any longer, I visited the medic and obtained a special ointment. Its application replaced the itchiness with a painful burning sensation, but eliminated the infestation within about a week.

Personal hygiene remained difficult to maintain and very low by today's military standards. Occasionally, we would rig a tub or shower or have access to a lake or river in which to bathe. More often, we would just wash with a little water and a bar of soap once a week or so, if we were not in combat. Lacking a toothbrush, I would squirt toothpaste on my finger to clean my teeth perhaps once or twice a week. There was generally only an opportunity to shave with my straight razor every couple of weeks.

Our basic gray-green German uniform consisted of a denim cotton tunic and pants worn over a cotton undershirt and underwear. In the woods or brush, this easily blended with the background environment, but out in the open steppe where there was no cover, you could not avoid sticking out like a camel silhouetted against a desert horizon.

Over our socks, we wore tight-fitting leather boots with leather soles. These were known as *Knobelbecher*, a term suggestive of the cup that is used to shake dice before they are rolled. While both the boots and uniforms were fairly durable, the divisional quartermasters still had to issue new ones to the enlisted men a couple of times per year as the old ones wore out. In 1941, I was issued riding pants made of a thicker fabric as well as a pair of riding boots that were of higher quality. The German Army required officers to purchase their own uniforms, but provided a clothing allowance as part of their pay package that helped to defray the cost. Officers could also receive fresh uniform items as needed in combat.

Generally comfortable in most climate conditions, our basic uniform was completely inadequate in the subfreezing conditions we confronted at Uritsk. Once the quartermaster finally distributed our thickly padded white uniforms a couple of months into the winter of 1941–1942, they only proved to be barely sufficient to keep us warm in the harsh Russian climate.

With only two uniforms, we laundered our clothes whenever our situation at the front made it possible. Wearing the same clothes and underwear for two or three weeks without changing, soldiers were almost always covered by itchy bites from the ubiquitous body lice, even in the cold of winter. You could feel them and see them crawling around on you. We would strip off our shirts to kill them, but could never rid ourselves of all of them. However, in contrast to the trenches and bunkers during the First World War, we experienced few problems with rats.

In such a stressful environment, it is not surprising that perhaps three quarters of the troops smoked tobacco. Although never smoking cigarettes in my youth, I started soon after the invasion of Russia when the fighting intensified. Because the supply of tobacco in our rations was inadequate to meet the demand, cigarettes became a currency when trading or gambling.

Gambling seemed foolish to me, but I frequently joined the other men in my bunker when they played a "thinking" card game called Skat at night. Our games helped keep me mentally alert in case of a Red Army attack. Like smoking, drinking, gambling, or other forms of relaxation, they also simply provided a temporary means of escape from the tension and tedium of war.

Most of the time we entertained ourselves, but the army provided occasional recreational activities for us behind the lines. Perhaps once every six months, we would even be given a day off from frontline duty, depending on the situation. The main center for recreation in the Leningrad area was Krasnogvardeisk. Though the small city was located just 10 or 15 miles south of Uritsk, I visited it only once for about 24 hours.

While the army organized soccer matches or other sporting events in Krasnogvardeisk where teams from different units would compete, many personnel from all services sought out the temporary companionship of females during their leaves. To meet this need, the army did not establish brothels, but it did bring in German women as "entertainment troops." According to rumor, the Luftwaffe was purported to operate two Junkers transports filled with women from occupied Europe who flew on a regular circuit of its bases to visit the pilots. Not interested in pursuing such liaisons during my visit to Krasnogvardeisk, I instead visited the German cemetery and a local theater presenting comedy routines and musical performances.

While we had lacked radios during our march into Russia, once we took up residence in our bunkers we frequently listened to the soothing *Volkskonzert* and other music programs on German armed forces radio. Sometimes, we would together sing the popular tunes like "Lili Marlene" or "Erika" that reminded us of home and the girls we had left there. At our rare religious services, we sang songs like "*Wir treten zum Beten*" (We Gather Together) and "*Eine feste Burg is unser Gott*" (A Mighty Fortress Is Our God) that provided us with spiritual comfort.

Despite the German Army's standard-issue belt buckles engraved with the phrase "*Gott Mit Uns*" ("God with Us"), religion and an inner spiritual faith never played a big part in most German soldiers' lives during the war. Military chaplains existed at the divisional level, but the troops usually only saw them at infrequent worship services or when they were behind the lines recuperating at a field hospital. Though chaplains sometimes led collective prayers at religious services before big battles, I knew few soldiers who prayed. If faith had played a bigger part in the lives of German soldiers, maybe they would have been more morally conscientious and held life in higher regard.

Despite regulations against it, it was not uncommon for German soldiers to ship looted Russian property such as icons or artifacts back to Germany. Most of the time, however, troops sent back items taken from the battlefield or from captured Red Army troops such as Soviet pistols or decorations. In general, the military authorities closed their eyes to such behavior. In my experience, parcels sent home were not even checked for stolen property.

When a soldier is fighting a thousand miles away from his native soil, mail from home provides a tremendous boost to morale. Because of military censorship, we could not write about our units, where we were, or our battles at the front. At the same time, letters to those back home provided us a momentary release from war's miseries and gave loved ones relief from their constant anxiety over the soldier's fate. Mail from my mother or occasionally another family member arrived at the front about three or four times a month.

By early 1942, the exchange of correspondence between Anneliese and I had increased to two or three times a month. Despite her continued engagement to the florist's son, I felt a growing sense of optimism that I could gradually entice her back to me. While we usually did not discuss her fiancée, she herself had begun expressing doubts about her future with him after becoming aware that he had a drug addiction and other problems. Even though I recognized that she was not yet prepared to break off her relationship with him, the tone of our letters to each other grew steadily more intimate in nature.

Like most soldiers, I read and reread these messages from home and devoted a large portion of my free time to writing letters in reply. In my experience, news from home was one of the most significant factors shaping a soldier's capacity in combat because it determined his state of mind and morale. Throughout the war, these letters were as important to sustaining our souls as food was to sustaining our bodies.

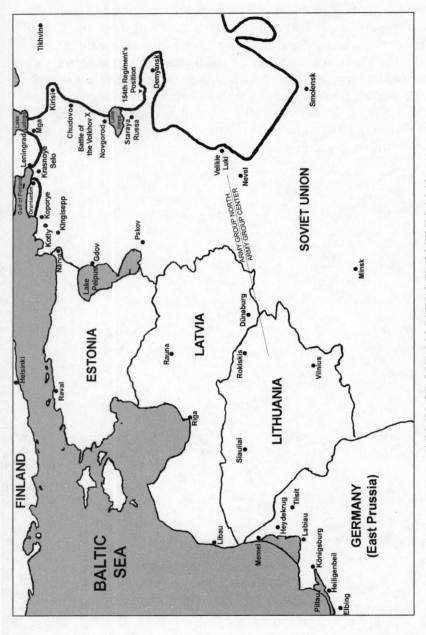

ARMY GROUP NORTH'S FRONT IN 1942

Heavy lines indicate the location of the front in Russia during 1942.

CHAPTER 9

COUNTERATTACK AT THE VOLKHOV

MARCH–AUGUST 1942

IN EARLY DECEMBER 1941, the Red Army staged a large-scale counteroffensive that pushed back the German forces of Army Group Center attempting to capture Moscow. The Russians followed up this counterattack with a number of other operations along the entire front.

On January 13, 1942, the Soviets began a major assault on German positions at the Volkhov River south of Leningrad. Their ambitious objective was to swing behind our forces farther north and break the siege of Leningrad. Within a few days, the attack covered half the distance to Leningrad, but Army Group North overcame the crisis and soon stabilized its front. The German high command then ordered the 58th Infantry Division and other units to the Volkhov front in order to cut off the enemy's offensive spearhead from its rear.

Pulled out of Uritsk in early March, our division's infantry immediately journeyed directly south on trucks. Meanwhile, our company and other heavily equipped units traveled south by train on a circuitous, roughly 200-mile route. Neither group knew that its destination was the Volkhov River; we only knew that we had to halt a Russian breakthrough. Arriving at a rail station south of the fighting, our heavy company reached the battlefield about a week after the infantry.

The German counterattack started on March 15. With temperatures still far below zero Fahrenheit, our infantry and other German forces advanced northward along the western side of the wide Volkhov River. Simultaneously, other German units were moving southward to link up with us and isolate the Soviet spearhead from its main lines to the east. By the time our two pincers met on March 19, we had trapped almost 180,000 Red Army troops in a *Kessel* (pocket).

While the battle raged about a mile distant, our heavy gun company and artillery units trudged through waist-high snow and dense forest to reach the gun position selected by the regiment's *Vorkommando* (advance team). Located on ground that was slightly elevated above the surrounding flat terrain, the wisdom of their choice would become apparent when spring weather arrived and low-lying areas reverted to swamp. As our forward observer, I took up my station beside the infantry on the nearby frontline, operating behind the log fortifications that formed the perimeter around the *Kessel*.

As soon as our howitzers fired the first ranging shot, it was apparent that the many tall trees in this virgin forest would pose problems beyond just obscuring my observation of enemy movement. If one of our shells prematurely collided with a tree on its ascent, its impact would cause the tree to fall or shower splinters that might injure or kill any friendly troops around it. On its descent, meanwhile, a round had to be on a steep enough trajectory to drop unobstructed onto an enemy target moving through the dense woods in the area. To overcome these obstacles, the barrels of the guns were raised to their maximum elevation of about 45 degrees and essentially employed as mortars, which proved modestly effective.

Following their encirclement, the Russian forces reacted rapidly. Even with the Red Army's numerical superiority in troops and tanks, they had to struggle fiercely to break out of the *Kessel*. The main axis of their counterattack breached our lines about half a mile north of my location at the end of another week of intense combat, reestablishing a link to their forces on the eastern side of the Volkhov through a roughly mile-wide corridor.

Using the old logging paths that formed a grid pattern inside this *Schlauch* (land bridge), the still largely isolated Red Army troops could now potentially receive a constant flow of reinforcements and supplies. From top to bottom, the passage contained three main *Schneisen* (logging roads) running east to west that we referred to respectively as *Friedrich Schneise*, *Erika Schneise*, and *Dora Schneise*.

These were intersected at right angles by *West Schneise, Mittel Schneise, Kreipe Schneise*, and *Süd Schneise*.

Once the new lines stabilized, I was about a half mile south of the Dora Schneise. The primary mission of our heavy weapons company was to support our infantry in a defensive capacity. As a secondary task, we also sought to harass the Red Army forces passing through the corridor as well as prevent them from widening the breach. Meanwhile, the combined fire of approximately 120 105-millimeter artillery pieces located on both sides of the corridor plus air strikes by Stuka dive-bombers relentlessly hammered the grid of *Schneisen* that ran through the gap.

Unlike the long lulls in the fighting at Uritsk, the air at the Volkhov was filled day and night with the incessant roar of artillery and the clatter of machine-gun fire.

BATTLING IN A SWAMP: April–June 1942

When the spring thaw arrived in early April, it swiftly turned the whole Volkhov battlefield into a muddy bog. The warmer weather was initially welcomed, but we would soon discover that conducting combat operations in the steamy heat of a swamp was even worse.

Though under constant bombardment from us, the Soviets somehow succeeded in constructing a narrow-gauge railroad track right through the middle of their *Schlauch* within a month's time. Upon its completion, this railroad became our principal target, but the storm of German shells and bombs could only hamper rather than halt movement through it. However, this disruption to the flow of traffic limited the corridor's value to the Russians, especially once the tree cover was obliterated.

During the course of a typical day, my work as F.O. ranged across some 50 yards of the frontline. Occasionally, I directed the fire of our guns on targets moving along the Dora Schneise, but it was very difficult to employ our firepower effectively because of the trees that shielded the enemy's movement. Most of the time our howitzers were focused on the area to our immediate front, leaving the *Schlauch* up to the divisional artillery.

At least once a day, there would be some type of suspicious movement in the brush along the enemy frontline, which in places was only 50 yards across from us. Whenever this occurred, I would urgently request a half dozen to a dozen rounds from our 75-millimeter howitzers. My objective was to prevent a concentration of large numbers of Soviet forces in order to preempt an attack before it began. The infantry around me would then sweep the location with machine-gun fire to eliminate any survivors.

Such massing of Red Army troops occurred relatively infrequently, but we faced a daily threat of infiltration. Scanning the tall grass and brush behind me, I was constantly on guard for enemy troops who might have penetrated our lines singly or in small groups. The persistent danger of an attack from any direction left us on edge and prone to fire at shadows.

In the swampy terrain, it was difficult for us to protect ourselves from enemy fire because we lacked our normal system of trenches and underground bunkers and instead had to operate behind the five-foot-high walls of thickly piled logs that ran along the entire perimeter. Deliveries of food and ammunition from the *Tross* up to the gun positions behind me were made under the cover of darkness to evade Russian observation and fire.

To avoid becoming bogged down in mud, all movement through the area, including foot traffic, relied on a network of "corduroy" roads and walkways, a term referring to their construction from fallen trees laid side-by-side. A narrow corduroy walkway linked the frontline perimeter to the gun positions about a half-mile back to the rear where our company slept and ate. Stepping off a walkway, you immediately sank into mud a foot deep.

When traveling these corduroy paths, I always clutched my submachine gun at the ready in case I encountered Russian infiltrators. For an enemy hidden in the grass, I would have been an easy target. This psychological strain generated by constant danger of attack from any direction at the Volkhov was even worse than that created by the threat of snipers at Uritsk.

In the rear, I would occasionally see Schütte or Sauke, but opportunities to enjoy a game of Skat or a smoke with comrades were almost nonexistent due to the amount of time I spent forward at the perimeter. Because of the regular need for my presence at the frontline,

I usually slept there as well. In both locations, we bunked in water-proof tents set up on a log foundation in order to keep us above the mud, though it was nearly impossible to remain clean or dry in such conditions.

The standing water around us generated swarms of mosquitoes from which there was no escape. Even with netting around our tents, they still ceaselessly hounded us. This compounded the persistent irritation from the lice on our bodies, making restful sleep almost impossible. With hot soup a rare luxury, our rations consisted of mostly crackers and canned tuna and sausage. Though our morale remained high, inadequate sleep, a poor diet, and the stress of combat left us physically weakened and mentally exhausted.

By the middle of May, the Red Army had decided to abandon its attempt to regain the offensive initiative at the Volkhov. Seizing the opportunity, we began an assault that pressed in around the entire perimeter of the pocket on May 22. By the end of the month, the 58th Division and other German forces had overcome determined Soviet resistance, resealing the *Kessel* a second time.

As the pocket was reduced in size, bitter enemy opposition persisted, though inside the encirclement, the already difficult conditions for the Red Army troops rapidly became worse. The Soviet artillery still continued to shell us from their positions on the east side of the Volkhov River, but the men within the pocket now lacked the ammunition and other provisions necessary to sustain major combat operations.

In desperation, the entrapped Soviet infantry conducted increasingly suicidal attacks against our positions, under pressure from the Red Army political officers called *Politruks*. Lacking an adequate supply of rifles for their men, Russian commanders ordered some soldiers to go forward unarmed and retrieve weapons from other troops as they fell. On one occasion, I watched with amazement as an enemy soldier ran directly toward my position without a weapon.

Prisoners reported to our intelligence that special Soviet units with machine guns were sometimes placed behind these hopeless attacks to make sure that soldiers obeyed the orders to advance. The enemy succeeded in organizing a couple of larger assaults that briefly penetrated our front, but most such attempts produced only terrible losses among their troops without accomplishing any purpose. Afterward, their bloated and decaying bodies lay scattered in the open ground just in front of us.

On my return to the front late one morning in June, I took up my regular observation post a few feet to the right of a soldier manning one of the powerful new MG-42 machine guns. Because the MG-42's exceptionally high rate of fire made it impossible to differentiate the shooting of its individual bullets, the machine gun produced a very distinctive noise, more closely resembling a cloth being ripped than a weapon being fired. Yet, perhaps its greatest asset was that the weapon would nearly always operate reliably, even in muddy conditions like those at the Volkhov.

As was commonly the case, the posted infantryman was unfamiliar to me and we engaged in little conversation, other than to remark on enemy movement. Less than a half hour after my appearance, a Russian attack surged toward our position, moving across the dense brush that occupied No Man's Land. Instantly, the alert gunner began to pour a non-stop fusillade across our front. Calling back a fire mission, I requested our 75-millimeter guns to drop shells in a curtain roughly 25 yards in front of our position, as close as I dared risk.

With the Red Army troops still closing on our location, I added my MP-40 submachine gun's fire to the torrent of bullets spilling from my comrade's machine gun. Despite no return fire and the lack of any clearly visible targets in the high brush, the gunner and I raked our weapons over the entire field in front of us as shells from our heavy guns began to slam down in support.

When the barrel of the MG-42 finally overheated from the relentless firing, the soldier yanked it off and tossed it into a puddle next to us, producing a cloud of steam. Locking a fresh barrel into the machine gun, he started blazing away again. Already, the gunner stood in a mound of empty shell casings.

Perhaps half an hour passed with no let-up in our fire. Upon emptying my third or fourth 32-round clip, I again ducked down behind the wooden walls in order to avoid exposing myself as a target during the 15 seconds it took to reload another magazine into my weapon. At that moment, I became aware that the machine gun had grown silent, but assumed that the gunner was also reloading or again switching the barrel of his weapon.

A glance to my right revealed the gunner crumpled on the ground beside me. A second later, I spotted blood running from a hole in his temple just under the rim of his helmet. The shot that killed him had not been audible in the din of combat, but its precision made it instantly obvious to me that it came from a sniper's rifle.

There is not much time to contemplate one's fate in the middle of a battle, but the thought flashed through my mind that it could have been me lying there with a bullet through my head, if I had not ducked down or my submachine gun's magazine had run out a few seconds later.

Crouching to keep my body hidden beneath the log fortifications, I sprinted over to the next infantry position 15 yards away to alert them to the loss of their machine gun support in that sector. While any regular infantryman would have had to hold his position and continue fighting, my latitude of movement as forward observer allowed me to depart that vulnerable area of the line and escape the fate of my unknown comrade.

On June 28, the relentless struggle at the Volkhov ended in a German victory three and a half months after our arrival. The Wehrmacht's High Command reported that German forces captured approximately 33,000 Red Army prisoners, 650 artillery pieces, 170 tanks, and 3,000 machine guns. Among those taken prisoner was General Vlasov, who eventually would lead units comprised of captured Russian troops who agreed to fight with Germany against the Soviet Union's Communist government. Viewed as a traitor by the Russians, he was executed after the war.

The German troops who went through the Volkhov also suffered during the months of fighting. Indeed, the condition of those of us who survived was often little better than that of our enemy captives. My own weight dropped about 20 or 25 pounds to an emaciated-looking 160 pounds, but many other German soldiers endured far worse health problems.

As I wandered over what had been the bitterly contested area of the *Schlauch* afterward, only a giant forest of stumps stretched to the horizon where the dense woods had once stood. The Soviet dead, or rather parts of their bodies, carpeted the churned up ground. The stench was indescribably ghastly.

The Battle of the Volkhov had been a terrible struggle in almost unimaginably miserable conditions, but our success reinforced our belief that Germany would eventually prevail in the East. That summer, a new offensive in southern Russia offered us further hope that final victory was not far away.

THE ORANIENBAUM POCKET
July 1–August 11, 1942

On July 1 1942, the 58th Infantry Division was transferred roughly 75 miles northwest to the perimeter of the Oranienbaum *Kessel*, roughly 15 miles west of our old position at Uritsk. The Soviet troops in this area had been cut off from the main body of Red Army forces further east during the previous summer's campaign and were now surrounded in a large semi-circular pocket with their backs to the Gulf of Finland.

Although the division occupied roughly 15 miles of the front at Oranienbaum, the general lack of action offered us a relative respite from combat. Just after our arrival, the company commander presented me with the *Infanterie Sturmabzeichen* commendation for close combat. As was the case with many other medals, this was received for an accumulation of combat service rather than for a specific action.

Although no major fighting took place at Oranienbaum, our heavy guns assisted in repulsing infiltration attempts by squads of Red Army soldiers about once a week. According to captured prisoners, the primary purpose of these raids was to seize one of our highly effective MG-42 machine guns that I had recently witnessed in action for the first time at the Volkhov.

Raiding parties also crossed No Man's Land from our side, just as at Uritsk. Ranging in strength from 12-man squads up to rare 100-man units, these teams conducted reconnaissance of the enemy's positions and attempted to capture prisoners for intelligence purposes. When these forays took place, I remained in constant readiness to call upon our company's guns to protect their retreat in case they encountered trouble. In most situations, this support was not necessary, but our howitzers helped rescue the situation two or three times.

Despite occasional fighting, the two-month deployment at Oranienbaum permitted our division badly needed time to recuperate and receive replacements. Our three and a half months of uninterrupted combat at the Volkhov had been unusual. In normal circumstances, troops engaged in intensive combat were permitted a rest after three or four weeks of heavy fighting.

On a relatively inactive front such as Oranienbaum, troops spent perhaps 80 or 90 percent of their time at the front. Despite rare rotations to the rear, we did sometimes have time to play a card game or write a letter in our bunkers. As in many other ways, our heavy weapons company was relatively better off than a regular infantry company in terms of the proportion of time that we spent on the frontlines versus time in the rear.

On August 1, the army promoted me to corporal (*Unteroffizier*). A week later, I was awarded the Winter Medal, which we referred to as the "frozen meat" medal, for surviving the bitter cold that had killed so many. More importantly, I was granted a long overdue three-week leave from duty on August 11.

Departing Oranienbaum, I set out on the roughly 1,000-mile journey back to Germany. Having last seen my family and Anneliese in November 1940, it was hard for me to believe that I was finally returning. While fighting in Russia, home had seemed a million miles away.

FIRST LEAVE FROM RUSSIA
August 11–August 30, 1942

When we reached the border of the German Reich at Tilsit in East Prussia, the military authorities required everybody on board the train to undergo a thorough delousing. All our clothes and belongings were treated with steam in a large chamber and we took long showers in hot water. Free of all pests, we proceeded into Germany. The sense of relief that I experienced upon getting out of Russia was overwhelming.

When I finally arrived in Püggen three days after my departure from Oranienbaum, my family gave me an even warmer welcome than when I had arrived home the first time from Belgium. After 20 months away from home, my sisters had grown so much that they were almost unrecognizable to me, particularly my 5 year-old sister Margarete. Playing with her was one of the highlights of my time at home.

The welcome and treatment that I received from my family made me feel like a conquering hero. My mother even laid out a spread of specially prepared foods for me in a separate dining room, which the rest of my family envied. During my meals, my sisters sang a plaintive song just outside the door, "Hear our quiet call for pastries for all."

Despite their best efforts, it was impossible to settle into the pleasant patterns of life with my family as I had done after the French campaign. When a soldier came home from the war in Russia, he was a different person. At a certain level, the psychological strain of living in constant danger during combat lingered inside me.

Though the old familiar routines of farm labor proved more therapeutic than my efforts to relax, it would ultimately take years to melt away the stress. Beyond this immediate tension, the fighting and killing had also perhaps affected my soul in ways that no amount of time would heal.

While the farm itself remained unchanged from my youth, much had changed in Püggen. By this time, the German government had begun sending prisoners of war and conscripted civilians to work as laborers in the nation's factories and on its farms to replace manpower serving at the front. Following Poland's defeat in 1939, several Polish POWs had arrived at our village. These had been joined by a larger number of French and Belgian POWs the next year.

As part of my family's continued targeting in retribution for its lack of support for the Nazi regime, local officials ordered my father, now a member of the *Volkssturm* (Home Guard), to serve as a guard for the village's 20 or so POWs. This duty required him to spend the night at the pub down the street from our house, since the prisoners were locked up at night in the pub's ballroom.

Since my father was about 50 years old, he probably would have found it difficult to cope with an escape attempt. Fortunately, he generally got along well with them and never had any problems. One of the Belgian POWs later told my father, "Well, Herr Lübbecke, you will not have to be a watchman very long. In the near future, you will be the prisoner and we will be the guards."

Under this labor program, the local authorities provided my family with a Polish POW named Sigmund, a factory worker from the Polish city of Lodz. Treating him as they would any German farmhand, my family worked beside him in the fields and never encountered any problems. Though government regulations stipulated that POWs should eat separately from German families, my mother ignored them and regularly set a place for Sigmund at our dining room table.

Eventually the authorities permitted the POWs to live out on the farms, if there was a space where they could be safely confined. Obtaining special permission, my family gave Sigmund a room in the *Altenteil* (my grandparents' former home). This positive experience with Sigmund was repeated later in the war with two Belgian POWs whom the government supplied to my family as farm labor. Despite such changes, life in Püggen still appeared almost normal and the war seemed far away for those not engaged in the fighting.

In the middle of my two-week visit with my family, I departed Püggen on August 21 to see Anneliese in Hamburg. Despite the passage of two years since we had last spent any significant time together, our increasingly frequent exchange of letters had brought us closer, though she still remained engaged to the florist's son.

Arriving in Hamburg, I met Anneliese not far from the florist shop in the *Arkade* across the Alster River from city hall, where she had been working since leaving her position at the shop in the city's main train station earlier that spring. In the half a day that followed, we quickly recaptured the intimacy of our early relationship as we talked and strolled around the city. Our time together was everything that I had imagined while I had been frozen in the snow at Uritsk and mired in the mud at the Volkhov.

From the moment I saw Anneliese again, I began to think seriously for the first time that she would make a wonderful wife, even if she was engaged to someone else. Unable to conceal my sentiments, I told her, "I am sorry. I do not want to interfere. But I still love you." What she chose to do was her decision, but it was important to me that she understood my feelings for her.

Just before I boarded the train to return to Püggen for the remaining week of my leave, Anneliese handed me a gold cloverleaf talisman, promising it would bring me good luck. Placing the gift in the breast pocket of my tunic, I felt confident that it was only a matter of time before we would get back together.

Yet, we both now recognized that a soldier's fate on the battlefield was very uncertain. Even with the widespread optimism over the German advances toward the Volga and the Caucasus that summer, it was clear that many soldiers would not be coming home to their loved ones.

CHAPTER 10

THE DEMYANSK CORRIDOR

SEPTEMBER 1942–MARCH 1943

NOVGOROD: September–November 1942

By the time of my return from my three-week furlough at the beginning of September, part of the 58th Division had been transferred about 70 miles south of Leningrad to a position on the north shore of Lake Ilmen, located only about 15 or 20 miles south of the Volkhov battlefield. When I reached my company, it had taken up quarters in deserted Russian homes on the southern outskirts of the ancient Russian city of Novgorod.

Our mission to help guard the far northern coast of Lake Ilmen against any potential amphibious operations from the Soviet-held eastern shore was a relatively easy assignment. Even if the Russians somehow managed to conduct a surprise amphibious landing in company or battalion strength, the natural defensive advantages of our position made us confident we could easily push them back into the water before they were able to establish a secure foothold. We remained vigilant, but there was little genuine concern about an attack.

On October 15, the 154th Infantry Regiment was redesignated the 154th Grenadier Regiment. This change nominally reflected the augmentation of its overall firepower through an increase in heavy weapons such as machine guns and large mortars. In reality, any increase in firepower could not fully compensate for the regiment's attrition of manpower that had reduced our overall strength by at least a battalion. Retaining a strong sense of pride in our unit, we saw little significance in the redesignation.

Despite our continued regular training exercises, our assignment to a quiet sector permitted us more time to relax. While the weather remained warm enough, some of us laid beside the shore of Lake Ilmen. It almost felt like an extension of my leave, as I sat in the sun reading letters from home.

Following my visit to Hamburg, the pace of my exchange of correspondence with Anneliese had increased. Within weeks, I received the news that I had been hoping for—Anneliese had decided to break off her engagement and build a relationship with me. Ironically, having just won back her heart, I proceeded to lose the gold cloverleaf charm she had given me for luck.

Though Novgorod was just a fifteen-minute walk from our position, I only once ventured into the city to wander its deserted streets. Typical of most Soviet communities, it was mainly filled with small wooden shacks and plain concrete buildings. Only the large bronze sculptures located in the central plaza near the town's city hall made a favorable impression on me.

My visit to one of the city's onion-domed churches so characteristic of Russia presented a mixed picture. While its exterior remained relatively intact, the church's dilapidated interior had been used to store grain or beets. This sacrilegious vandalism reinforced my view of the Communists as barbaric atheists who posed a grave danger to Europe's Christian civilization.

Meanwhile, other soldiers from my regiment took advantage of our location on the lake to go fishing. Instead of using rods or nets, they would toss standard kilo-sized blocks of explosives into the water, causing stunned or dead fish to rise to the surface for easy retrieval. In a tragic incident, four soldiers fishing this way were killed when they accidentally blew up their own boat. Even during the quietest moments in Russia, death never seemed far away.

DEMYANSK: November 1942–February 1943

As part of its general counteroffensive in the winter of 1941–1942, the Red Army had staged an assault against German lines south of Lake Ilmen. By early February, the enemy had succeeded in isolating our units holding the areas around Demyansk, forcing the troops there to be supplied by air.

In late April, the Wehrmacht counterattacked and forced through an overland route to the isolated troops, but the roughly four-mile-wide and seven-and-a-half-mile-long supply corridor remained precarious. At the end of November 1942, the 58th Infantry Division joined other German divisions transferring south of Lake Ilmen to help protect this vital, but still vulnerable land bridge to the Demyansk pocket.

With another Russian winter already upon us, our division moved into an area just above the Pola River along the north side of the *Schlauch* in the hilly terrain known as the Valdai Heights. However, as was usually the case, most of us lacked any knowledge of our geographic location and were only aware of our immediate tactical situation.

The fighting at Demyansk remained fairly constant, though in our area it lacked the intensity of what we had endured at the Volkhov. In resisting several large assaults and frequent smaller raids against our lines by the Red Army, we sometimes yielded or seized ground in tactical retreats or advances, but the frontlines remained relatively stable. While these operations were of much greater consequence, it was the small, personal encounters that most stood out for me.

Reaching our newly assigned post on a low ridge along this corridor, my communications specialist and I joined a group of other soldiers in a large bunker near the front that served as the living quarters. Because it was impossible to dig out an underground bunker or trenches in the frozen, rock-hard earth, it had been constructed above ground with snow camouflaging the log walls. A snow wall facing the Russian lines offered additional protection. Nearby, there was also a small observation tower.

In spite of our efforts to create a secure position, we soon began to be plagued by sniper fire from a Soviet sharpshooter. Fearful of getting hit, we were forced to remain inside the confined space of the bunker during the daylight hours. After this situation had persisted for several days, I finally grew frustrated and decided to do something about it.

Grabbing a Mauser rifle, I made my way from our bunker to the snow rampart. Crouching down on my knees, I carved out a small aperture through the wall with my hands. Scrutinizing the winter landscape, there was nothing that gave away the location of the enemy sharpshooter.

Suddenly, a shot burst through the snow wall, passing just over the top of my helmet. Accepting my defeat in our brief duel, I pulled my rifle from the hole and quickly ducked back into our bunker. As far as I was concerned, we would have to learn to live with the threat of the sniper.

Soon afterward, I was surveying the enemy lines from the observation tower when I observed a Russian soldier walking out in the open through the snow about 500 yards away from our position. As I shouted down a fire mission, an infantryman aimed a small 50-millimeter mortar and dropped a round into the tube.

When the shell impacted about 50 feet from the Russian, he appeared to be startled. Suddenly realizing his perilous situation, he took off running through the deep snow and never stopped. Despite the gauntlet of fire created by the half-dozen mortar rounds falling around him, he somehow escaped unharmed. Sometimes war seemed more like a harmless game rather than the deadly struggle it really was.

My turn as the quarry would come a few weeks later at another frontline bunker, located perhaps a mile from our previous position.

The morning after my arrival there, I awoke to discover an overnight snowfall had built upon previous accumulations to leave a powdery cushion a foot deep. Leaving the bunker with a field telephone, I trudged a short distance through the picturesque winter landscape until I reached a good observation point. Concealed by my white camouflage, I remained standing in order to better survey the surrounding terrain.

Without even lifting my binoculars, a quick scan of the enemy position immediately revealed a couple of Red Army bunkers. Protruding six feet above ground, the structures were plainly visible from my position less than 100 yards away. Though fresh snow now partially covered the layer of protective earth piled onto the bunkers, they appeared to be of recent construction and clearly posed a direct challenge to our control of the area.

Selecting the closer and larger of the two, I called back firing coordinates to one of our 150-millimeter howitzers, requesting a single round on the roughly 30-square-foot target. In a couple of minutes, an explosion threw up a cloud of snow about 20 yards to the left of the bunker. After adjusting the distance and direction, the second round landed 10 yards to the right. Advancing a little closer to better observe the target, I made a further correction and requested a delayed fuse.

This round found its mark. Just after it smashed through the roof of the bunker, there was a loud whoosh of air as the shell with the delayed fuse detonated inside the structure a second later. The only thing observable externally was a little white smoke that drifted out through the roof.

Before I could call back the targeting coordinates for the second bunker, enemy mortar rounds suddenly began bursting in the snow around me. Despite my camouflage, a Soviet observer had somehow spotted me during the twenty minutes that had passed. Now I was the prey.

Moving clumsily through the snow, I headed for cover in our bunker a dozen yards away. Just over halfway to the entrance, a shell exploded right behind me. I felt a rush of air, but the deep snow partially absorbed the force of the blast, probably sparing me from serious injury.

Gaining the relative safety of our bunker, I asked an infantry soldier inside whether I had been hit. Examining the back of my padded jacket, he confirmed that it was perforated with tiny holes caused by metal splinters from the mortar round. During the next half-hour, he painstakingly removed the small shrapnel fragments from my skin. Once again I had been lucky to avoid more serious injury.

Because the precision involved in targeting enemy bunkers was a great challenge, it became my favorite task as forward observer. My success in knocking out perhaps a half dozen of these structures over the previous year had earned me a reputation as a bunker-busting specialist inside the 13th Company. The destruction of the large bunker on the Demyansk corridor, however, had drawn me unwanted attention from the enemy.

Around this time, the Red Army had begun to deploy loudspeakers on the frontlines to spout propaganda and threats delivered in perfect German. Perhaps a week after my successful elimination of the bunker, a soldier from one of the regular infantry companies asked me if I had heard the Russians calling out my name over the loudspeakers.

Replying that I had not, he informed me that these broadcasts were threatening me personally, announcing "Lübbecke, when we catch you, we'll cut off your nuts!" Apparently, a captured German soldier had identified my role in destroying their bunker.

From experience, I regarded this warning very seriously. In at least one recent instance, the Russians had castrated a sergeant and a corporal captured from one of our regiment's infantry companies. We discovered them the next day, dead from loss of blood.

Such brutality reinforced our determination to avoid being taken prisoner by the Red Army at all costs, even if we had to take our own lives to escape that fate. This mentality was totally different than the mindset we possessed during the French campaign. If surrounded by French troops, I would have surrendered with confidence that I would be treated humanely.

Realizing that the isolated position at Demyansk was a strategic liability, the army's high command began withdrawing equipment in early February 1943. On February 17, it officially ordered the evacuation of the pocket to begin. Though under intense pressure from Soviet forces, the German Army conducted an orderly retreat. The 58th Infantry Division pulled out of the area on February 24.

NOVGOROD: March 1943

At the beginning of March 1943, our division returned to the north coast of Lake Ilmen to occupy a new defensive position near Novgorod, not far from where we had served the previous fall guarding against potential amphibious operations. Now the thick winter ice covering Lake Ilmen provided a hard crust across which Russian forces could carry out "land" operations.

In the weeks that followed, however, the Red Army's attacks across the frozen lake proved disastrous failures because of our ability to spot their approach across the flat surface at a great distance. Even under the cover of darkness, the Soviets found it difficult to move across the ice since we could illuminate the area with floodlights when we heard anything approaching.

When the Russians made their attempts, the heavier artillery pounded them so effectively that they generally never even came within range of our company's guns located a couple of miles from the shoreline. As the artillery shells shattered the lake's ice shell, men and equipment would slide into the freezing waters below.

In a battalion-sized attack against the regiment positioned next to us, the Red Army employed a number of large motorized sleds, apparently intending to cross the frozen lake before our forces could react. This particular assault did succeed in reaching our lines, but the enemy was soon repulsed with heavy casualties.

The relative security of our position at Novgorod allowed us a little time to relax. Among the German troops, perhaps the most readily embraced feature of Russian culture was the *banya* (bathhouse), typically built about 50 yards behind a Russian home. After steaming ourselves inside, we would exit the *banya* to cool ourselves in the snow. On one of these occasions, someone started a snowball fight. Still naked, we engaged in a running battle in the frozen winter landscape, momentarily forgetting the real war.

Despite the Wehrmacht's successful evacuation of the Demyansk pocket to more defensible positions, and small tactical victories like those we achieved at Novgorod, our previously high morale slowly began to decline in 1943. For Army Group North, the war had definitively shifted to a defensive struggle to hold the gains achieved in 1941, while the Soviets now held the military initiative.

We were also aware of the catastrophic fate of the German 6th Army at Stalingrad far to the south. After being encircled by the Red Army in November 1942, its survivors were finally forced to surrender in February. So great was the magnitude of the calamity that even Göbbel's Propaganda Ministry did not attempt to conceal it. Also, while the war in Russia took a mounting toll of casualties among German troops, our families back home began to increasingly suffer from Anglo-American bombing raids.

Yet, after two years of war, we remained deep inside enemy territory and maintained faith in Germany's ultimate triumph. Our experience at the front left us wholly convinced that our army was still superior in terms of both our troops and equipment. Our generals and other officers also retained our full confidence and gave us a tactical advantage on the battlefield. Furthermore, we believed that German industry would continue to supply us with qualitatively better weapons than those of the enemy.

Even after Stalingrad, we believed that we could still win a defensive struggle by not losing. The Red Army would gradually exhaust itself in its bloody assaults against us that produced only minor gains or no advantage at all. It seemed to me that the Soviet Union would eventually have to accept a negotiated peace that would leave Germany with much of its territorial gains.

LEADERSHIP AND TACTICS

Just as Stalin controlled everything in the Soviet Union, Hitler held supreme power in Germany. Only after the war did it become clear to me that Hitler had engaged in a constant struggle against the Wehrmacht's general staff for control of military decision-making. As the war progressed, he increasingly subordinated the generals and the army to his whims.

Unaware of Hitler's bungling and the political conflicts at the top, we never questioned the military decision-making until late in the war. Witnessing the skilled leadership exercised in the field, German troops at the front held the officer corps in high esteem. Yet, even if tactical decisions by field officers remained unaffected, political meddling at the level of corps command or higher produced many poor strategic decisions.

In the Red Army, the intervention of the Communist political leadership in military operations was even more pervasive. Unlike the Wehrmacht, the Red Army installed *Politruks* (political officers) down to the company level and empowered them to make final decisions on lower level tactical matters about how and where to fight.

Although the Russians possessed many capable military officers well-versed in military tactics, the presence of these *Politruks* limited their effectiveness on the battlefield. This political interference largely explains Germany's tactical superiority. As the *Politruks* gained more influence over military decisions later in the war, they caused the Red Army a lot of unnecessary casualties. Based upon my experience in combat and the intelligence we obtained from captured enemy troops, I would judge that perhaps a quarter of the Red Army casualties can be blamed on the interference of the *Politruks*.

It was also apparent to German troops at the front that the Soviet political leaders and officers regarded an ordinary soldier's life as a commodity without much value. They never hesitated to expend the lives of their men in operations that had a minimal chance of success.

The Red Army sometimes, or possibly most of the time, fortified its troops with vodka to instill a sense of confidence in soldiers who often faced daunting odds. As we witnessed at the Volkhov, there were instances where a portion of the Red Army troops in an attack would even begin moving forward unarmed, with orders to retrieve weapons from those who were killed in the advance. The NKVD, the Soviet secret police, would set up machine guns behind the attacking infantry to prevent any retreat. With no alternative, these troops would advance forward against our well-defended positions to be slaughtered or captured.

If captured, the Russian soldier would generally continue to resist. Attempts to threaten a prisoner with a firearm during interrogations would frequently produce only a smile. Strangely, only the threat of a beating with a club or some similar weapon would tend to make the man fearful.

In addition to the ethnically Slavic troops, growing numbers of Mongolians from the eastern parts of the Soviet Union began to appear in Red Army units after 1943. While not afraid of the typical Slav, we feared these Mongolians, who were especially tough and brutal adversaries in combat.

At the start of the war, we often viewed and treated the Soviet soldier as a primitive brute. As we came to know the enemy, however, the natural courage and toughness of the Red Army soldier won him our respect. Whatever their views on Communism, it soon became clear to us that the Russian troops were willing to sacrifice their lives to repel the German invaders who had occupied their motherland.

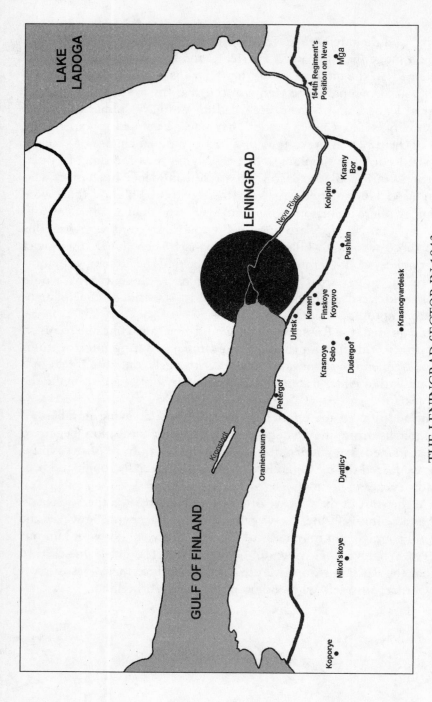

THE LENINGRAD SECTOR IN 1943.

Heavy lines indicate the fronts north and south of Leningrad and the Soviet-held Oranienbaum pocket.

CHAPTER 11

HOLDING THE LINE AT LADOGA

MARCH–SEPTEMBER 1943

KRASNY BOR
Late March–April 24, 1943

Though we still maintained our siege lines close to Leningrad, a Red Army offensive in January 1943 succeeded in opening an overland supply route into the city along the southwestern shore of Lake Ladoga. In mid-March, the Soviets began the Second Battle of Ladoga in another push against the German lines east of Leningrad.

At the end of March, the 58th Infantry Division was pulled out of Novgorod and traveled some 60 miles north of Lake Ilmen to help bolster this threatened sector. When our division reached the frontline near the town of Krasny Bor, just south of the Neva River, we were placed into a reserve position behind the Spanish Blue Division, which was fighting in Russia as a German ally.

By this time, the 13th Company had gone through a couple of further changes in leadership. With Second Lt. Münstermann and his successor, Second Lt. Jürgens, both promoted to command battalions in our regiment, Second Lt. Reichardt had now been placed in charge of our company. Perhaps in preparation for future promotion, Reichardt designated me to serve as the informal liaison between our heavy weapons company and the Spanish forces stationed in front of us.

Beyond coordinating the use of our heavy guns to support the Spanish in case of a Soviet attack, I dealt with any other issues that might arise between our company and their division. There was a generally good relationship between the German and Spanish troops, but we felt uncertain about the Spanish soldiers' capability on the battle-field. Their heavy losses in the preceding months of combat in this sector reduced our confidence in their ability to resist a serious Red Army attack.

When Soviet artillery fire began to pound the Spanish positions a couple of days later, our company immediately went to the support of the Spanish troops with our howitzers and recently issued 105-millimeter mortars. Despite our best efforts, the Russian assault sent a portion of the Spanish troops reeling backward.

In response to the crisis, our regiment's seasoned infantry quickly moved forward and counterattacked to prevent the initial enemy penetration from developing into a full-scale breakthrough. Within a couple of hours, our troops had forced the Red Army to retreat and had stabilized the frontlines.

In the weeks of relative quiet that followed, we were permitted some much needed rest behind the front. As in other regions of Russia, the villages around Krasny Bor were mostly only a stretch of road with houses along either side. The Red Army had burned down many homes and villages during their scorched-earth retreat early in the war, but a few structures close to our position remained intact.

A group of us from my company were temporarily quartered in one of these surviving Russian homes for a few nights. Though usually billeted in unoccupied residences, in this instance we shared the small house with its residents, two women in their thirties or forties and their children. In fact, these were the first Russian women I had since we had been stationed in Uritsk over a year earlier. As was usually the case with the Russian civilians we encountered, they appeared almost apathetic about our presence.

During this period of relative quiet at Krasny Bor, a number of soldiers in my regiment made use of a nearby Russian *banya* to relax. This led to unexpected tragedy when soldiers from the Spanish Blue Division decided to engage in target practice with a machine gun in the same location. Opening fire, they accidentally killed all four Germans who had been relaxing inside the bathhouse. Although this incident naturally caused some bitterness toward the Spanish, most of us had grown so accustomed to death that we were almost desensitized.

SECOND LEAVE FROM RUSSIA: April 24–May 15, 1943

Three and a half weeks after our arrival at Krasny Bor, I received my second furlough from duty in Russia and departed on April 24 for the long trip home to Germany.

Despite the warm welcome that I received from my family, coming home from the fighting in Russia remained a difficult experience. Over the first week or so, I could not connect to civilian life at all. During the day, my mind was still at the front as if I had never left. My nights were filled with dreams of combat. Only a couple of weeks into my leave did I slowly begin to readjust, but by then, of course, I had to return to the front. Still, whatever difficulties I experienced, it was always wonderful to be home.

On May 8, Anneliese came to Püggen for her first visit with my family. Since breaking off her engagement to the florist's son, our relationship had continued to grow more intimate. On walks around the farm, we talked about our future plans. Though marriage was still not imminent, it was already apparent to my family that eventually we would wed.

Everyone in my family thought very highly of Anneliese. My sisters treated her like a sister and my mother adored her. Only my father expressed any concern about our plans. He liked Anneliese personally, but had been trying to convince me that a man with my prospects could make a better marital connection by pursuing a woman from a wealthier background. His concern for my financial future reflected our own family's monetary difficulties during the Great Depression, but I did not agree with regarding marriage from a purely material point of view.

Upset that he was attempting to meddle in what was a highly personal matter, I told him bluntly, "Dad, this is my decision. I love this woman and am going to marry her. You are not going to interfere." He never again questioned my judgment.

At this time, Anneliese was still working at the flower shop across from Hamburg's city hall. However, the previous January she had volunteered to enter training as a Red Cross nurse, feeling she had a patriotic duty to make a more direct contribution to the war effort. Shortly after her visit with us, she would start a three-month training course at a hospital in Hamburg.

As Anneliese headed back home and I set out on the journey back to the front on May 12, we parted knowing that it was not only me who would soon be at risk.

KRASNY BOR: May 15–July 24, 1943

If readjustment to life at home was difficult for me, the separation from loved ones to return to the front was infinitely worse. As my train traveled down the miles of track, it was impossible not to dwell on the memories of Anneliese in my arms and the time spent together with my family, uncertain if I would live to see them again.

Those first mid-May days back at the front at Krasny Bor were among the worst that I experienced as a soldier, especially since I was going directly into combat. Normally, the familiar pattern of trench warfare would again become my daily reality after about a week or so back at the front, but on this occasion my efforts to leave home behind failed. When a soldier's mind is focused on thoughts of home, he can become careless and highly vulnerable to injury or death. In an effort to compensate for my distraction, I sought to exercise an especially high level of caution during this period.

Even though our lines at Krasny Bor shifted little, our company fought in a number of small and large actions against the enemy forces posted across from us. During this period the Russians would some-times stage attacks that seemed designed to acquire our food supplies as much as to occupy our positions. When the Soviet troops broke into our trenches, we would often fall back a couple of hundred yards while they went into our bunkers to pilfer our food stocks. With time to regroup, we would organize a counterattack that threw them back out of our positions, almost as if we were operating on a tacitly agreed schedule.

Of course, some days stand out. On Sunday June 17, I turned 23. Normally, birthdays at the front received little recognition. On this occasion, Second Lt. Reichardt, the company commander, took note of mine and presented me with a bottle of cognac. He also used the rare calm at the front to hold our first church service since the start of the war in Russia almost two years earlier. Such respites from the conflict never lasted long.

Sometimes the war would strike unexpectedly. As I was walking among some large trees behind our lines on a quiet day, I heard the distant boom of an enemy artillery piece. Keeping my ears tuned to the whistle of the incoming round, I suddenly realized that it was coming close, very close. Instantly flinging myself flat, I pressed my body down into the rain-soaked earth. In that brief moment while I awaited its impact, life or death seemed equally possible.

My ears had not deceived me. The shell landed only three or four feet away from my prone body, but fortunately plunged deep into the mud before detonating. Incredibly, the explosion left me covered with mire, but otherwise unhurt.

Even when we slept, combat often filled our dreams. One night, I came partially awake in our bunker, mistakenly believing in my still semi-conscious state that we were under enemy attack. Snatching a hand grenade, I yelled, "The Russians are coming!"

Fortunately for me, my communications specialist was fully alert and managed to yank the grenade from my hand before the pin was removed. Because we were down in a bunker, there was no way I could have gotten rid of it in time. In that confined space the blast would have killed us both. Even though my assistant was my subordinate, rank mattered little in such a situation. At that moment, he was simply a comrade who was looking out for me, just as I would look out for him.

As the weeks at the front passed, my time at home came to seem like a far-off dream, though Anneliese remained constantly in my thoughts. For her twenty-second birthday on June 29, I arranged to have a dozen red roses sent to her. It was as much an expression of my hope for our future together as it was a token of my deep affection.

While my correspondence to her was mostly devoted to expressing my feelings, I would sometimes make passing mention of our combat operations in terms that would pass the censor's scrutiny. In a letter to Anneliese on June 20, I referenced a dual between our howitzers and Soviet artillery. Writing on July 10, I noted that our howitzers and mortars had successfully repulsed an assault by the Russians against our position. Such engagements were routine for us and otherwise soon forgotten.

AT THE NEVA: July 24–September 4, 1943

On July 22, the Red Army initiated the Third Battle of Ladoga, renewing its struggle to break the German siege lines east of Leningrad in the area close to the lake. Two days later, our division was rushed the 15 miles from the Krasny Bor sector to a key position beside the Neva River in an area known as the Sinyavino Heights. This placed us about four miles southeast of Lake Ladoga and three miles northwest of the critical rail junction of Mga.

The 58th Division soon experienced some of its heaviest fighting of the war as the Soviet 67th Army attempted to seize the high ground from us. The struggle on August 4 was particularly brutal. The 154th Regiment's attempt to regain the ground it had lost had to be broken off after the counterattack met with stiff enemy resistance and heavy losses. On August 8, we experienced more tough fighting that tied me down in a foxhole for hours.

On a generally quiet day a short time later, a strange episode occurred as I was tramping along a dirt road on the way from my frontline position to my rear bunker about a mile behind the front. As I approached the area just behind our howitzers, a young German second lieutenant wearing an unsoiled uniform came strolling up the road toward me from the north. This immediately struck me as odd since the German Army had no units located in that direction.

While I was baffled by his presence in the area, the officer did not appear nervous or exhibit any suspicious behavior. As we passed one another, he cordially returned my salute and I dismissed my apprehensions.

Two hours later, Soviet heavy artillery slammed 50 or 60 shells into our position with pinpoint accuracy. Only our deeply dug set of entrenchments prevented the bombardment from causing any casualties or damage to the howitzers.

Instantly, my mind flashed back to the mysterious German officer. In retrospect, I concluded that he must indeed have been a Russian agent gathering intelligence. His close-up scouting of our position would explain the enemy's ability to target our camouflaged position so precisely. Convinced of my failure to identify a spy, I silently vowed to be far more wary of anything unusual in the future.

On an afternoon a few days later, I headed up to the frontline to join my close comrade Sergeant Schütte, who had begun interchanging with me as our company's F.O. Becoming suspicious about the unusual quiet that followed the recent artillery attack, he warned me that the Red Army might be preparing another assault.

Deciding to study the enemy position myself, I climbed up the branches of a pine tree at the edge of the forest about 100 yards behind our trenches. In case any targets appeared, I hauled along a field telephone. Perhaps half an hour after I reached my perch about 20 feet up, four Soviet T-34 tanks suddenly appeared from the northeast and began a slow advance across the flat ground directly toward my location in the tree. Soldiers were riding on top of the tanks, which were followed by a large number of additional infantry on foot. While our company's heavy guns were not designed to serve in an anti-tank role and lacked armor-piercing rounds, I knew from long experience that it was possible to accurately target the fire of the guns into an area about ten square yards in size.

With a chance to halt the advance before it progressed any further toward our regiment's position, I used the field telephone to direct one of our 150-millimeter guns to fire a round against the closest T-34, about 500 yards to my front. Falling just to the left of the target, the first shell's blast knocked the enemy troops from the tank but failed to damage the vehicle. After redirecting the howitzer to shift its fire to the right, the next round fell short of the tank. The next shell landed very close, missing the T-34 by only a few feet.

Receiving a further correction, the gun crew fired a fourth round. When the shell detonated against the turret, the tank instantly ground to a halt. Seconds later, a small plume of white smoke began to drift from the vehicle.

Shifting my attention to a second T-34 about 20 yards behind the destroyed one, I called in a fifth round. Smashing into its treads from the side, the shell's explosion immobilized the vehicle, forcing its crew to jump out and run for cover. The third Soviet tank in the group immediately ceased its advance while the fourth one began to retreat.

As this assault ended, a larger group of around fifteen tanks momentarily came into view 1,000 yards behind the scene of the attack before moving out of sight behind a hill. Unsure whether this larger armored force would renew the advance, I telephoned back to headquarters to make our new regimental commander, Colonel (*Oberst*) Hermann-Heinrich Behrend, aware of the situation.

"Where are you?" he demanded before I could even speak.

"I am in a tree right behind the front line," I responded with some trepidation.

"What the hell are you doing up there?" he yelled back, obviously concerned that I would place myself in such a vulnerable position.

Informing him that we had stopped an armored attack probing our defenses, I warned that significant tank forces were massing behind it and might conduct another assault.

After requesting details on the number of tanks and their location, he indicated that he would pass along the intelligence to divisional headquarters and he then hung up. Once their initial thrust was halted the Soviets did not, however, attempt to renew their attack on our sector of the front .

Despite my thrill at knocking out the tanks, there was still a danger that the enemy would spot me the longer I remained in my exposed position. Yet, climbing down the tree in the daylight would greatly increase the risk of attracting the attention of a Russian sniper or machine-gun crew. In this dilemma, my only choice was to wait for the cover of darkness.

When dusk finally fell about an hour later, I made a rapid slide down the trunk and headed for safety in the rear. Reaching the gun crew, I passed along news of our small triumph. In a war filled with many combat engagements, hitting a moving target with indirect fire from guns in the rear was a rare and memorable accomplishment.

Over the course of the war, most of the casualties in our regiment resulted from Russian artillery and mortars, to a lesser extent from small-arms fire. About this time, however, we also began to endure our first bombing and strafing raids by Soviet aircraft.

During the daytime, we occasionally faced a threat from Soviet ground-attack planes like the Illyushin-2 Sturmovik. At night, we confronted the menace of the Polyarkov-2, nicknamed the *Nähmaschine* (Sewing Machine) for the loud rhythmic clattering of its engine.

The noisy approach of the *Nähmaschine* was audible at a great distance, but it was virtually impossible to target them in the darkness.

Flying a couple of hundred feet overhead, the pilot and copilot would search for any flicker of light that would reveal the location of our lines or rear camps.

Despite efforts to black-out everything on the ground, there was bound to be someone who would light a cigarette or use a flashlight that the enemy could spot. Once locating a potential target, the Soviet pilots often cut their engines in order to glide silently over the spot before dropping their bombs on the unsuspecting targets below.

The day after one of these nocturnal raids by a *Nähmaschine*, not long after the tank battle, I was again up front operating as forward observer. Immediately after directing one of our 150-millimeter howitzers to fire a round against an enemy target, I instead heard an enormous boom from the direction of our heavy guns in the rear.

The mystery was soon revealed. A misfiring shell inside the barrel of the howitzer had caused an explosion that detonated the shells stacked next to it, killing the five-man gun crew and obliterating everything in the vicinity. Though unable to get back and observe the scene myself, I was told that only a large crater remained.

This malfunction could have resulted from faulty workmanship or sabotage in the manufacture of the shell, but I was convinced it resulted from the phosphorous dropped on our position during the previous night's air raid. A corrosive particle of the phosphorous could have burned a small hole in a shell that went undetected during its loading. Unfortunately, a sudden change in the battlefield situation within hours of this accident forced my company to pull back from the position without conducting an adequate investigation.

Earlier combat in the area of the Leningrad siege had primarily involved stationary trench warfare similar to that experienced on the Western Front in the First World War. In contrast, the combat near the Neva was more fluid, also more bloody. Frequently, there were sudden shifts in the frontlines as both sides in turn retreated and counterattacked.

As always, the 13th Company experienced a much lower casualty rate than the 154th Regiment's regular infantry companies, since the majority of our personnel served in the rear handling our heavy weapons. Even though my assignment as forward observer placed me on the frontline, my freedom to avoid or pull out of more hazardous areas gave me a significant advantage over the regular infantry, as the earlier incident with the sniper at Volkhov demonstrated.

Back in Germany, where Anneliese was completing her nursing training, she and other civilians had begun to experience firsthand the horror of war. Frequent Allied air raids by large bomber formations now often forced her and the other members of her household to take refuge in the basement of her father's home in Hamburg.

At the end of July 1943, I heard on the radio that the Allies were repeatedly targeting Hamburg with powerful air strikes. Employing hundreds of planes in the first of a series of massive area bombings of German cities, the enemy dropped large numbers of incendiary bombs that ignited multiple blazes. Heat and strong winds soon whipped these into a firestorm of unprecedented scale that killed about 40,000 people and devastated much of the central part of city.

In the aftermath of the attack, all mail to Hamburg stopped for a couple of weeks, leaving me deeply concerned. A long three weeks later, I received word that Anneliese and her family had survived. By the time her letter reached me, Anneliese had meanwhile completed her basic nursing training and been transferred up to a hospital at St. Peter-Ording on the North Sea coast, a location where she would be much safer.

Composing a letter to Anneliese, I conveyed both our difficult conditions at the front as well as my concerns for her. "We are in the most northern part of the Eastern Front on a large river [the Neva]. We are in foxholes [and] life is really miserable. We don't get any sleep. I await a letter from you concerning the bombing of Hamburg on 25th and 26th of July, 1943." It would be months later before I learned what she had personally experienced.

Despite the hardships in Russia, I still expressed an abiding optimism about the outcome of the conflict. "We don't have very much of our younger years [left to us], but this will change when the war is finished. We here on the front are very positive that we will win the war."

My words also sought to reassure her by painting a brighter future for us after the fighting had ended. "All that we are going through now will be compensated by our mutual love. After our victory, we will make up for all these missing moments and hours."

CHAPTER 12

OFFICER CANDIDATE

SEPTEMBER–DECEMBER 1943

ORANIENBAUM TO NEVEL
Early September–October 31, 1943

At the beginning of September, the 58th Division received orders to prepare to transfer 40 miles westward from the fiercely contested Ladoga area to the relative calm of the Oranienbaum pocket, roughly two years after our previous posting there.

Before making the shift to a new position, a *Vorkommando* would be sent ahead to determine the placement of the guns and other equipment. As a recently promoted sergeant (*Feldwebel*), I was assigned to head the team by our company commander, Second Lt. Reichardt. On September 8, the day before the remainder of the division arrived, I wrote a letter to Anneliese describing the view from our new location near the coast: "I can see the Baltic Sea, the towers of Leningrad, and the hills of Finland."

In the midst of a conversation with Reichardt the day after my letter, he abruptly asked, "Do you want to be an officer?" Though it had been apparent that he had been grooming me for greater responsibility, the sudden question still caught me off guard. Despite my surprise, I responded instantly with an enthusiastic, "*Jawohl, Herr Leutnant!*" With my acceptance, I became an officer candidate, finally earning the chance to pursue a leadership role to which I had long aspired.

Two days later, on September 11, Col. Behrend, our regimental commander, decorated me with the Iron Cross First Class for bravery in recognition of my role in halting the tank attack near the Neva

153

River as well as a number of other combat actions. In our company, the Iron Cross First Class was awarded to only a few soldiers so it was a distinct honor that I felt privileged to wear.

Excited to share my news, I decided to try to give Anneliese a phone call from my frontline bunker at Oranienbaum. Since the communications network was restricted to military needs, I was aware that my effort might be blocked, but figured it was worth a try. Using our field telephone, I reached the regimental switchboard and was patched through to the division. The divisional operator, in turn, placed a call to the hospital in St. Peter-Ording where Anneliese was working. Much to my disappointment, I learned that she was already off duty that day. I tried to phone her again, but never reached her. My failure to speak to her left me even more anxious to see her again.

Before entering a military academy back in Germany, officer candidates had to fulfill a short tour of duty in charge of an infantry squad. On September 18, I was assigned temporary command of a squad of about a dozen men in one of the regular infantry companies, comprised mostly of men from the Hamburg area.

Removed from my familiar role and comrades, this new assignment placed me in a role for which I felt unprepared, among soldiers I did not know. Naturally, I greeted the task without much enthusiasm, but accepted it as a necessary step in the process of becoming an officer.

Larger events soon took us into action. Intelligence in early October revealed that the Soviets were massing two armies before the German front at Nevel, located about 150 miles south of Leningrad. As the junction point between Army Group North and Army Group Center, it was a particularly vital sector of the front.

Responding to this imminent threat, the high command directed additional forces to the Nevel area from across the northern front, including the 58th Division. Together with the rest of the 154th Regiment's infantry, my squad spent October 2 to October 6 aboard trains on a circuitous 300-mile journey south from Oranienbaum.

The expected Russian offensive commenced on October 6 and quickly broke through at the seam of the two German Army Groups. The newly arriving 58th Division played a key role in halting the enemy's advance just north of Nevel, but its hastily organized counterattack was unable to regain control of the town.

When the train carrying my infantry squad and other elements of the 154th Regiment reached the Nevel area, we joined the desperate fight. After the infantry company's commander outlined my assignment on a map, I met with my men to explain what we could expect as we moved into our frontline position. "Listen closely, this hill ahead of us is under Russian fire. When we reach the top of it, the Russians will be able to see us. Get over the top and onto the other side where we'll have cover again."

Shouting, *"Auf gehts!"* ("Let's go!"), I led them forward. Advancing over the treeless crest of the hill, we immediately encountered machine-gun fire and dashed for cover at the bottom. Given our vulnerability in this situation, I was relieved to execute the mission with only one wounded man.

Upon reaching our frontline, I instructed my squad to dig trenches and haul up logs to create a rampart. In the midst of constructing these defenses, a group of several German Stuka dive-bombers appeared up in the sky.

With sudden alarm, we watched as they began to plummet toward us. Gaining speed in their descent, the sirens mounted under their wings screeched louder and louder. The planes were coming right at us! Only at the last minute did they veer off to deliver their bombs on an enemy target about 150 yards to the front of our trenches.

A short time after we took up our post, a flock of sheep wandered into the No Man's Land running between the German and Soviet lines. In the fading light just before sundown, one of the men in my squad brought down one of the sheep with his rifle. Once it was dark, a couple of my men hauled the lamb back into our lines, where it was skinned and roasted over an open fire. Having gone without fresh meat for a long time, we all savored a rare feast of mutton.

Our satisfaction did not last long. Apparently, the meat was cooked inadequately. Everyone in my squad soon began to experience stomach cramps and had to run for the bushes. At the end of my own two-week bout of diarrhea, I swore an oath to myself that I would never touch mutton again.

Because of casualties suffered by the infantry company's officers in the intense combat, I was shortly assigned the command of a full platoon of roughly three-dozen men. Lacking bunkers in which to take shelter, we huddled in our holes in the already freezing weather.

During a firefight on October 12, a bullet passed through the left arm of my overcoat. While only slightly grazing my skin, the injury nonetheless required me to seek first aid and bandages from our medic, temporarily pulling me off the frontline.

With a brief moment to contact Anneliese, I penned a letter. The following line conveys the extent to which my feelings for her sustained me. "It is because of your existence and love that life in combat here on the Eastern Front is made bearable."

After a couple of days back up at the front with the infantry platoon, new orders arrived on October 16 reassigning the infantry command to someone else and directing me to remain in the rear area. Running increasingly short of officers, the army perhaps took this measure as part of its larger effort to ensure that officer candidates would not die in battle just before returning to Germany for training at one of the five *Kriegsschulen* (war academies).

Though my brief stint in command of regular infantry troops proved a positive experience, there had not been enough time for us to develop any sort of bond. While the troops treated me with the respect due anyone superior in rank, they were otherwise indifferent to me.

Likewise, I felt little personal attachment to them and missed my old comrades back in the 13th Company. Working as a forward observer gave me a greater sense of responsibility, knowing that the whole regiment was depending on my skills to provide them with fire support from our heavy guns.

On October 17, I received orders from Col. Behrend to attend a ten-day course. Conducted a few miles behind the frontlines, it was designed to help prepare officer candidates who would soon be entering a *Kriegsschule*. Having obtained the official status of *Fähnrich* (junior officer candidate), I finally departed Russia on October 31 for the long train trip back to Germany.

PARTISANS

To defend against attack by Soviet partisan forces, the front and rear railcars of the train were mounted with light anti-aircraft guns.

Although sabotage of the railroad tracks along our route delayed the trip a couple of times, we otherwise crossed through occupied Soviet territory without encountering significant partisan activity.

Despite the interference with its logistics that the German Army faced from enemy partisans, most of the time our division did not have much difficulty obtaining supplies at the front. The worst supply problems had actually resulted from the weather during the bitterly cold winter of 1941–1942. Since that time, the Wehrmacht had succeeded in adequately meeting our needs for food, ammunition, and other essential supplies. Even letters and parcels from home arrived promptly.

Although we did not notice any change in the availability of our supplies at the front, soldiers returning from leave in 1943 began to report that the partisans were becoming a significant problem in rear areas. They eventually grew so powerful that the German Army deployed whole divisions behind the lines to conduct counterinsurgency operations to secure the rail links to our army at the front. Even with these efforts, the partisans frequently succeeded in disrupting our rail network and impeding the movement of troops and supplies.

Up at the front, we placed a large part of the blame for the growing problem with the partisans on the brutal way the *Generalkommissariat* (Nazi political officials) ran the occupation behind us. These Nazis in the *Generalkommissariat* were known as *Goldfasanen* (Golden Pheasants) because of the golden brown color of their party uniforms and their arrogant and corrupt misrule.

Most of the German soldiers around me felt a deep bitterness at the suffering that these *Goldfasanen* intentionally and unnecessarily inflicted on the Soviet civilian population. This ideologically inspired cruelty led many of the occupied peoples that had once welcomed us as liberators to shift their support to the partisans working for a Communist victory.

RETURN TO GERMANY
October 31–December 7, 1943

Because my orders did not immediately require me to report to the 58th Division's reserve base in Oldenburg, Anneliese and I had made plans to spend four days together in St. Peter-Ording, in Schleswig-Holstein, where she had been posted as a nurse. On November 3, I finally reached the small town and took a hotel room.

Despite windy, cold and wet weather that time of year, Anneliese and I still enjoyed strolling around the scenic resort area and watching the waves crash against the coast. After all we had been through during the previous six months apart, we were simply happy to have time together again.

On November 8, I returned south to the reserve base in Oldenburg, which served as the 58th Infantry Division's primary processing center for soldiers departing and returning from the front. There was little for me to do, but Anneliese was able to follow me down from St. Peter-Ording for a two-day visit.

Just after she returned to St. Peter-Ording, Anneliese began experiencing stomach pains and underwent an emergency appendectomy on November 17 at a hospital in Tönning near St. Peter-Ording. Before returning home to Püggen for my three-week furlough before the start of my training at the *Kriegsschule*, I made a trip up to Tönning to spend a little time with her in the hospital.

Reaching home the next day, my family gave me their usual warm welcome. As always, my sisters wanted me to carry them on my back and play games with them. Despite such light moments, it was clear to me that life in Germany was growing harder.

Beginning in the winter of 1943–1944, the local authorities required children to bring a piece of peat coal to class each day in order to help heat Püggen's one-room schoolhouse. If the supplies ran out, my sisters and the other students would have to bundle up in their coats throughout the day to stay warm.

By this time, Marlene had completed her elementary schooling and had entered an upper level school in nearby Salzwedel, where her main teacher was a strong Nazi. Aware of our family's lack of support for the Nazis, this teacher caused Marlene many difficulties, especially for her failure to use the "Heil Hitler" salute in which the arm is thrust out. Politically handicapped and under constant scrutiny, Marlene had to work extremely hard to achieve a measure of academic success.

Her experience reflected the broader treatment that my family received because of its unfavorable attitude toward the Nazis. For example, when my family sought permission to butcher one of our pigs, it encountered problems obtaining authorization from the local farmer who had been granted such decision-making powers because of his Nazi loyalty. Likewise, when the higher authorities issued a directive requiring Püggen to supply a certain number of animals for slaughter or horses for transportation, this same Nazi farmer made sure that my family was the first one required to surrender the necessary livestock.

In other ways, my family's experience was typical of that of other German families. Like many of them, my parents risked losing more than one son in the war. Earlier that year, the army had drafted my younger brother, Otto. When he completed his basic training, he was stationed with an infantry division in northern France, in the area south of Normandy. Because his twin Hans had suffered a childhood accident in which a wagon wheel ran over his left leg, he was unable to serve at the front, despite his desire to do so.

When we were away at the front, my mother would anxiously await letters from Otto or me each day. While eager to hear more news on the military situation, my mother did not trust the information presented by the tightly controlled German media.

Although risking harsh punishment for tuning into enemy broadcasts, she would regularly get out a small radio she kept hidden away and scan the dial for the BBC's distinctive classical music call sign. Though occasionally joined by other members of the family, she frequently would sit alone in a back room listening to their German language program in an effort to obtain a clearer picture of the war. Closely following military developments on a map, my mother knew where the frontlines ran and sometimes even where our divisions were operating.

Upon her release from hospital in Tönning on November 27, Anneliese was granted leave from her nursing duties and went home to Hamburg, where I joined her for four days. During this visit, she arranged for me to stay with her "Aunt" Frieda, a sweet elderly woman who was a close friend of her father's and who had somewhat taken on the role of mother to Anneliese since she was growing up without her own mother. She resided in a two-bedroom apartment in the Winterhude suburb of the city, located behind the popular delicatessen that she ran selling coffee, chocolates, and other desserts.

Like Aunt Frieda's apartment, the house that Anneliese's father shared with his sisters in the suburb of Wandsbek had escaped major damage in the bombing raids, but the magnitude of the devastation in the heart of Hamburg was astonishing. In tears, Anneliese finally described her horrible recollections from the previous summer.

In the aftermath of the bombings, she had only been able to reach the hospital where she had been training as a nurse with great difficulty. Once there, she treated many terribly burned civilian casualties. The giant inferno caused by the bombing had generated such intense heat that the asphalt roads had melted into a sticky tar. People trying to escape the firestorm became stuck and burned like torches.

In the tragedy's grim wake, we found it difficult to appreciate fully our limited moments together. The war was now everywhere and impossible to escape. Yet, even as the situation at home and the news from the front grew more ominous, a surprising sense of optimism about the outcome of the war still prevailed among all those I knew.

Göbbel's speeches promising the imminent arrival of miracle weapons, more advanced than anything Germany's enemies possessed, inspired hope that our fortunes would soon change.

CHAPTER 13

KRIEGSCHULE

DECEMBER 1943–MAY 1944

WHEN I ARRIVED FROM Püggen to commence my officer training at the *Kriegsschule* in the suburbs of Dresden on December 8, the old Saxon city was still beautiful. There was no hint of the terrible fate that awaited Dresden later in the war, when an Allied incendiary bombing would kill about 60,000 civilians.

In acknowledgement of our service at the front, the war academy tried to make our experience as officer candidates as agreeable as possible, providing us with comfortable rooms in the barracks and good meals in the mess hall. At the same time, the academy's staff kept us constantly busy with a variety of tasks.

From morning until noon, we attended classes on leadership skills, tactics, and other military theory. Our instructors also taught military etiquette, such as proper conduct for an officer in the company of a woman and appropriate dining manners.

In the afternoon, we carried out field training with weapons in the rolling hills of the academy's firing range at Königsbrück. Our instructors would assign us a platoon with a couple of 75-millimeter guns in order to assess our leadership skills and our ability to handle the howitzers in a variety of offensive and defensive tactical scenarios.

Because most of the soldiers we were commanding possessed frontline experience, the exercises were not too challenging. In fact, because of my years in combat as a forward observer, I was often able to pass along practical advice to the instructors.

On weekday evenings, we would study in our rooms after a meal in the academy's mess hall. Although the academy arranged no dances or other social activities for us on weekends, I sometimes attended operas and operettas with other officer candidates at Dresden's renowned Semper opera house.

Despite increasing numbers of officers from middle class origins, Germany's officer corps was still filled with many blue-blooded aristocrats—"Von so-and-so"— who had been educated at the nation's elite institutions. The majority of these high-born officers were decent men who treated the other soldiers with respect, but there were a few who held very superior attitudes toward others not of their social class.

While most of the 'Vons' were fellow Prussians, I was not from an aristocratic background and despised those officers who treated common soldiers like myself in a condescending manner. My experiences with one particular Prussian aristocrat illustrates the character of this arrogance.

The same first lieutenant who had once led his horse into our barracks at Lüneburg in a drunken display of insolence had since achieved the rank of captain and been placed in command of a battalion-sized unit in the regiment.

At a regimental staff meeting I attended after becoming an officer, the captain exhibited his disdainful attitude toward the enlisted men. When several other officers entered the bunker to join our group, he said with undisguised distaste, "Shut that door! It smells of ordinary people out there."

Relatively few officers from aristocratic backgrounds acted so haughtily, but this captain's attitude reflected the importance of class in German society at the time. If someone had a 'Von' in front of their last name and was well educated, they would typically sail right through the hiring process when seeking a job. This same sort of favoritism similarly applied in granting military promotions, though the Wehrmacht was not generally a class-based institution in other respects.

Once becoming a German officer, you were accorded respect because of your rank rather than because you were a Prussian, a Nazi, or possessed some other privileged background. Interestingly, I never witnessed any particular cultural clash between officers coming from aristocratic Prussian backgrounds and those coming from less privileged circumstances. In my experience, it would be more accurate to say that the aristocrats separated themselves from everyone else, just as they did in civilian life.

A couple of weeks into our training, Anneliese surprised me with a telegram announcing her impending visit to Dresden at the end of December. During this unanticipated but very welcome visit, Anneliese and I crammed as much as we could into our time together. In the couple of days before the New Year's celebration, we wandered through the city's famous rambling baroque complex of pavilions and galleries called the Zwinger, watched a play at the opera house, and called on some of my distant relatives.

Anneliese and I also dropped by a number of Dresden's jewelers in order to select a shop to craft our engagement rings. Because it was impossible to purchase anything made of gold during the war, the customer had to provide the jeweler with an adequate amount of gold to fashion the desired item. Several weeks after we supplied our collected gold to the jeweler we had settled on, the shop delivered an attractive pair of rings to me.

On January 6, our cadre of officer candidates traveled 25 miles south from Dresden to the mountain resort of Altenberg for a week of training in downhill and cross-country skiing. The evenings included entertainment by a talented troupe of female dancers and a youth choir singing local folk songs, but our daytime "recreation" was far more demanding.

In a scenic winter setting among snow-covered trees, our instructor spent the first couple of days teaching us the basics of downhill skiing. Though I had cross-country skiied in Russia, this type of skiing was completely new to me. Once our instruction ended, we headed up to the slopes.

Waiting in single file at the top of a ski run, we watched each man in turn disappear from sight, uncertain what lay beyond our view. Finally, the instructor ordered me to push off. Building up speed as my skis carried me down the slope, I came over a hill to confront a ski jump located directly in my path. There was no way to avoid it. Racing down the ramp in a crouch, I was sitting on my leather riding britches by the time I left the end of the jump. And that was how I crash-landed in the soft snow at the bottom.

A couple of days later, our instructors ordered us to ski down an icy bobsled run. On my attempt, I managed to ski about 20 or 30 yards. By that point, I was traveling too fast to navigate the turn. In desperation, I threw my arms around a large tree growing beside the run to keep from breaking my neck.

Soon after our return to the academy in Dresden, we were faced with another test of courage. About ten o'clock one night, our instructors ordered us to put on our swimming trunks and come down to the school's large indoor pool. On our arrival, we lined up at the bottom of the ladder leading to the 33-foot-high diving platform.

One at a time, each officer candidate was directed to ascend to the top. Once there, the instructor switched off the lights and ordered the man to jump down into pitch-black darkness. While some of my fellow officer candidates were very hesitant to obey the order, I simply dropped into the pool feet first when my turn came, figuring that our instructors would not want to eliminate future officers.

With these types of training methods the German Army was instilling an unconditional obedience to orders, whatever obstacles might exist or whatever doubts an individual might possess. Such challenges perhaps also made my promotion to *Oberfähnrich* (senior officer candidate) on March 1 a little more meaningful.

A few days before our training concluded, we learned that Adolf Hitter would personally deliver an address in Dessau to officer candidates from across Germany. Even with my deep discomfort with the Nazi regime, it was impossible not to feel a sense of anticipation during the 100-mile rail trip from Dresden.

The subsequent announcement that the Führer would not be able to attend and that instead Admiral Dönitz, the commander-in-chief of the *Kriegsmarine* (German Navy), would speak to us was met with widespread disappointment. Even with my childhood interest in submarine warfare, I found his oration uninspiring.

Back at the *Kriegsschule*, our graduation on March 15, 1944 involved no fanfare. Instead, the academy's commanding superintendent simply delivered a short, inspiring speech and wished us well. Though the field training had been of little practical utility and could not begin to match what I had learned through years of combat, the theoretical aspect of our instruction had been interesting and helpful to me as I prepared for a new leadership role. If nothing else, it was simply a relief to have several months away from the bullets and shells at the front.

On my arrival in Oldenburg from Dresden the day after graduation, I reported to a captain, who told me to return the following morning. When I finally received my second lieutenant's shoulder boards the next day, I eagerly headed straight to a Wehrmacht tailor to make the necessary changes in my uniform. Although uncertain what lay ahead of me upon my return to the front, I had at last achieved my long-sought ambition to serve as a leader.

ENGAGEMENT TO ANNELIESE AND FURTHER TRAINING
March 17–May 13, 1944

Receiving a two-week furlough on March 17, I made the short trip from Oldenburg to Hamburg, anxiously anticipating my imminent engagement to Anneliese. She was already in the middle of a month of leave from her nursing duties and was waiting for me when I arrived.

Rather than spending my three nights at Herr Berndt's house, I again stayed with Aunt Frieda in Winterhude. However, Anneliese and I took our meals back at her home in Wandsbek in order to give me an opportunity to spend a little time with her father and her other relatives who lived there.

On March 18, Anneliese and I placed our newly crafted rings on one another's fingers at Aunt Frieda's home. There was no real celebration of the occasion, but we shared the news of our engagement with her father and telephoned my family back in Püggen.

In the middle of a war in which our future together was so unsure, Anneliese and I agreed that we should delay our marriage until peace was achieved. Facing a return to the Russian front in a few weeks time, I did not know if I would even live to see my twenty-fourth birthday. Though it was difficult for me to tie another person to my uncertain fate, her promise to marry me would give me a sense of hope in the dark days that lay ahead.

While our decision to wait was based solely on our concerns about what might happen in the future, we were also aware that we would need to obtain authorization from the army and other government

agencies when we did decide to marry. Beyond the normal bureau-
cratic red tape, we faced an additional complication because Anneliese's mother possessed the Jewish surname of Salomon.

This had been her mother's maiden name as a result of her childhood adoption by the family of a Jewish butcher in Hamburg. When
the authorities saw the name, they refused to grant me permission to
marry Anneliese without further investigation. Challenging such racial
restrictions was impossible, though I did not see how the government
had any right to interfere with whom I chose to marry, even if
Anneliese had been Jewish.

Leaving Hamburg a couple of days after our engagement,
Anneliese and I spent the next few days with my family in Püggen. On
March 24, she departed our farm to spend a week at home before
reporting for duty in Leer, Germany. After obtaining her orders in Leer
on April 4, she made the 250-mile trip to her newly assigned hospital
in Beverlo, Belgium.

At the end of March, I traveled 60 miles west to Munster, where I
entered a two-week training course for company commanders. It
included additional classroom instruction as well as field training at a
large proving ground nearby. This gave us an opportunity to observe
firsthand the performance of new weapons such as a highly accurate
210-millimeter rocket launcher.

Following another two-week furlough from duty in Püggen, I
arrived on April 30 for a week-long course at the officer's riding academy in the town of Soltau, a little west of Munster.

Waking at dawn, we began by leading our horses at a trot around
and around the sawdust covered floor of a large building. This was
followed by an exercise in which we practiced repeatedly jumping
onto the horse's back while the animal continued to move around the
ring. Beyond the constant riding, our instructors also taught us other
potentially useful skills, such as how to make a horse lie down in order
to shield ourselves in the midst of a firefight.

By the end of the second day, areas of the flesh on my buttocks and
thighs had become rather disgusting raw wounds. Each night they
would crust over before painfully reopening during the following day's
riding. Other than this physical discomfort, the experience at Soltau
proved generally agreeable. While many of the men found the course

arduous, my previous work with horses on our farm made the training relatively undemanding for me.

On the completion of this last element of my required officer training on May 8, I spent three days at the 58th Division's reserve base in Oldenburg. To my great satisfaction, Anneliese was able to join me after receiving a short furlough following an Allied bombing raid that had struck her hospital in Beverlo. Although she had not been injured in the attack, the prospect of further air raids nonetheless caused me to grow increasingly concerned for her future safety.

During her stay in Oldenburg, we had planned to get a hotel room together. However, when I approached the hotel's manager for a room, he inquired whether we were married. When I responded that we were engaged to be married, he informed me that unmarried couples were not permitted to share a room and instead required us to pay for separate rooms. The war had brought many changes, but it did little to alter Germany's traditionally conservative social conventions.

At the end of our brief time together on May 10, Anneliese returned to Belgium. Shortly after her arrival, she was shifted 20 miles east from Beverlo to the Belgian town of Genk. At the hospital here, she would soon be helping to treat a flood of casualties from France.

At the end of a final visit to Püggen from May 10 to 13, I said my goodbyes to my family. Heading back to the Eastern Front as an officer, I had no idea where I would be assigned, nor whether I would ever return home.

Little did I anticipate the hammerblows about to befall the Wehrmacht in the following month of June. During the summer of 1944 Germany would face an escalating series of crises that would-steadily increase the suffering and hardship at the front and at home.

CHAPTER 14

RETURN TO THE FRONT

MAY–OCTOBER 1944

WHEN MY TRAIN REACHED Tilsit at the border of the German Reich on May 15, there was a cable waiting for me at the Wehrmacht's central leadership reserve depot from Col. Behrend, commander of the 154th Grenadier Regiment.

His message requested my return to the regiment to take charge of my old heavy weapons company, replacing the already departed Second Lt. Reichardt. Since I could have been assigned to any company in Army Group North, his appeal for me to receive command of my old unit was excellent news as far as I was concerned, though it was a completely unexpected action over which I had no influence.

Granting Behrend's request, the army promptly issued new orders returning me to the 13th Company. Boarding the next train out of Tilsit, I embarked on the 250-mile trip to rejoin the 58th Division at the front, now located in northeastern Estonia. The journey offered me further time to reflect on developments on the Eastern Front over the previous half year.

In January 1944, the Red Army had executed an offensive that brought an end to our long siege of Leningrad and forced Army Group North into a general retreat to the west. This orderly withdrawal in the northern sector was part of the larger shift in the strategic situation that had taken place after Stalingrad.

Although there was no decline in the fighting capability of the individual German soldier, there were ever-increasing personnel losses that Germany could not replace. Meanwhile, the Red Army was steadily increasing its quantitative superiority in manpower and mate-

169

rial and regaining its territory lost early in the war. There was hope that by shortening its length of front the Wehrmacht could in some measure compensate for its inferiority in personnel, while at the same time shortening its own supply lines and lengthening those of the enemy.

As the 154th Regiment pulled back to the northwest from Nevel with the rest of the 58th Division that winter, it split up into smaller formations in order to conduct a more effective fighting retreat. Under mounting pressure, the detachment of regiments, battalions, and even companies from their larger formations had become more commonplace. With few reserves available, the Germany Army deployed these newly created "fire brigades" to plug gaps that opened along a fluid front and to respond to other crises.

By February 1944, the 154th Regiment had reassembled and joined the 58th Division at a location near Narva in northeastern Estonia, where it took up a position in a previously constructed network of defenses that ran between the Baltic Coast and Lake Peipus. Operating from this fortified "Panther Position," the 154th Regiment helped to repulse Red Army attacks around the town of Sirgala, about 15 miles east of Narva and our old Plyussa battlefield of 1941.

Upon my arrival at the 13th Company's position on May 20, I immediately assumed the role of acting *Kompanieführer* (company leader). Within a month, Col. Behrend confirmed me in this position. Normally it would have been held by a captain rather than a second lieutenant, but the desperate shortage of officers had now made my situation relatively common in the German Army. As the only officer in the company, I was forced to run my platoons with sergeants who normally commanded squads.

Senior Sgt. Jüchter was still in charge of the *Tross* (rear area) and Staff Sergeant Ehlert continued to lead the communications platoon, but now I was their superior. The camaraderie that I once enjoyed with many members of the company as an enlisted man was no longer possible. Addressed as *"Herr Leutnant,"* a certain awkward distance appeared between myself and the other longtime veterans of the company like Willi Schütte.

Yet, as a result of the discipline and respect for rank instilled by army training, we soon adjusted and became accustomed to the changed relationship. While there was deference to my rank and a distance between us off the battlefield, the old comradeship would return during combat or if one of them was wounded. My relationship with the men in the 13th Company may have also been helped by the fact that I continued to spend about the same amount of time at the front as the enlisted men.

Though there were few casualties in the company during the first two months after my return, the intense fighting over the preceding months had reduced the unit to about 200 men. This strength was significantly less than the complement of between 250 and 300 troops we had maintained in the first couple of years of the war in Russia. Fortunately, the relative calm at the Panther Position permitted us to restore our depleted strength to some extent as we received replacements and the return of wounded troops from convalescent leave.

The fact that the Wehrmacht drew most of the men filling its divisions from a single region enhanced camaraderie and cohesion within a unit, but it could also lead to significant tension when the army had to send outsiders as replacements or when units from different regions had to act in close cooperation.

While interaction between troops from different regions could lead to problems, a few strangers from outside northern Germany performed very successfully in our company. In particular, an Austrian private first class from Vienna surprisingly proved to be one of the best soldiers I would command in combat. His relaxed manner caused me some initial concern, but he executed orders promptly and always remained calm when the bullets were flying. You could never predict someone's behavior in combat.

As an officer, I was issued a Luger pistol for my sidearm. While only firing it a couple of times in combat, it proved a good weapon and fairly accurate up to a range of 20 to 30 yards. Later, I obtained a Spanish-made Astra Model 600 pistol that would serve as my favored sidearm. In some instances, I also carried a Mauser rifle or MP-40 submachine gun, though I preferred the rifle in action due to its much greater range and accuracy.

With my new rank, I acquired the services of a soldier who took care of my clothes and delivered my meals from the company field kitchen. The company had few motor vehicles, but there was a

Citroën at my disposal and, fortunately, a designated enlisted man to serve as my driver. Because my family had not possessed an automobile or truck when I was growing up, I had never learned to drive nor obtained a license.

My position also entitled me to make use of a horse named Thea and receive the services of her handler, although I would seldom ride her unless we were on the march and conditions were quiet. With a farming background, my knowledge of horses often proved greater than that of the soldiers charged with their care. On one occasion, when a sergeant was experiencing trouble taming a particular horse, I leapt up on it and rode around in circles until the horse became submissive.

Despite my responsibilities of command, Anneliese remained constantly on my mind. While suffering many difficult and painful experiences as a soldier, the worst part of the war for me was my separation from her and the uncertainty of whether we would ever see each other again. Our letters were filled with expressions of our yearning to see each other, our wish to marry, and our desire to enjoy a normal life. Beyond conveying our love to one another, we also shared the hope that the war would soon end. In the face of ever-darker news, we sought to reinforce each other's morale about the outcome.

Working as a nurse in Belgium, Anneliese mentioned her frequent sightings of the massed bomber formations flying overhead on the way from England to Germany or on their return. Having witnessed the horrible fate of Hamburg, she would wonder which city would next face devastation.

She also conveyed news from her correspondence and phone conversations with my brother Otto, who was posted relatively nearby her in France. Soon after the long-anticipated landings by the Western Allies on June 6 1944, she and my family became greatly concerned when they lost touch with him. Three months of uncertainty passed before they finally received a note from the Red Cross indicating Otto had become a POW following his capture on August 30.

Yet, though my anxiety over my brother's fate eventually lifted, my concern for Anneliese's safety only intensified, especially when I learned that the area around her hospital in Genk had been bombed in mid-June.

THE DÜNA: mid-July–August 7, 1944

There had been only limited action along the Narva sector of the Panther Position since my arrival in late May, but an urgent crisis on the Eastern Front soon developed to the south. On June 22, the third anniversary of our invasion of Russia, the Red Army commenced a massive offensive that virtually annihilated Army Group Center, killing or capturing hundreds of thousands of German troops.

The destruction of one of the Wehrmacht's three army groups was a strategic disaster at least equal to Stalingrad that gravely undermined Germany's entire position on the Eastern Front. With the southern flank of Army Group North almost unprotected, the high command rapidly assembled units from around the northern front to deploy down to southern Latvia in mid-July.

As we were preparing to pull out of the Narva area, the division supplied my company with about two-dozen 210-millimeter rockets. These were capped with a variety of different warheads, including one type that spread small steel ball bearings dispersed by a high explosive; another variety that spread shrapnel dispersed by an explosive compressed air canister; and a third that used an incendiary naptha material.

With our departure imminent, it was necessary to expend or destroy any remaining ordinance that would have been difficult to haul with us, in order to prevent it from falling into enemy hands. After witnessing a test-firing of these rockets a few months earlier at the company commander's course in Munster, I was also simply interested to assess their combat effectiveness.

Lacking the necessary equipment to fire the rockets, I came up with the idea of using their shipping crates as launching tubes. Working behind a hill that hid us from enemy surveillance, we constructed two sets of simple wooden supports and then chopped down a couple of five-inch diameter trees for crossbeams.

Leaning one of the shipping crates against a crossbeam at the appropriate firing angle, we aimed the ersatz launcher by sight at a target in the Soviet lines. After connecting one of the rocket's electric trigger mechanisms to a hand-operated electrical detonator normally used to set off mines, we carefully loaded the weapon into the improvised launching tube. On ignition, it flashed through the air and exploded right on target.

Following this success, I issued orders to similarly prepare our entire stock of rockets for launching, setting their built-in timing mechanisms in order to produce a short delay between each rocket's firing.

When the detonator handle was twisted, the rockets began racing across No Man's Land to their designated targets on the edge of a nearby woods. In an awesome display of concentrated firepower, the explosive warheads' detonations tossed trees into the air, while the incendiary warheads instantly ignited a blaze across a wide swath of forest.

Though we were uncertain exactly what Russian forces were arrayed across from us, these rockets had obliterated whatever was there. With the proper launching devices, the rockets would have been highly effective weapons, but we never received any further supplies.

Leaving the Panther Position, the 58th Division transferred about 100 miles west to Reval, Estonia.

Generally, we moved these longer distances by train and shorter distances by horse or by foot. Despite some attempt to motorize the 58th Division during the course of the war, the process had been very inconsistent. While lacking any trucks when we fought in France, the Wehrmacht subsequently issued us a number of Bedford trucks captured from the Allies after that campaign had ended.

From about the end of 1942, we began to receive a large number of German-made motorized vehicles in Russia. This effort to motorize our division soon halted and we received no further vehicles after mid-1943. Once the army stopped supplying us with new vehicles, we thought it somewhat amusing to find ourselves increasingly on horses once again as our existing trucks were destroyed or immobilized from a lack of spare parts.

Motorization had mixed results in the conditions we experienced in the Soviet Union. When the spring and fall *rasputitsas* (rainy seasons) turned many Russian roads into a mud resembling quicksand, horses sometimes proved superior to trucks. Often, the mud was so deep that our Panzers would have to haul the trucks out. Even in good weather, you could never drive very fast on primitive roads while hauling a 150-millimeter howitzer.

On reflection, I believe that many commentators have overestimated the significance of our lack of mechanization, especially once Germany had been placed on the strategic defensive. Horses did not require petrol for fuel nor steel and industrial plants to be produced, so in this sense helped preserve Germany's resources for more vital weapons and ammunition. Whatever the relative merits of horse-drawn versus motorized transportation, our division was again relying almost exclusively on horses to haul our guns and other equipment by the time I returned to the front in mid-1944.

Soon after arriving in Reval, our division made the 150-mile journey by train south to Dünaburg, located beside the Düna River in Latvia. At the end of a 30-mile march west to the town of Rokiskis in neighboring Lithuania, we engaged in an intense battle with advancing Soviet forces on July 17, but failed to hold the city. Adopting a defensive posture, we entrenched in a nearby position about 75 miles southeast of Riga, Latvia.

Though no longer a forward observer, I continued to operate close to the front as an officer. Confident of my horsemanship, I probably also took some unnecessary risks. On a quiet day, I decided to take Thea out for some exercise, but ended up straying too close to the enemy's position.

Suddenly bullets began whizzing through the air around us. It was a scary moment for me, particularly since captured Russians had told us that Red Army troops had standing orders to shoot first at those German soldiers who wore the form-fitting pants and boots typical of German officers. Swinging Thea around, I jumped her over a fence and galloped to the rear. Once again, my life had been spared.

In addition to visually monitoring the enemy's frontlines, we listened for any change in the volume or type of noise emitted from their position. Sometimes the change was subtle, but at other times it was obvious. At our first position close to Rokiskis, the sound of female laughter echoed across No Man's Land. Calling back to our guns, I ordered a few rounds be dropped in that direction. Following the short barrage, the front became completely silent.

Late one night soon afterward, a sudden torrent of heavy machine-gun fire erupted from our frontlines about 50 yards ahead of my bunker. Confirming my suspicions, an infantryman arrived moments later to report that a Soviet attack was coming directly toward our position.

With our troops in urgent need of fire support, I moved outside the bunker and contacted the teams manning our three 105-millimeter mortars, aware that the vertical trajectory of their fire made them more effective than our howitzers among the Düna's tall trees. Uncertain how close the Russian assault had penetrated, my initial orders directed a barrage of mortar rounds into an area about 100 yards to our front.

When several salvos produced no diminishment in the intensity of the battle, I pulled the curtain of shells 50 yards nearer to us. The concentration of fire from our machine guns immediately made it clear, however, that the enemy had advanced even closer. Cutting the range back to coordinates 25 yards ahead of our frontline, I ordered a final bombardment, fearing that any further reduction might risk hitting our own troops.

As the mortar rounds slammed into a rectangular zone roughly 25 by 75 yards, the Soviet assault was finally halted. Rather than spreading out as they normally would in a daylight attack, the Red Army troops had clustered together in the darkness, amplifying the deadly results of our barrage. Our infantry later told me that just one of these rounds alone had killed ten to twenty Russians. The total enemy death toll from the 30 or so mortar shells must have been in the dozens.

One afternoon a few days later, I was resting in my bunker about 100 yards behind the front. Lieutenant Colonel (*Oberstleutnant*) Werner Ebeling, who had just become the acting regimental commander, entered and asked, "Lübbecke, do you have something to drink?" Pleased to have a chance to talk with him, I grabbed a bottle of cognac from under my bunk.

Almost immediately, three more officers I knew from the regimental staff appeared and demanded, "Is that all you have?" Happy to share my stock, I produced additional bottles.

The problem with this situation was the German custom of toasting. When a toast is made, everyone present must empty their glasses, turning them upside down as proof of their consumption. At the end of a long afternoon of toasts, we were all so drunk that we could barely walk.

Departing the bunker, we somehow stumbled the mile and a half back to the *Tross*, no doubt resembling a bunch of drunken sailors. Locating our quartermaster, we obtained a barrel of salted herring and ate the fish right out of the top of it.

My impression is that we eventually wandered back up to the front, but I was too drunk to recall exactly. The following day, my head was aching with one of the worst hangovers I had ever experienced. For the rest of my life I have not been able to smell cognac without feeling ill.

BACK TOWARD RIGA: August 7–October 5, 1944

Shortly after our drinking party, advances by the Red Army threatened the German forces near Rokiskis with encirclement, forcing us to make our first major retreat in the Düna region on August 7. Withdrawing to the northwest over the course of the next couple of days, the 180 or so remaining men in my company established a new position near the western turn in the Nemunelis-Memele River. This placed us about 40 miles northwest of Rokiskis and roughly the same distance southeast of Riga.

When we reached our new position, I ordered a single round to be fired at a particular set of coordinates to our front, as was standard procedure. When our howitzer boomed behind me, I waited for the expected explosion in our front.

Instead, there was a blast right behind me and I realized that the shell had fallen short. Immediately afterward, an enlisted man came running up to our position yelling, "Those sons of bitches—they shot me!"

Uncertain whether the misfire resulted from a mistake on my part in calculating the range or an error by the gun crew, I did not volunteer that I might have been to blame for this incidence of "friendly fire." Luckily, the man's wound was slight and no one else was injured.

As August progressed, the situation on the Düna front grew more fluid and we were increasingly on the move. Red Army attacks across a wide front against outnumbered German troops led to the increasing use of ad hoc "fire brigades" assigned to block Russian penetrations. Their effective deployment was hampered by uncertainty as to whether the enemy was in front of us, to the side of us, or to our rear. To avoid being outflanked and encircled, there was ultimately no alternative but for the whole frontline to steadily pull back.

Acting as one of these emergency "fire brigades," our heavy weapons company sometimes occupied an area of the front separate from our regimental infantry or even in support of units from another division. While none of the main Soviet assaults struck our company's sector of the front, we frequently engaged in numerous smaller combat actions.

Whereas in offensive operations we used our guns to reduce the capability of the Soviet forces to resist an advance, in defensive actions we sought to break up concentrations of Red Army forces before they advanced or during an attack. When this failed, we sought to limit the enemy's ability to closely follow our retreat.

When orders came to pull out of a position, our gun company was always the first part of the regiment to pull out since we required more time to load our equipment and also traveled more slowly. The regiment would leave a rearguard of the two or three infantry squads with machine guns supported by a couple of 75-millimeter howitzers or 105-millimeter mortars from our company. When this infantry rearguard pulled back, the remaining gun crews received little time to load their equipment and get on the road ahead of the pursuing Russians.

Throughout the Baltic region, there were a few large depots where the Wehrmacht had accumulated enormous quantities of supplies to support the operations of Army Group North. These stores of war materials and food often had to be hastily destroyed or simply abandoned because of the speed of the Red Army advance. Frequently, there were large clouds of black smoke billowing up into the sky behind the frontlines just before we retreated.

The loss of these depots caused certain types of supplies to grow tighter, but it also meant that we sometimes received delivery of large amounts of rare luxuries. In one instance, the army sent our division numerous bottles of Hennessey cognac that would otherwise have been lost. Under the constant threat of a Soviet attack, there were few opportune moments to allow the men to drink freely. Now more alert than ever to the dangers posed by excessive drinking, I kept the liquor supplies tightly rationed.

At a location further along in our retreat through the Düna region, there was a rare occasion when the divisional artillery coordinated with our heavy weapons company to jointly strike a target.

While our heavy weapons company supported the regimental infantry's operations closer to the front, the artillery normally concentrated on targets in the enemy's rear area. The forward observer for the regiment's heavy gun company typically worked in close proximity and often exchanged ideas with his counterpart in the division's main artillery regiment, but their distinct fire support missions meant that they almost always operated independently.

In this particular instance, our division's intelligence had become suspicious that the Red Army was massing forces in a roughly ten-acre wooded area to our front. To destroy whatever was there, the artillery command requested our company to join them in a barrage on the Soviet position.

With my long experience as an F.O., it was possible for me to calculate almost down to the second how long it would take for the shells from our howitzers and mortars to reach a particular target. Coordinating with the artillery's F.O., we sought to precisely time our barrages in order to deliver the maximum possible intensity of fire on the unsuspecting Soviet forces hidden in the forest.

Orchestrating the barrage from our guns by my watch, I first ordered the firing of our 105-millimeter mortars because it takes longer for their rounds to reach the target due to their high trajectory. This was closely followed by the firing of all of our 150-millimeter and 75-millimeter howitzers.

In about half a minute or so, hundreds of shells from our guns and the artillery simultaneously slammed into the woods. This devastating cataclysm of fire undoubtedly annihilated any Russian forces that might have been massing there. In such circumstances, it was impossible not to feel pity for the enemy.

A few lines from a series of letters to Anneliese during our steady retreat that August exposes my darkening mood at the Düna. With an almost fatalistic attitude about the future I wrote, "You and I will fulfill our duties to the end." With survival uncertain I penned, "God-willing, we'll see each other again."

Yet, our love left me with hope that I expressed to her with the words, "I am grateful to have you, Dear Annelie." When she sent me a lock of curls from her hair in a letter at the end of August, I placed them in my breast pocket as a talisman.

Meanwhile, the speed of the Allied advance through France and into Belgium forced a sudden evacuation of her field hospital in Genk on September 8, 1944. In the chaos that followed, the medical personnel had to make their own escape.

After hitching a ride to back to Germany, Anneliese received a temporary leave from her nursing duties. Because of the air raids on Hamburg, she went to stay at my family's farm in Püggen until she was called back to service.

About this time, refugees fleeing the Soviet threat in the east and the bombing raids on the larger German cities began to appear in Püggen and other rural areas in greater numbers. My family welcomed distant relatives into our home from all over Germany, but there were also many strangers who knew no one in Püggen. Perhaps because of my family's long antagonistic relations with the Nazis, the local authorities assigned 20 or so of these refugees to our farm.

Every unoccupied room in the house was turned over to the refugees. Lacking enough beds, my family piled straw for the guests to sleep on. To help meet the need for food, my family even butchered some of our pigs. The presence of refugees placed an especially heavy daily burden on my mother, who worked hard to make sure that everyone was provided with cooked meals and other basic needs.

Despite my family's lack of Nazi sympathies, my sisters were pressured to attend regular meetings of the *Bund Deutscher Mädchen* or BDM (League of German Girls), the Nazis' female youth organization. In what apparently was an intentional attempt to prevent the girls from attending church services, the BDM held these sessions on Sunday mornings.

While my sisters were on their way to a meeting in a neighboring village late in the war, a low-flying Allied aircraft suddenly appeared and began strafing everything on a nearby road, causing my sisters to spring for cover in a ditch. There were similar stories of Allied fighter planes breaking away from the bombers to attack people working in the fields. Although the rural areas in Germany escaped the Anglo-

American bombing raids that targeted cities, even there residents did not completely escape death from the sky.

On both fronts, the war was drawing steadily closer to the Fatherland and no one would be left untouched.

CHAPTER 15

RETREAT INTO THE REICH

OCTOBER 1944–JANUARY 1945

"FORTRESS MEMEL"
October 5, 1944–late January, 1945

Upon being issued orders to retreat from Latvia to the German port city of Memel on October 5, most of the regular infantry from the 58th Infantry Division headed by truck to Riga's harbor and then set out aboard ship on the short sea voyage down the Baltic coast. Before their departure, Lt. Col. Ebeling assigned me temporary command of all the 154th Regiment's horse-drawn equipment, of which my own heavy weapons company comprised only a part.

Directed to deliver the detachment to Memel by road, I led the three-mile long column out of the Riga area on a 100-mile trek to the southwest. During the first part of the march, Soviet aircraft made frequent strafing runs that forced us to scramble for cover off the road, but the raids diminished once we left the area around Riga.

When our slow-moving procession had traveled a little more than halfway to Memel, a Red Army thrust reached the Baltic Sea ahead of us, blocking our planned overland route to the city. New orders redirected me to lead the column toward the German-controlled port of Libau in northwestern Latvia, from where we would sail down to Memel by ship.

Riding my horse Thea out in front of our column soon afterward, I heard a voice from behind me ask, "Where are you going?"

Caught off guard, I spun around to see an officer's staff car moving just off to the left side of my horse. Inside the vehicle sat Field

Marshall Ferdinand Schörner, the commander of Army Group North.

Startled by his sudden appearance, I nonetheless managed to snap off a salute and reply, "Libau, as far as I know, Sir."

Schörner had a reputation for ruthless discipline and for making surprise appearances all over the front. The story went that when his driver made some error, Schörner ordered him to stop and demoted him right on the spot. The next time the driver did something that pleased Schörner, he again ordered the car to stop and promoted him back to his original rank. Fortunately, I avoided the Field Marshall's displeasure and was ordered to continue with my mission.

Our column finally reached the harbor in Libau on the afternoon of October 15. Using cranes to hoist the heavier equipment, everything was loaded aboard ship in a matter of hours. Evacuating by sea that night, our blacked-out vessel hugged the Baltic coast on the roughly 35-mile voyage south. Behind us, the trapped divisions of Army Group North would fight on until the end of the war.

In the morning, our ship docked in "Fortress Memel," as Nazi propaganda referred to the city in an effort to inspire its defenders. We were now under the command of Army Group Center and back inside the territory of the Greater German Reich, about 25 miles from where the 58th Division had begun its advance into Russia three and a half years earlier.

By the time we arrived, our battered regimental infantry had already helped to repulse a number of fierce Soviet assaults against Memel. Forced to rely on only machine guns and other light weapons to this point, they urgently sought the fire support of our heavy weapons. Within a few hours of docking, our company's guns and other equipment had been unloaded and we set out for the frontlines six or seven miles from the harbor.

After passing through the edge of the city, we immediately deployed in position behind the infantry, firing a series of ranging shots to establish our zones of fire. Attacks struck our position the next day, but no major offensive followed. In the ensuing weeks, the Red Army mounted only company and battalion-sized operations against our defenses, and even these grew increasingly intermittent.

Though it usually stayed fairly quiet in our sector, Russian assaults elsewhere around Memel pushed the German lines slowly back toward the city during the following weeks. Despite persistent enemy pressure, most German units in Memel were soon transferred south-ward in response to more urgent crises. In the end, only our division and the 95th Infantry Division remained to man the city's defenses, but that proved enough to hold it.

While the Red Army's high command had other priorities, they may also have concluded that dislodging us was not worth the cost, just as we had eventually given up trying to eliminate the isolated Soviet pocket at Oranienbaum on the Gulf of Finland. A cornered enemy fighting for their lives is tough to overcome.

Throughout the siege, I occupied a bunker halfway between the frontline and Memel, while the rest of the personnel in my company were stationed at a farm a mile or two closer to town. With its civil-ian population evacuated to the west, the city itself became a virtual ghost town.

During one of the breaks in the fighting, I entered a nearby vacat-ed home to savor the luxury of a bath for the first time in months. There was even an occasional opportunity for me to hunt jackrabbits, which our company cook would convert into a delicious meal.

About nine o'clock one morning, I was still resting in my bunker after a late night when Lt. Col. Ebeling unexpectedly appeared at the entrance. Still not dressed, I sprung out of my bunk and saluted, but he did not appear impressed. My relationship with our regimental commander was good, but it was embarrassing to have been caught sleeping at such a late hour in the morning.

Around this same time, a more serious incident occurred. Since the men in my company had not fired their rifles for a while, I decided to find a suitable area for them to conduct target practice. A hill located near our company's billet on the farm seemed the natural choice. The fact that the bunker housing the regimental headquarters was situated on the other side of the hill never entered my mind.

After about five minutes of shooting, there was an urgent call from the regiment ordering my troops to cease fire immediately. Stray bul-lets were soaring over the hill and whizzing through the air around the regimental bunker. Though the soldiers in my company were profi-cient in the use of our heavy weapons, most of them, unfortunately, were not skilled marksmen with their rifles.

On the city streets near the farm where our company was garrisoned, my men posted signs with the words *Einheit Lübbecke* (Unit Lübbecke) to direct anyone seeking our location. Typically, the letters sent to soldiers at the front did not indicate the name of the company and regiment since this was militarily valuable information. Instead, the letter's writer addressed the intended recipient's *Feldpost* number (postal number in the field), which remained constant throughout the war.

Perhaps because the military situation had deteriorated so greatly, increasing numbers of our letters home passed through censors during this period. Despite this scrutiny, I never felt limited regarding what I could communicate. Likewise, I felt that I received a clear sense of what was happening with Anneliese and my family as well.

THE CHALLENGE OF LEADERSHIP

On January 20, 1945, the army elevated me from *Kompanieführer* (company leader) to the more permanent status of *Kompaniechef* (company commander). My satisfaction at this promotion was reinforced when the men in my company honored me with an informal celebration at the farmhouse where they were quartered. Ultimately, the respect of the soldiers I led in combat was even more important to me than the approval of those above me. This elevation in my command status was soon followed by a promotion in rank from second lieutenant (*Leutnant*) to first lieutenant (*Oberleutnant*) on January 30, but by then other events would intervene.

The burden of my duties as a company commander were much lighter in Memel than they had been when we were in action at the Düna, but there were increasing manpower problems. By late 1944, the declining pool of replacements in Germany made it impossible for the Wehrmacht to provide us with an adequate number of troops to make up for our losses. As in the rest of the German Army, I could only reorganize my remaining 150 men in an effort to fulfill our combat mission as effectively as possible.

Though leading men in combat was something for which I felt well suited, there were many additional non-combat duties for an officer to perform. When soldiers under my command were killed, it was my responsibility to send letters notifying their wives and families back home. Despite the routine sentiments contained in such letters, I always felt this duty to be the most difficult in my service as an officer.

Yet death is an inevitable reality of war. The side that wins the field at the end of a battle controls the treatment of dead and wounded. Often, the fate of those listed as missing is never known. Though concerned for those lost in battle, the unit must look to its immediate needs. The enemy is not interested in an accounting of your casualties and the fighting moves on. The bodies of the dead lie in the woods and rot. It is terrible, but it is an ugly side of war that is often forgotten.

During the latter part of the war, combat on the Eastern Front grew even more brutal. When the Soviets won battles after 1943, they would sometimes shoot our wounded and leave our dead unburied. In those situations, only those who could walk would be sent off to the POW camps. Ultimately, the treatment of soldiers depended on when and where a battle was fought.

In my experience, the Wehrmacht never issued orders that forbade German troops to take prisoners. I never personally witnessed German troops shoot wounded or surrendering Red Army soldiers, though these things could have happened. While we did not necessarily bury the enemy's dead, especially when the front became fluid, to the best of my knowledge German forces provided medical care to the wounded Russian troops and sent all those who surrendered back to POW camps, even if the conditions in these facilities were utterly inadequate.

Though German troops did not always behave properly, a military code of conduct was strictly enforced. As commander, I sometimes administered disciplinary action for the troops in the company who failed to obey it.

One case involved the court martial of a sergeant who was one of my oldest comrades. After being drafted into 13th Company with me back in 1939, he had worked his way up to command a gun crew operating one of our 75-millimeter howitzers. Finding a family's silver belongings buried in a yard near Memel, he ordered one of his men to dig them up and pack them in a parcel for shipment back to Germany.

When the crime came to my attention, I enforced military procedure and sent him back to the division to receive his sentence. Last that I heard, he ended up in the punishment battalion that we called the *Himmelfarhtkommando* (roughly, the heaven-bound force), a unit so named because they received the most dangerous combat assignments.

Although lacking the subordinate officers who would normally assist the company commander, I did receive some limited support from the regimental command staff as well as from our "mother of the company," Senior Sgt. Jüchter, who was in charge of the *Tross*. His assistance was invaluable in carrying out my many mundane but nonetheless essential administrative chores, such as requesting supplies, ammunition, and hay for our horses.

My other tasks included issuing authorizations for furloughs, based on Jüchter's determination as to who was due one, as well as sending up requests for decorations or promotions. On my recommendation, two men in the company returned to Germany for officer training. The downside of this action was that I lost a couple of my better men.

By my estimation, about fifty percent of the troops were married, a proportion that had increased since the beginning of the war when a larger percentage were young volunteers. At this time, divorce was frowned upon in German society. Married couples typically pursued a divorce only when there were severe and irreconcilable problems, but war tended to worsen these problems as well as create new ones. The separation of soldiers from their wives and girlfriends at home sometimes exposed these women to unscrupulous men who would take advantage of the situation.

During my year in command, there were at least four situations where I had to respond to legal papers requesting me to verify that a particular soldier had not been on leave during the previous ten months before his wife had a baby. This confirmation would provide either the soldier or his wife grounds for a divorce.

Separately, I had to respond to about five or six sets of court papers from wives seeking divorce from soldiers in my unit. Calling the soldier into my bunker, I would ask him to tell me man-to-man what had happened.

When a soldier learned for the first time that his wife wanted to end the marriage or was having an affair, it would rip his guts out. Naturally, such traumatic news would also have grave repercussions on the way the man behaved in combat. The end of a relationship with a wife or serious girlfriend usually caused a sense of psychological torment that exceeded even the emotional suffering that resulted from the death of a close comrade.

Dealing with these situations only reinforced my own concerns about Anneliese. As I wrote to her in a letter at the time, "The price of war goes way beyond the battlefield."

ANNELIESE

At the end of two months with my family in Püggen following her evacuation from Belgium, Anneliese received new orders on November 9 transferring her to a hospital run by the *Kriegsmarine* in Zeven, located about 100 miles northwest of Püggen between Bremen and Hamburg. Her previous service as a nurse had been in military hospitals run by the German Army, but the *Kriegsmarine* now provided her with a different uniform and issued its own regulations governing the conduct of medical personnel.

Following a couple of months working in Zeven, Anneliese was transferred further north to a hospital in Altenwalde, a suburb of the city of Cuxhaven located at the juncture of the Elbe River and the North Sea. While she spent most of the next nine months based in Altenwalde, she was later detached to the hospital in neighboring Süderdeich, further up the Elbe.

Earlier in Belgium, and later in northern Germany, Anneliese was exposed to other perils besides Allied bombing. As an attractive 23-year-old nurse in a military hospital, she worked in a harsh environment for which her upbringing had left her wholly unprepared. She was lonely and vulnerable without me or a family to provide her with any love or support.

My concern for her safety and well-being in that environment caused me immense stress. Despite her engagement to me, Anneliese was forced to continually fend off advances from the soldiers and sailors whom she encountered daily as well as from the doctors with whom she worked. In several letters, I warned her to be cautious and guard against the predations of such men.

In a previous letter to me written on July 20, 1943, Anneliese expressed the pain she still suffered because of the absence of affection in her childhood: "You had such a happier youth than me. It is so hard for a girl without a mother's love." Now, she was a woman on her own without the benefit of a mother from whom she could seek advice about men and the dangers they might pose to her.

As a result of the lack of love in her youth, Anneliese had a deep need for affection as an adult. This made her a natural target for aggressive males pursuing female companionship, especially when such a man dishonestly promised that he only sought her innocent company. In this regard, her environment at the military hospital was more hazardous than my situation at the front where there were no women who might divert our attention.

Realizing the inherent risk to her, it was extremely difficult for me as a 24-year-old man to endure our separation while simultaneously performing my duties as a company commander. Several lines from my various letters reflect my anxious efforts to reassure her of my love and to encourage her to remain strong.

"How many times a day do I think I about you?"

"The biggest problem I have is missing you, Annelie."

"Mutual love overcomes all separations."

"Our love gives us peace in these sorrowful days."

"The remembrance of our past times together hurts badly."

"My thoughts are always with you far away, my love."

"I cannot describe with words my love for you."

"I am thankful that God showed me the way to you, Annelie."

Ultimately, my upbringing imparted to me a strength of character and self-control to bear my burdens. Lacking a similar upbringing, Anneliese was less able to cope with our separation. As I would later discover, there would be consequences.

While my deep apprehensions persisted, Anneliese and I had decided that we no longer wished to delay our marriage until after the war. We now only awaited the necessary official permission, following the completion of the required investigation into the Jewish surname of her mother. Indeed, we had already plotted out our imminent wedding in Hamburg down to the last detail in a series of letters.

Using some cloth purchased when I had been on occupation duty in Belgium, I had hired a tailor in Hamburg to make me a suit. Anneliese had meanwhile purchased her wedding dress. We planned to have a covered carriage pulled by two white horses to carry us to the ceremony at the church and then deliver us to a wedding reception at Aunt Frieda's apartment. Afterward, we would celebrate our honeymoon at a Hamburg hotel.

On January 23 and 24, 1945, the division and then the regiment signed the Marriage Allowance Paper, providing us with the last of the official documentation that we needed. Since I was next in line for a three-week leave from duty, I pushed my concerns about Anneliese's situation from my mind and looked forward impatiently to our impending marriage.

EVOLVING VIEWS ON THE WAR

Throughout the war, German soldiers had regular access to the news through the weekly issues of the divisional newspaper and armed forces radio, but the heavily censored information offered us only a general picture of what was happening in Russia and the wider war.

My general lack of concern about Germany's declaration of war against America during the winter of 1941 in Uritsk had been typical. At that time, the United States seemed too far away to make a difference in our struggle against Russia, but it turned out that American industry would provide crucial material support that helped the Red Army recover from its early disasters.

Reports of the surrender in Stalingrad in early 1943 sparked much more concern among the troops, but most of us still remained confident that Germany would ultimately win, or at least obtain a favorable peace settlement. The surrender of Italy, Germany's main ally in Europe, in September 1943, only inspired us to fight harder to obtain this ultimate victory. Even with the news of our steady retreat from Russia, almost everyone at home and at the front still fully expected that we would win the war as late as mid-1944.

This persistent optimism partly reflected the power of the Nazi-controlled media to shape perspectives and opinions among the German public. There were also rumors, grandly reinforced by

Göbbels, that Germany was developing secret wonder weapons to ensure ultimate victory. When our new *Vergeltungswaffe* (Vengeance) missiles began striking England in the summer of 1944, they appeared to give credence to the rumors, though their effect may have been exaggerated.

While the regime's reports, exhortations, and propaganda skillfully manipulated the public's hopes and fears, I believe that Germans also allowed themselves a certain amount of self-deception about the situation in order to sustain their morale in the face of overwhelming odds.

Soon after my return to the front from Germany in May 1944, we learned about the Allied landings in France. This was not necessarily considered bad news because for years the Allies had been targeting our cities with air raids, as though they were hesitant to again confront the Wehrmacht on the ground in France. It was hoped that once they had staged the landings we could then force another Dunkirk, eliminating the threat from the West for the foreseeable future.

When the expected repulse of the Allies failed to materialize within the first couple of weeks, it was apparent that Germany now faced a second front. Perhaps if Germany had possessed more veteran divisions like the 58th on the Western Front, the D-Day landings would have failed, but by then experienced troops were in short supply.

Before the war, there was a deep resentment toward the West that stemmed from the harsh treatment meted out to Germany in the Treaty of Versailles. By the time the Western Allies landed in France on D-Day, I had come to see the current conflict against the Western powers as more like a game compared with the brutal nature of our struggle against the Russians.

A German soldier captured by the Western Allies expected to survive, but one captured in Russia did not. Upon learning of my brother Otto's capture by the Americans in the summer of 1944, I was not concerned because I knew he was safe. From my perspective as a soldier on the battlefield, the war with the American or British troops in the west was a struggle between civilized foes, while the war against the Red Army in the east was generally perceived as a clash with a barbaric mortal enemy.

The view toward the Western Allies inside Germany was different.

Because the German people expected the Americans and the British to conduct the war in a more humane fashion and to follow the Geneva Convention, they were surprised and embittered at the Anglo-American bombing of cities that claimed the lives of hundreds of thousands of German civilians. Rather than breaking their spirit, the attacks probably made most Germans more determined to resist.

Although the troops around me in Russia still did not pay too much attention to events on the Western Front, the success of the Allied invasion of France in June increased our pessimism. Even while still writing to Anneliese that there was "no doubt that we will prevail in this war," my doubts were growing.

During the previous summer's retreat through the Düna in the wake of the destruction of much of Army Group Center, I had begun to think for the first time that Germany would lose the struggle, even if we really did possess wonder weapons. Recognizing the increasing inevitability of Germany's defeat, I admitted to Anneliese in a letter, "I gave up expecting the impossible." With the Wehrmacht retreating on all fronts, Allied willingness to reach a negotiated peace appeared more and more remote. Uncertain what would happen next in the war, we were increasingly fighting for our survival in the hope that we could somehow eventually make it back to Germany.

In the second half of 1944, political discussions became commonplace among the troops for the first time in the war. We realized that something must be wrong with Hitler and the Nazis. Most of the time, you could express yourself more freely with comrades at the front than back in Germany. Of course, you still needed to be careful with whom you shared your opinions. If you openly stated, "Hitler is an idiot," it would undoubtedly land you somewhere very unpleasant.

A few weeks after the Allied landings in France, a German officer-led assassination attempt on Adolf Hitler failed. Like some of the troops around me, I felt disappointed that the plotters had botched the effort. Not all German troops supported assassination, but there was certainly a widespread negative attitude toward the Nazi leadership and a growing indifference to Hitler's fate.

When the Nazis issued an order on July 23, 1944 that required all units in the Wehrmacht to adopt the Nazi Party salute, the 58th Division declined to obey this command, instead maintaining the traditional soldier's salute used in most armies. Perhaps on the basis of our combat record, our refusal was not punished.

If our unit had been given some hard-core Nazi troops, they would have received a rough time from the other men. We were patriotic soldiers fighting for Germany, not a bunch of Nazi brownshirts fighting for Hitler. Most of the soldiers I knew did not support the Nazi Party, even if the practical result of our military effort was to maintain the Nazi regime in power. It is an irresolvable dilemma when you want to serve your country, yet oppose its political leadership.

While my own hostility toward the regime increased, Anneliese condemned the German officers who had carried out the plot against Hitler as traitors, retaining her deep belief in both the Führer and German victory. Even during the last months of the war, Anneliese remained absolutely convinced that Germany was building miracle weapons that would rescue us. When she told me in a letter that a framed photograph of Hitler hung on the wall of her room, my reaction was one of utter disbelief.

Though many Germans shared her commitment to the regime, I considered such faith to be completely ludicrous. Yet, whatever one's feelings toward the Nazi government, we were all engaged in a fight to the bitter end. Unlike the First World War's negotiated armistice, this war would be decided on the battlefield.

Because the Nazi eagle resembled a vulture, Germans had sometimes jokingly referred to it as the *Pleitegeier* (the bankrupt vulture). The reference implied that the Nazis, for all their bombast and early successes, were not leading Germany to a bright future, but rather to a calamitous fate.

CHAPTER 16

CATASTROPHE

SAMLAND: Late January–April 13, 1945

On January 13, the Red Army began a major new offensive into East Prussia. This assault to the south of Memel quickly threatened to isolate us from the other German forces in the region. The cancellation of all furloughs wrecked my plans to marry Anneliese. No further successful communication with her or my family would take place for half a year, despite our mutual attempts to send letters.

The evacuation of German troops from Memel to the Samland region of East Prussia began in the last week of January. Traffic departing for the southwest jammed onto the long sandy neck of the Kurische Isthmus, located between the Baltic Sea and the Kurishe Bay.

As Soviet forces moved to block the exit from the Kurische Isthmus into the Samland, the last elements of the 58th Division rushed to pass through the escape route. German artillery held off the enemy's advance just long enough for all of my division to reach the Samland. Linking up with the main body of German forces, we immediately went into combat in the bitter cold of the East Prussian winter.

The mission of the newly designated Army Detachment Samland was to defend East Prussia and provide a shield for German civilians fleeing the Soviet onslaught. Our immediate objective was to relieve the city of Königsberg, which was surrounded by the Soviets at the end of January. While the 58th and other German divisions would make a push toward the city from outside, troops within would simultaneously attempt to break out in the direction of the relieving forces.

The attack began early on the morning of February 19. Joined to a lesser extent by our company's heavy guns, our division's artillery conducted a devastating barrage against the Soviet rear in preparation for the assault by our infantry. Placing my old comrade Schütte in charge of directing our heavy guns in the rear, I took my usual place at the front, where I could get a better sense of what was occurring.

As our regiment's attack advanced in the direction of the Soviet frontlines in a wooded area, I moved forward beside three or four German *Stürmgeschütze* (tracked armored vehicles with 75-millimeter guns), which were crossing the open terrain of rolling hills. Simultaneously, our infantry began advancing about one or two hundred yards to my right.

Unfortunately, our shelling of the enemy's position had failed to crush their ability to resist. Within moments of the start of our assault, the *Stürmgeschütze* began to be picked off one after the other by Soviet anti-tank guns concealed along the line of trees about a hundred yards ahead of us.

Suddenly alone among the smashed vehicles, I cautiously began to move back toward my company's gun position 300 yards behind me. Long before I reached it, my company's 75- and 150-millimeter howitzers retaliated for the destruction of the vehicles, pouring a barrage of a couple of hundred rounds into the tree line.

The infantry's offensive meanwhile pushed on about five miles before losing momentum. In the process, it revealed that our strike had taken the Red Army by surprise, preempting an assault they had been preparing to make against our own lines a few hours later.

The Soviet concentration of American-made high-velocity anti-tank guns at regular 20-foot intervals at the edge of the forest might have been optimal in an offensive operation, but their close deployment also served to magnify the destructive impact of my company's guns. Similar results had been achieved in the rear of the Russian lines by our artillery. All that remained of a couple of Red Army divisions were the remnants of their forward headquarters and the wreckage of other equipment. The attack was a success, but it would be the last hurrah for us.

As the coordinated assault of Army Detachment Samland hit the enemy forces arrayed along the front, German units within Königsburg succeeded in punching a six-mile-wide corridor through the Red Army units encircling the city. Refugees who had been trapped inside the city when it was initially surrounded quickly began streaming through this escape route. The tragic plight of civilians forced to flee westward cast my mind back to the parallel scene I had witnessed in France in the summer of 1940, though the danger to those who fell under Soviet control was greater.

In the small area that we had liberated from Soviet occupation, we received firsthand accounts of atrocities committed by the enemy troops. In one of the worst incidents, we heard that every sister in a Catholic convent for blind nuns had been raped. Word of such barbarity helped inspire our efforts to hold our ground as long as possible before retreating. It also reinforced the urgency of evacuating all German residents to the west as rapidly as possible, employing force if necessary to make them depart.

Directed to assist in this mission, my company joined other units behind the lines in loading civilians aboard a couple of trucks sent over by the division. Arriving at a farm only a few miles from the front, we encountered an elderly couple in their seventies. The wife boarded the truck but her husband refused to leave, insisting, "I am going to stay here and I am going to die here." Obeying our orders, I commanded my soldiers to forcibly haul the man onto the truck, but it was a gut-wrenching moment. If my parents had been similarly forced to abandon our farm in Püggen, I knew it would break their hearts.

Beyond trying to shield the civilian population, we were now simply fighting for our own lives with a desperation born from hopelessness. There was no place to retreat and no more illusions that some miracle would rescue Germany. We had no choice but to accept whatever fate held in store for us. While my basic instinct to survive persisted, I felt a deepening sense of resignation that the end for me could come at any time.

In these critical circumstances, the army began to employ a number of *Volkssturm* units at the front. These were comprised of older veterans from the First World War, including some who were grandfathers in their sixties. Many of them were local farmers who had remained to defend their homes after their families were evacuated.

Despite their age, they were seasoned soldiers who fought surprisingly well against overwhelming odds.

The Wehrmacht also began sending our division untrained replacements from the Luftwaffe and Kriegsmarine who completely lacked any type of combat experience. When a group from the Luftwaffe appeared at our company's position in the middle of a night lit by tracer fire from machine guns and rocked by the explosions of artillery rounds, it was obvious that they were scared stiff. Nonetheless, I ordered one of my men to take the new troops up to the front where we needed every available body.

Before the night ended, one of the new soldiers came back with a bullet wound through his hand that was obviously self-inflicted. As a veteran, I recognized that the man lacked training for combat and had simply acted out of fear. Following military regulations, I ordered the man to be sent to the rear to face a court-martial, but it was a duty that I despised.

During the struggle in the Samland, Lt. Col. Ebeling proved himself to be a highly capable commander. More than anyone else in our regiment, his leadership and tactical skill were essential in slowing the Red Army's advance, even if the enemy's numerical superiority made it a battle that we had no chance to win.

On March 24, Ebeling issued me a verbal promotion to the rank of captain (*Hauptmann*), but informed me that I would probably never receive a written confirmation in the chaos.

Subsequent to promotion to captain, all previous commanders of the 13th Company had quickly moved up to command a battalion of four infantry companies. Because officers were expected to lead from the front and infantry units bore the brunt of the fighting, their life expectancy was not high. The war did not last long enough for me to determine whether my destiny would have been the same.

FISCHHAUSEN: April 13–16, 1945

Following the surrender of Königsburg, a new Soviet offensive on April 13 brought about the collapse of the German defensive front in the Samland. In the aftermath, all German units began withdrawing westward toward the Frische Isthmus. Bordered by the Baltic Sea on the north and the Frische Bay on the south, this narrow, sandy strip of land provided the only remaining overland escape route west, similar to the function that the Kurische Isthmus had played for the German units evacuating Memel less than three months earlier.

A merciless Soviet artillery and air bombardment pursued our retreating forces, which were now mere shadows of what they had been in 1941. Our battered division was down to a few thousand men, while the 13th Company retained only about 100 men, a couple of dozen horses, one 150-millimeter gun, four 75-millimeter howitzers, four 105-millimeter mortars, and several supply wagons. Since our retreat to Memel, the intensity of the fighting had prevented me from riding Thea and I was now on foot.

Whenever the shellfire increased or enemy planes appeared overhead, we would run for cover. Resuming the march when the threat diminished, our ears remained tuned to the incoming rounds, attempting to determine each shell's trajectory and potential danger. Even if we could almost guess when and where a round would impact, it was an intensely nerve-racking and exhausting experience.

Beyond the artillery shelling and bombing, we also now regularly endured attacks from a Red Army weapon that German soldiers called "the Stalin Organ" and the Russians called the *Katyusha*. Serving a combat role similar to the artillery, this multiple rocket launcher had been brought into increasing use over the second half of the war. After hearing the distinctive high-pitched whir of rockets firing off in quick succession, we could watch their contrails as they raced through the air toward us. The Stalin Organs proved particularly dangerous because of their capacity to devastate a wide area in a very brief period, much like our new 210-millimeter rockets.

As our column was traveling down the road late in the afternoon of the second day of the retreat, the sound of a Stalin Organ firing its rocket salvo instantly sent everyone scrambling for cover. Eying one of the abandoned earth-camouflaged ammunition bunkers that lined the road, I made for the entrance 20 feet away. Just before I passed through the doorway, a piece of shrapnel from one of the rockets struck my temple in the exposed area just below my helmet.

Although leaving the side of my face bloodied, the wound proved minor and our medic had my head bandaged up within a couple of minutes. When I returned to the road, a private from my company came stumbling toward me. In a calm voice, he asked, "Will you tell my wife about me, sir? I am going to die now." Since the soldier did not appear to be wounded, I disregarded his concern and responded, "You're not going to die."

Afterward, I began to wonder if my dismissal of his distress had been too hasty. I could have made more effort to learn about his condition. He might indeed have suffered a fatal shrapnel wound that was not immediately apparent. In addition to providing him with medical attention, I could have made some effort to reassure him. Though never learning his fate in the mounting chaos, my failure to aid a man who was possibly dying still pains me today.

Everything that we had endured in the preceding weeks would only foreshadow the events that occurred two days later, a dozen miles to the west. On April 16, the artillery of four Soviet armies combined with several hundred aircraft to unleash the culminating attack designed to annihilate the remaining German forces in the Samland. What ensued was the greatest catastrophe that I personally experienced during the war.

Our company had reached the small town of Fischhausen that morning. A key junction for roads from the north and east, it was located at the top of the narrow peninsula leading to the Frische Isthmus. The Red Army artillery that continued to pound us from a couple of miles to the east had now been joined by Soviet planes swarming through the skies overhead at an altitude of only 500 or 1,000 feet.

Scouting the route ahead for my men and guns, following about twenty yards behind me, I proceeded along the narrow main road into town. The shelling and bombing began to increase dramatically, probably doubling in intensity from what it had been on the road outside town. Between the unceasing barrage and the congested mass of units, the traffic had ground completely to a halt. In the growing disorder, the troops struggled to maintain control of their animals.

Keeping close to what was left of the abandoned one and two story homes along the street, I refrained from entering inside the dwellings that had not yet been destroyed, fearing that they might collapse if struck with a direct hit. Instead, whenever a new round whistled toward me or a plane appeared headed in my direction, I ducked behind the corners of the houses or into doorways. While the deafening explosions of shells and bombs constantly hammered the entire area, I would periodically break cover to press a little further ahead as my instincts dictated.

By the time I had advanced perhaps half a mile into Fischhausen, the hurricane of artillery fire and bombing on this chokepoint was creating an indescribable hell of carnage and chaos like nothing I had ever witnessed during the long years of war.

Wrecked equipment from the remnants of the four or five divisions was jumbled everywhere. The shattered, blackened corpses of men and horses in various stages of death lay strewn on the street. Only the increasing thunder of the barrage spared me from the pitiful moans of the wounded and the whimpering of dying animals.

The horrific scene overloaded my already shell-shocked senses, leaving me completely numb and utterly despondent. At that moment, I fully expected my life to end.

But I was not prepared to die. My sole purpose became to escape this nightmare and gather any other survivors from my company.

By this point, the bombardment had grown so heavy that it was clear I had to leave the main road or be killed. Unable to contact my men behind me in the chaos, I could only hope they would likewise realize that their only chance of survival was to leave behind the horses and guns and somehow make their own way out of Fischhausen.

Reaching a side alley off to the left, I headed a couple of short blocks to the edge of town. When I came to the southern outskirts, I resumed my course to the west, proceeding along a route that paralleled the main road located about 30 yards to my right. Remaining close to the houses for cover, I moved cautiously along ground that was slightly elevated above the bay about 100 yards away. Though the bombardment here was less concentrated than along the main street, shells and bombs continued to crash around me.

On reaching the far side of town, I moved back toward the main street about half a mile beyond where I had turned off to the shore. As I approached it, a Soviet Yak fighter plane came streaking toward Fischhausen, strafing everything in its path as it flew low above the road.

Spotting a row of foxholes next to the street, I instantly dove into one for cover. Yet, instead of sliding down to the bottom of the five-foot-deep hole, I remained where I could observe the action, compelled by an insatiable curiosity to know what was happening around me.

Evidently having seen me take cover in the foxhole, the Yak pilot angled his aircraft directly toward my position. With my eyes protruding slightly above the rim of my foxhole, I felt almost mesmerized by the bright muzzle flashes of the fighter's machine guns as it hurtled toward me through the sky.

Bullets began pelting the ground in front of me, spewing a cloud of dirt into my eyes and shattering into a hail of shrapnel that sprayed my face. As the plane roared low above me, I reeled backward in pain to the bottom of the foxhole.

A moment later, my brain began to evaluate my condition. My wounds felt slight, but my eyes revealed only blackness when I opened them. Huddled in the foxhole, I wondered anxiously whether my blindness would be permanent.

At the end of a couple of long, apprehensive minutes, my sight began to return, though I was still barely able to see through the crusts of blood and dirt.

Hauling myself up from my foxhole, I staggered onto the main street and surveyed the scene around me with hazy vision. Despite the steady rain of shells, a few troops were in the process of rendering their surviving artillery pieces inoperable by disabling the barrels, unable to haul them further after the horses had been killed.

Only an hour or so had passed since I had first entered Fischhausen about a mile back, but during that time most of what remained of the German Army in the Samland had been destroyed. With the Red Army's capture of the area imminent, my only course was to search for any survivors from my company and seek new orders. The disaster at Fischhausen signified an end to much that I had known, but it also marked the start of my almost miraculous escape from Russian captivity.

Stumbling westward from the town as shells sporadically fell around me, I soon located a small remnant of men from my company beside an empty ammunition bunker a couple of miles away. My subsequent hunt for Lt. Col. Ebeling proved nearly fatal when a squadron of Russian bombers pounded the area in which I was searching. Only just managing to take cover in a trench at the last second, I again eluded serious injury from my second air attack in a few hours.

Perhaps ten minutes later, I finally came across Ebeling attempting to organize a new defensive line in an effort to resist the enemy's expected advance from the east. However illusory, my new written orders directed me to return to Hamburg to serve as part of the leadership cadre for a new division. While offering me a chance to escape back to central Germany, these orders also required me to transfer most of the surviving troops at the bunker to another division, an action which caused me lasting grief since it likely meant either death or captivity for them.

Two days afterward, on April 18, Senior Sgt. Jüchter and I made our way westward toward Pillau, under intermittent Red Army artillery fire. Crossing the narrow channel separating Pillau from the Frische Isthmus, we journeyed three dozen miles south by truck to an area on the Gulf of Danzig. From there, we boarded a ferry that took us to the port of Hela, isolated at the end of a long peninsula.

Jüchter's death in a Russian artillery barrage two and a half weeks later reinvigorated my efforts to seek a way off Hela. The following day, I linked up with a Silesian infantry unit ordered to sail for central Germany. That night, we boarded a German destroyer heading west. All those who remained behind fell into Soviet hands.

OCCUPIED GERMANY IN 1945

CHAPTER 17

THE PRICE OF DEFEAT

MAY–JULY 1945

PRISONER OF WAR

"*Herr Oberleutnant, der Krieg ist vorbei*" ("Lieutenant, the war is finished"), a sailor's somber voice announced to me in my bunk on the morning of May 9, just hours after our destroyer had departed Hela.

Germany's unconditional surrender had officially come into effect at 2301 hours Central European time on May 8, though the process had already commenced several days earlier. On May 4, the British had accepted the military surrender of all German forces in Holland, northwest Germany, and Denmark in a ceremony held at the training area near Wendisch-Evern where I had undergone much of my drilling during boot camp.

On the night of May 4, Admiral Dönitz, with British consent, ordered all available warships to sail across the Baltic Sea to the port of Hela and the Weichsel River Estuary near Stutthof. Their mission was to evacuate as many German soldiers and civilians to the west as they could in the short time that remained before the final surrender. The last of these ships, including the destroyers *Karl Galster* and "25," left Hela at midnight on May 8. Only by chance had I joined the troops of a Silesian infantry regiment boarding one of those destroyers that night.

Though our small convoy of ships was still closer to territory occupied by the Red Army on the morning of May 9, we were determined to avoid surrender to the Russians. Ignoring Soviet demands for us to proceed directly to one of the ports under their control, the commander of our small convoy contacted the British for instructions. In addition to allowing the convoy to proceed to the Danish port of Copenhagen, the British authorized our commander to resist any attempt to force him to do otherwise.

Our failure to obey the Russian demand to sail for a harbor under their control brought an assault by a group of Soviet patrol boats later that morning. With German sailors firing every available weapon aboard the destroyers, the enemy boats quickly broke off the attack and escaped into the fog. Though not witnessing the engagement, the loud thumping of the ship's guns was audible to me in my cabin below deck. It would be the last time I heard the fire of heavy guns in combat.

Years later, Lt. Col. Ebeling told me he had been evacuated at about the same time aboard a tug pulling a barge crammed with about 200 troops. As they were crossing the Baltic Sea, a storm struck. The tug survived, but all those on the barge drowned in one of those countless tragedies of the war's final days.

When our destroyer arrived in the harbor at Copenhagen that afternoon, all personnel were ordered to disembark down a gangplank onto the dock. At a checkpoint there, waiting British soldiers would relieve us of any weapons as we began our internment as prisoners of war.

While still aboard ship, I withdrew my Luger pistol from one of my tunic's pockets. To make the weapon inoperable, I removed its firing pin and tossed it overboard into the harbor. Replacing my superior Astra pistol in the holster with the now useless Luger, I then slipped the Astra into my tunic pocket, anticipating that I might need it for some unforeseen eventuality. Last, I took off my Iron Cross First Class and dropped it into one of my pockets.

Reaching the checkpoint, I handed the Luger to the waiting English soldier. Much to my surprise, he angrily shouted at me in perfect unaccented German. With a hate-filled expression, he proceeded to rip the officer's shoulder boards and decorations from my uniform leaving me stunned and humiliated.

Without another word, he gestured for me to move on. Retaining my composure with great difficulty, I resigned myself to my new status as a POW. In retrospect, I suspect that the soldier might have been a Jewish-German immigrant to Britain who took indirect revenge on me for the bitter experience he had endured before departing Germany. Otherwise, in my experience, the British troops behaved correctly and professionally, though they appeared to be wary of us.

From the checkpoint, I immediately joined about two or three thousand German soldiers piling aboard a large freighter. Recognizing no one, I mostly kept to myself during the 20-hour voyage south. However, I felt an obligation to do what I could to assist other German officers attempting to maintain military discipline among the enlisted troops, a problem which had become a mounting challenge.

Another officer told me that an ad hoc court-martial committee comprised of four or five colonels had conducted a trial and issued a death sentence against an enlisted man who had attacked a German officer aboard ship. Attaching a heavy base plate from a mortar to the convicted soldier's back, they shot him and threw the body overboard.

When we entered the small harbor of Heiligenhafen in the Schleswig-Holstein region of northern Germany the next day, British troops were again waiting at the end of the gangplank, this time to hand-pump a delousing powder on us before we marched off to internment.

The harbor was located about three or four miles from the entrance to a sprawling, open-air POW camp established in the region's rolling farmland. Like sheep herded into a pen, hundreds of thousands of surrendered German soldiers crowded into a roughly 30-square-mile area around the small villages of Gremersdorf, Nanndorf, and Altgalendorf. A few British soldiers patrolled the boundary of the territory, but the perimeter remained unfenced.

Inside the internment area, the British delegated to Wehrmacht officers the responsibility for maintaining order among the interned troops. They even authorized us to carry sidearms, apparently unconcerned how we might have retained such weapons.

Upon reaching an isolated farm, I was charged with the supervision of an improvised company of a couple of hundred men from the ship. While making little effort to assert control over my assigned soldiers, I soon realized that it would be difficult to maintain even minimal discipline, even with an Astra in my holster.

Shortly after our arrival at the farm, one of the soldiers passed by me with his hands in his pockets, neglecting to make any effort to salute. When I protested, "Where is your salute?" He simply laughed at me and walked away.

Though I called out to him twice, he continued to ignore me. This complete lack of respect for my rank left me furious, but he perhaps recognized that an officer was not likely to shoot a man for gross insubordination in the existing circumstances. Or maybe he was simply apathetic about his fate.

Following Germany's defeat after six years of fighting, most of us indeed just felt numb and utterly powerless to control our own destiny. There was no sense of relief about the end of the war, only a somber resignation to our circumstances and anxiety about the future. The Germany we had known was gone. There was no leadership. There was nothing.

Escape from the camp would have been a simple matter, but nobody attempted it. There was no place to go when the whole of Germany was under occupation. Furthermore, anyone who succeeded would lack the necessary discharge paper from the British that would provide a man with the legal status necessary to obtain employment. It also reflected the German respect for rules and authority as well as our submissive psychological state following defeat.

On the farm, a large, empty wooden cow barn provided the company with adequate shelter. There were few opportunities to wash or shave, but the lack of food was by far our primary concern. The British supplied each of us with a daily ration of four or five crackers about the size of a small piece of bread, but this inadequate diet made hunger our constant companion. At one point I became so desperate to fill my stomach that I began eating dandelion leaves, having learned in my childhood that these were edible.

When the men asked me if they could set up a primitive kitchen, I told them to go ahead, while we scrounged the area for something to cook. Discovering a little barley at a neighboring unoccupied farm, we intentionally burned the grain on our improvised stove in an effort to give it some flavor. The taste was awful, but it at least it provided us some needed nutrition.

The scarcity of food in the camp meant that everyone lost weight. At 6 feet tall, I generally had maintained a weight of 180 pounds throughout the war. At the end of a couple of months in the camp, I dropped to an emaciated 150 or 160 pounds and again began to wonder about my survival.

No recreational activities were organized, but there was no interest in such things anyway since most of the men had little energy and wanted to keep to themselves. There was finally the time and peace to write to the families of my soldiers who had died in the last weeks of the war, but I lacked names, paper, and addresses.

Even if the fate of many of the troops in my company was uncertain in the chaotic conditions of the final days and weeks of fighting, I knew that at least some of those listed as missing had actually been killed. It saddens me greatly to think that none of these families received any closure regarding their loved ones who never returned.

Reflecting on my own survival through years of combat, I am convinced of divine intervention in my fate. Despite four minor wounds over the course of the war, our medics were able to treat all my injuries at the front and never even needed to send me back for more extensive care at a field hospital. God simply had other plans for my life and spared me.

Of course Anneliese and my family remained unaware of my survival, just as I remained ignorant of their fate. Writing letters at the camp was generally impossible, but the Red Cross provided all POWs with a couple of postcards to notify our families shortly after our arrival. In separate cards, I jotted short notes to Anneliese and my family, informing them that I was alive and in relatively good health in a British POW camp in Schleswig-Holstein, hoping that the postal system would manage to deliver at least one of them amid the postwar chaos.

Through the course of the summer, a number of the soldiers on the farm had received notice of their release from the camp and been sent to the exit area for processing. In late July, I learned that my turn would soon come. Aware that there would likely be British checkpoints where I would be frisked, I decided to bury my Astra pistol and *Soldbuch* to prevent their potential confiscation.

Just before leaving the farm, I walked into some woods about a mile away. After carefully wrapping the items in waterproof material, I buried them and covered the hole with earth, marking the spot with a rock. A year later, I would return to retrieve the package.

When I arrived at the exit processing center for the huge internment area, I was stunned to run across Otto Tepelman, my old childhood friend from Püggen. It turned out that he too had served in Russia and escaped capture by the Red Army. Despite the presence of Soviet occupying troops in Püggen, he now planned to return to our village.

Because former Wehrmacht officers were still being shipped to POW camps in the Soviet Union after the war, I knew that my own return would be too risky and decided to claim Lüneburg rather than Püggen as my hometown. Just before Tepelman's discharge, I wrote out a short note and asked him to deliver it to my family personally, since I was still unsure whether they had received my Red Cross card.

My own departure came only a few days later on July 27, which was fortunate since the small exit area of the camp lacked any shelter other than a network of holes dug into the ground. As we prepared to leave, the British placed me in charge of two dozen other German troops who were returning to Lüneburg. We were soon loaded aboard three trucks driven by British soldiers under the command of a corporal.

Meanwhile, a couple of days before our departure, Anneliese had learned of my survival and internment, after finally receiving my Red Cross card. Determined to see me again, she immediately left her nursing duties in Süderdeich without even seeking permission from her superiors, who were now under British supervision. Walking to a crossing point on the nearby Elbe River, she smuggled herself aboard a ferry.

When it docked on the eastern bank, Anneliese somehow acquired a bicycle for the 100-mile journey to my internment area in Schleswig-Holstein. Utterly exhausted, she finally reached the main gate of the camp, only to learn that the British had released me the day before her arrival.

For the time being, I remained ignorant of these events. At the end of our roughly 100-mile trip south from the camp to Lüneburg, I directed the British driver of the leading truck to head for the employment office in the center of town. After the men piled out into the courtyard in front of the building, I lined them up before issuing my final orders: "The war is finished. Go home."

And so, at the end of July 1945, at the age of 25, I was once again a civilian after six years of war.

FOREIGN OCCUPATION

Until they received the short note delivered by Otto Tepelman, my family still had no idea where I was, or if I was even still alive. In fact, they had received none of the letters that I had mailed since departing Memel nor the Red Cross postcard, so this note would prove to be the first word from me since January.

Though my youngest brother Hermann had been adopted by my Aunt and Uncle Stork, my family was also naturally concerned for his fate as well. Drafted as a 16-year-old about six months before the end of the war, he had been sent to serve with an anti-aircraft battery in the Berlin area. Fleeing west just ahead of the Red Army, Hermann swam across the Elbe River and reached the home of his adopted parents in Lüneburg shortly after the end of the fighting.

Even while Otto remained a POW, my family felt comforted knowing that he was at least safe. Interned in the United States, he spent most of his time picking oranges and grapefruits in Arizona and California. When so many German families lost two or three sons and brothers, it is truly remarkable that the three of us survived the war.

Following Germany's defeat, the victorious Allies divided the country into Soviet, American, British, and French zones of occupation. They also reduced Germany's European territory on an even greater scale than after the First World War. Under the Treaty of Versailles in 1919, parts of the three large agricultural provinces of East Prussia, Pomerania, and Silesia had been transferred to the new Polish state while Alsace-Lorraine went back to France. In 1945, all of Pomerania, Silesia, and Brandenburg east of the Oder-Neisse Rivers went to Poland, while East Prussia was divided between Poland and the Soviet Union.

Beyond territory, the Russians also shipped whole industrial facilities from Germany to the Soviet Union as war reparations. In one case, a huge steel mill in Salzgitter near Braunschweig was dismantled and shipped to Russia by train. Because the railroad gauges changed size in Poland, all train cargo had to be unloaded and switched over to other trains at the junction points.

When this dismantled factory arrived, the German POWs carrying out the transfer randomly divided up the equipment among different trains heading east so as to make it virtually impossible for the Russians to reassemble the factory. It was but one small measure of resistance against a tide of Soviet looting.

On a much smaller scale, the Western Allies also took advantage of their position at times. For example, the British chopped down thousands of trees in the Lüneburg area and sent these back to the United Kingdom by the shipload. Germans were more accepting of the West's occupation of Germany than they were of the Soviet occupation, but when the Western Allies did something like that people became bitter. "They won the war and now they want to take the rest of what we have." It was only after the passage of two or three years that most Germans in the west would come to view the Americans and the British as allies in the emerging Cold War against the Soviets.

At the end of April 1945, American troops had occupied Püggen and required all civilians to vacate the village while they used it as a base for further operations. My family camped out in one of the farm's meadows, eating food they had carried with them and sleeping in our wagons. After ten days, the Americans pulled out of the village, though they remained in charge of the area around it. While no fighting occurred in the area around Püggen, the evacuated homes were in bad shape, mainly as a result of the actions of the Allied POWs who had been liberated.

During this period immediately after the war ended, numerous former German soldiers wandered through the countryside trying to reach home. In an effort to help, my mother frequently provided the men with food and civilian clothes so that they could avoid drawing attention from the occupying armies.

At the end of June, British troops briefly replaced the Americans in the area around Püggen, just ahead of the scheduled July 1 transfer to Soviet control that had been agreed upon by the occupying powers. Everyone in the village was fearful.

Most of the refugees who were living in Püggen chose to head west with the departing British to escape Russian occupation. Many local residents decided to join them, taking only their horses and wagons and leaving most of their belongings behind on their farms. After debating whether to depart for the west, my family finally chose to stay and take their chances.

Immediately after the British withdrew, Red Army troops began to patrol the border between the eastern and western zones, which was initially marked only by stakes. For a bottle of schnapps, they would allow those who had not yet departed to cross over. Meanwhile, those who had decided to stay on their farms awaited the arrival of the Soviets with great anxiety.

As the ragtag Russian Army troops entered Püggen accompanied by small ponies pulling little four-wheeled wagons, they appeared to the residents more like a column of Gypsies than an army. Though the appearance of the Soviet forces who came later somewhat improved, my mother later told me that she felt an initial sense of surprise and disappointment that such a rabble could have defeated the modern and disciplined German Army.

At first, the Red Army attempted to portray themselves as liberators who had rescued the Germans from Nazi tyranny, but Russian animosity toward the German people soon became evident, especially when soldiers had been drinking. The Soviet troops mostly remained invisible during the daytime, but they would come out at night and harass those who had not fled to the west. They would check German homes for weapons and force the families to prepare meals for them using the best food still available.

If Russian troops were present, German women would hide because of their constant fear of being raped. When they made their initial visit to our home, only my mother's intervention somehow dissuaded the soldiers from going upstairs where my sisters were hiding. Even after the initial period of occupation, females could only move safely around the village and the surrounding area if they had the protection of at least a couple of German males.

While rape had been widely tolerated by the Red Army leadership during the war, some officers gradually began to impose harsh field discipline against troops who violated German women under Soviet post-war occupation. In one case in Thüringen, a Russian officer allowed a German female to identify the soldier who had raped her.

He then shot the guilty party on the spot as a warning to the other troops.

Of course, Germans living under Red Army occupation faced other dangers as well. Because the Nazi secret police had searched the homes of anyone suspected of disloyalty to the government, my mother expected the occupying Soviet forces to do the same. Fearful that our family could be placed in jeopardy if the occupiers learned that one of their sons had fought in Russia, she had wisely collected the spare uniform, Walther pistol, and military decorations that I had left at home and tossed them into the outhouse behind the pig barn.

However, she had hidden my officer's dagger under a mattress in one of the bedrooms, perhaps recognizing its sentimental value to me. When the dagger was discovered in a Russian search of our home, my family was taken for questioning at the local Red Army headquarters in Püggen. They were only released after undergoing an extensive interrogation.

Perhaps the greatest risk for civilians came in situations where they encountered Russian troops while they were alone. Stories circulated about individuals who had been intentionally run down by Soviet trucks while innocently bicycling down the road. The situation was also perilous for those who lived outside the main local village. In the evenings, these families often came into town to avoid risking a nocturnal visit to their isolated farms.

In their absence, however, Red Army soldiers would sometimes plunder their farms, seizing animals and all the property they could haul away. If the animals were too weak to move, the troops beat them. In some extreme instances, they even set the remaining animals loose in an act of sheer hooliganism. In the winter of 1945 to 1946, many stray animals wandered around the landscape.

Every village was governed by a Russian commissar with the assistance of native German Communists who often proved harsher than the foreign occupiers. Under the commissar's direction, leaflets were printed which specified the provisions that the German farmers were required to deliver. These items included food, clothes, and, most importantly, woolen blankets. If the commissar-appointed German *Bürgermeister* (mayor) failed to fulfill these measures, the Russians would simply go into the farms and seize what they wanted.

After awhile, the confiscation of farms over 100 hectares began. Once the Soviet authorities issued an order to vacate, the owners had only a few hours to pack a suitcase and leave their property. One family had to depart their farm at five o'clock in the evening on Christmas Eve. If the owners failed to vacate, they would be placed in concentration camps. In these circumstances, most owners crossed over to the western zone.

Frequently, the new owners were already waiting out front of the farm to take control of the property. These new owners were selected by German Communists with the assistance of the Russians. For farms 100 hectares or larger, there were typically 10 to 15 new owners, consisting mainly of those who had previously worked as hired laborers or were simply good Communists.

Every new family looked out for its own interests, which often led to serious clashes with the other new owners. Due to the high production quotas demanded by the Communists, some of these new owners did not stay very long. Generally, they departed in the dark of night, taking every portable item they could. Those who stayed ran into other problems since all machinery and other equipment was tailored for the operation of larger farms rather than smaller plots.

Because the Communist authorities gave the new owners more rights than the remaining established farmers in a village, disputes among them were common. This conflict was magnified by the quota system. While the quotas for the new owners who were natural supporters of the Communists actually decreased from year to year, the established farmers had to meet ever larger quotas.

With a growing portion of the harvest delivered to the Communist authorities for distribution in Germany or shipment to the Soviet Union, there was a diminishing amount left over to feed the farm families and their animals. In particular, there was a constant shortage of butter, eggs, and meat.

The psychological stress was perhaps even worse than the shortages. Farmers remained constantly anxious that they would be unable to fulfill the unrealistically high quotas for grain, meat, eggs, and the like. The great fear was that their failure to meet the designated quotas would lead to their deportation to a Siberian labor camp.

Unable to meet the burden imposed on them, some of these families who had farmed a piece of land for generations ultimately decided to flee to the west as refugees. In other cases, children left for the west while their parents stayed behind on the farm. If someone was caught trying to escape, they could be sent to Siberia, thus succumbing to the very fate they had sought to avoid. This was the reality of life under postwar Soviet occupation.

CHAPTER 18

POST-WAR GERMANY

REBUILDING OUR LIVES
July 27–December 24, 1945

After dismissing the men outside the employment office in Lüneburg, I set out on the five-mile walk to my uncle's farm in Hagen. Dressed in the same uniform I had been wearing since Fischhausen, it was strange to be returning to the place where I had first received the telegram ordering me to report for training almost six years earlier. So much had happened.

Arriving at the front door of the familiar home, I knocked. When the door opened, my aunt stood before me with an expression of deep disappointment on her face. In a sorrowful voice, she said, "And I thought it was Heinrich."

My aunt and uncle's oldest son Heinrich had achieved the rank of captain in the artillery. In the last weeks of the war, he had been on his way back to the front from a furlough when he was ordered to take command of one of the ad hoc units formed to help defend Berlin. Only sometime later did my aunt and uncle learn that he had been killed during the Russian assault on the city.

Despite their natural concern for Heinrich's fate, my aunt and uncle tried to make me feel welcome. To my great relief, they passed along a card from Anneliese that she had sent to their home when she learned that I was alive. It was the first time that I had any word from her for over six months.

Following a couple of days in Hagen, I caught a train to Hamburg.

217

When I reached Anneliese's home in the suburb of Wandsbek, her father greeted me warmly and told me that he himself had just recently returned home after duty with the *Volkssturm* in Belgium and Germany. He generously invited me stay in the house that he shared with his relatives while I waited for Anneliese to arrive and sought a place of my own to live.

After years in combat, terrible nightmares regularly plagued my sleep. Shortly after my arrival at the Berndts' home, I had a dream that I was trapped in a bunker in Russia and began pounding the wall beside my bed. Because the nearby explosions of Allied bombs during the war had loosened its plaster, the wall quickly gave way under my unconscious hammering, collapsing onto my bed and the floor in a pile of dust and debris.

Hearing the loud noise, everyone in the house awoke and rushed to my room. Upset and embarrassed by the episode, it was hard for me to explain the damage. While I continued to suffer the psychological effects of post-traumatic stress, I knew many other former soldiers who found it much more difficult to cope. Only with the passage of five or ten years did the war gradually fade from my thoughts and dreams.

Following her failure to find me at the POW camp, Anneliese had returned to Süderdeich where she obtained an official discharge from her nursing duties on August 6, 1945.

When she came through the door to her father's home in Hamburg later that day, she flung herself into my arms. Holding each other tightly in a long embrace that I will never forget, we both cried tears of joy and relief. It was my love for her and my hope for this moment that had kept me going through the darkest moments of the war. Against all odds, we were together again at last.

Soon after our emotional reunion, I learned the fate of the money that I had saved during the war. Throughout my years of service, I was paid a fixed salary according to my rank as well as supplemental pay for combat duty. Because I was almost always in combat, I was able to use the supplement to provide my spending money at the front, while the army deposited my regular pay into the army bank in Bremen. Since 1941, I had been saving these funds to pay for college after my discharge from the army.

When the war ended, however, the army collapsed and the bank disappeared. I never saw any of that money. Perhaps it would have been wise for me to have shifted it somewhere else, but by the time I realized that Germany's defeat was likely I was more concerned about staying alive than protecting my money. Still, it was very hard for me to accept that all my savings had simply vanished. With our families able to offer little assistance, Anneliese and I would be building new lives almost from scratch.

Before entering the Wehrmacht in 1939, I had already finished about a year and a half of the two-year apprenticeship required of everyone who wanted to pursue an engineering degree program. In case my educational plans did not work out, I now decided to complete the longer four-year apprenticeship necessary to obtain the status of journeyman (licensed professional) electrician before attending college. While the electricians guild waived a year of my journeyman's apprenticeship in compensation for my years of military service, my remaining year and a half as an apprentice provided an hourly pay that only allowed a very meager standard of living.

Soon after Anneliese returned, I found a job as an apprentice electrician with the A. Lehmann Company, which subcontracted me to Blom and Foss, the largest shipbuilding company in Hamburg. After a fifteen-minute train ride from my new apartment to the harbor, I would take a short ferry ride to the shipyard.

Arriving for work one day, my foreman ordered me to wait in front of the high-voltage electrical breakers while he went next door and flipped on the power. As he intended, the thunderous noise produced by the sudden surge of current scared the heck out of me. With an occasional prank to liven things up, the work was interesting and I learned a great deal.

During my days at the shipyard, I sometimes watched demolition crews across the harbor preparing to raze the giant concrete bunkers that had been built to protect German U-boats from Allied bombing raids. When they finally detonated the charges, the concrete roof was lifted up by the explosion, but only crashed back down into place.

Only after several attempts did the demolition effort succeed. It was natural to feel a certain pride in the quality of German workmanship, but I now realized that we needed to harness our energies and skills to more peaceful and productive pursuits in the future.

Meanwhile, Anneliese had taken an apartment located just across the street from her father's nursery, where she was now working on an informal basis. Her apartment was also only a few blocks away from my own apartment, which made it easy for us to spend our free time together.

One afternoon, Anneliese and I paid a visit to Planten und Blomen, a pleasant park in the center of Hamburg. As we strolled through it, we witnessed a scene that left us shocked and embarrassed. Behind nearly every second bush, British occupation troops could be seen making out with German girls. Some couples were kissing; some had one partner laying on top of the other. It was a crude spectacle. We would never have dreamed of conducting ourselves that way in public.

That fall, a rumor began to circulate through the city that appeared to place our plans to marry in jeopardy yet again. According to the word on the street, the British occupation authorities planned to issue an order on January 1, 1946 that would strictly prohibit all marriages between Germans for the following three years in order to reduce Germany's population. When the rumor persisted, Anneliese and I began to think that there must be some truth to it.

Concerned that we might have to wait years, we decided to advance our marriage plans to December 22, 1945. We set aside our more extensive plans for a big wedding, but I did manage to hire a covered carriage with two white horses to convey us to the church for the very small ceremony in the morning.

Afterward, the carriage took us to an intimate reception with Anneliese's family and my brother Hermann in Aunt Frieda's apartment, where I had just rented a room. While my sister Marlene had not been able to extend her recent visit to Hamburg in order to attend the wedding, she presented us a pork roast from our family's farm to celebrate the occasion before crossing back to Püggen in the Soviet Zone.

Given my limited financial means and the devastation of postwar Germany, my effort to arrange a suitable honeymoon proved difficult. Much of Hamburg was flattened into rubble after the war, but one hotel still stood among the ruins in the center of the city, on the

Mönkeberg Strasse, not far from the main train station. When my telephone call received no answer, I headed down to the hotel and asked the manager if I could reserve a room for us.

Initially informed that no rooms were available, I explained that we were getting married and needed a place to stay on our honeymoon. "Oh, that's different," the hotel manager replied. For two nights after our wedding, my new bride and I thus enjoyed a luxury suite with all the amenities, starting with a long bath in hot water that was still unavailable where we lived. It was a happy start to our life together.

In the last months of the war, Anneliese may have suffered a sense of emotional confusion and mental turmoil similar to that which I experienced after the destruction of my company at Fischhausen. With no letters from me following our retreat from Memel in January, she had no way of knowing whether I had been captured or killed. Given the huge scale of German losses, it was completely understandable that she would believe I was gone from her life. In such a situation, her sense of isolation and vulnerability could only have deepened. Despite these wartime trials, our love for each other only grew and strengthened during the years that followed.

STRUGGLING TO SURVIVE
December 1945–August 1949

As soon as the Allied powers in the western part of the country gave the Germans the authority to begin rebuilding their economy and industry, conditions started to improve. Although life gradually became better, the overall economic situation in Germany remained bleak in the years following the war. Even the rationing begun during the war continued for a year or two under Allied occupation. This limited the quantities that we could purchase of various products in short supply, such as food and clothing, as well as access to housing and transportation.

Following our wedding, Anneliese moved into my room in Aunt Frieda's apartment. Fortunately, the Winterhude suburb of Hamburg where Aunt Frieda lived and ran her delicatessen was one of the few parts of the city that had not been completely bombed out.

Even renting a room from her, our financial circumstances were exceptionally tight. After our marriage, Anneliese stopped working in her father's nursery. Even though we could have benefited from the extra income, married women rarely worked outside the home at that time. In any case, there were few jobs available.

As her husband, it was now my responsibility to provide for Anneliese. Despite our constant efforts to economize, my small income severely limited the amount of food we could afford. While our diet was supplemented by produce from Mr. Berndt's nursery, our persistent hunger made me resort to other options.

One weekend, I took a train from Hamburg 100 miles south to the small town of Gifhorn, located near the farm of a distant relation. Reaching his home, I pleaded for my relative to sell me a few potatoes. Though grudgingly agreeing to my request, he made it clear that he did not welcome my visit. Like many farmers, he lacked much sympathy for those who came out from the cities looking for food.

That night, I arrived home to my wife and Aunt Frieda with a sack full of potatoes, exhausted and humiliated. This terrible situation was far worse than anything that my family endured during the Great Depression. After an additional journey to Gifhorn, it was clear by the fall of 1946 that we needed to find another way to meet our need for food.

Though my sister Marlene had risked several trips across the Iron Curtain to bring us food parcels from Püggen, it had been over two years since I had last visited with my family there. Naturally, I was anxious to see them, but crossing the border into the Russian-occupied zone was a perilous venture that until now Anneliese and I had avoided. Our hunger now left us no choice.

In spite of the danger that lay ahead, Anneliese fell asleep on my shoulder as our train rolled down the track on the 75-mile trip from Hamburg to the crossing point at Bergen an der Dumme. After it pulled into the station late that September afternoon, we made a short walk down the *Bahnhofstrasse* to the border, where we waited.

Nightengales were singing around us as Anneliese and I joined a number of other people crossing at dusk. Though barbed wire and mines had not yet been placed along the frontier, the Red Army heavily patrolled a two- to three-mile-wide security sector in which only local residents were permitted. About halfway across this frontier zone, a voice cried out, *"Stoi!"* (Stop!) in Russian, immediately sending a cold chill through me.

The two Soviet soldiers who approached us couldn't speak German, but one of them gestured to Anneliese that she could proceed into the Russian zone, while motioning me with his hand to come with them. Since the troops were armed with submachine guns, it was pointless for me to resist or attempt to run. Trying to maintain my calm, I told Anneliese to leave me before they changed their minds.

After a moment's hesitation, she headed into the forest, casting a frightened look back toward me with tears in her eyes. One of the border guards then shoved me with his submachine gun and we marched off. Just after dark, we came to a large stone farmhouse about a mile or so from where I had been captured. After I had been deposited in the living room, the farmhouse grew quiet.

As a former Wehrmacht officer, it was certain that I would be sent back to the Soviet Union as a POW if they checked the name on my documents against their records from the war. Earlier that year, the Russians had placed one of my distant cousins under arrest. A medical student at a German university in the Soviet zone, he had been sent to Siberia for two years with no explanation. If they treated him this way, I could only imagine how they might treat a former German officer.

After three or four minutes passed silently, I tested the door and discovered it had been left unlocked. Swinging it outward, I then circled behind it to hide. When no one came to check on me in the moment that followed, I decided to gamble on a dash into the night. Hearing my escape, angry shouts erupted from my Russian captors.

As I bolted into the pitch-black woods, the troops began blindly spraying bullets from their submachine guns, lashing the brush and pine trees around me. Long accustomed to the sound of gunfire, I never considered halting. Instinctively moving into a crouched posture to minimize myself as a target, I continued to sprint ahead, seeking to put as much distance as possible as between me and the farmhouse.

Afraid that Soviet patrols in the area had been alerted, I raced breathlessly through the woods in the direction of the village of Hohendolsleben, about three or four miles away, hoping that Anneliese had headed to my aunt's home there. Exhausted, it was a huge relief when my wife met me at the door. We clung to each other for a long time, aware that I had one again dodged a terrible fate.

Despite my escape, there remained a real threat that German Communists in the village would discover me and inform the Russians of my presence. This danger was magnified by the fact that the family was under political suspicion due to my uncle's involvement in the Nazi Party, even though he himself was already confined in a British camp.

Early the next morning, the local Communist officials made an unexpected visit to the house on a random inspection for contraband items. Racing upstairs to the attic, I concealed myself under a large pile of old clothes, while Anneliese remained downstairs with my aunt. As the search and questioning persisted, my anxiety mounted that they might come up to the attic. Even when the officials finally departed a half hour later, I knew that it was still not safe and that I was placing my aunt at grave risk.

The next day, Anneliese and I cautiously traveled the 15 or so miles from Hohendolsleben to the relative safety of my family's home in Püggen, where we could more easily stay hidden from local informers. A couple of days later, we warily recrossed the border with two backpacks crammed with all kinds of food, fortunately encountering no further incidents. Given the risk of capture and imprisonment, I would only make one further journey to our farm.

Even with the underlying concern that our presence would draw the attention of the Communist authorities, Anneliese and I fell into the routines of farm life with surprising ease during our second visit to Püggen late in the fall of 1946. After spending most of the day with my father and sisters passing the harvested bundles of grain through a leased threshing machine, my father suggested that we quit and finish up the following day. Since it was still just late afternoon and only about an hour of threshing remained, I convinced him that we should go ahead and complete the job.

Soon afterward, the tractor engine driving the threshing machine began to shoot out sparks that ignited the highly combustible straw nearby. In spite of our vigorous efforts to quench the fire, the whole barn was soon engulfed by flames. Though we succeeded in preventing the blaze from spreading to the other buildings, it nonetheless proved to be the worst disaster that we ever experienced on our farm. Because I had urged my father to finish the job, I naturally felt responsible, but there was nothing I could do.

In the spring of 1947, after convincing me that she would be safe traveling alone, Anneliese made the border crossing to Püggen to retrieve another backpack of food for us. Her willingness to face the hazards involved reflected both daring as well as a little naiveté. While her first solo journey across proved uneventful, her second trip soon afterward ran into trouble.

Following her return, Anneliese recounted to me how she had almost stumbled into a Red Army patrol the previous night near the border. Fortunately, the troops did not see her and she was able to hide in a nearby farmer's barn. In the morning, the farmer had come out to feed his cows and discovered her. Despite the risk to himself, he allowed her to leave without revealing her presence to the Communist authorities.

After hearing the story of her close call, I refused to allow her to attempt any further expeditions across the Iron Curtain. When I consider the danger now, it is difficult for me to understand how I could have consented to place my wife in such jeopardy even once. Indeed, my willingness to countenance the risk to her safety is the best illustration of the desperation we felt during those years.

In April 1947, I finally entered the electrical engineering program at the Federal Engineering College in Hamburg. Although I had been permitted to work and receive wages as a journeyman electrician for several months before entering school, I only officially passed the qualifying exam to become a journeyman in July. While a journeyman's income was more than adequate to support my family, I realized even before beginning my college studies that I could not work even part-time as an electrician if I planned to be a full-time student.

After attending the first semester of college in Hamburg, I spent the remaining four semesters at a different college in Wolfenbüttel, just outside the city of Braunschweig. With me now unemployed and Anneliese unable to find work, I was forced to request a loan of 1,000 Marks from my Uncle Stork, who owned an Opel auto dealership in Lüneburg. Even with these funds, our overall living conditions in Wolfenbüttel were slightly worse than they had been back in

Hamburg, where we had at least received occasional produce from Herr Berndt's nursery.

Though we greatly appreciated Marlene's delivery of a couple of packages of food from Püggen, her efforts did not fundamentally improve the food situation for Anneliese and me. Sometimes, I was driven to take desperate measures. On two occasions I pawned our wedding rings that the jeweler had crafted while I was in Dresden. On another occasion when there was no money, I snuck into a farm field about a quarter of a mile from our apartment to pick beans. It was stealing, but I was determined to do what was necessary to feed us.

While my family in Püggen still had enough to eat, they faced increasing tribulations as the Communist government intensified its control over farms. To prevent the consumption of animals without official permission, officials began visiting farms regularly to conduct counts of the livestock. During one of these inspections, my sister Christa snuck two small lambs into her bedroom, only barely managing to muffle the noise of their bleating.

My family also experienced more targeted harassment from the Communist government. Though the official pressure (or intimidation) partly resulted from our family's failure to fulfill the unrealistically high quota of crop production a couple of times, it also stemmed from my father's willingness to speak publicly against the Communist Party in Püggen.

In the postwar years, my father regularly made annual visits to see my uncle and other family in Hagen. While he was away on one of these visits in late 1948, our local Lutheran Church pastor, Herr Schmerschneider, visited my mother and warned her that my father would likely be arrested upon his return from the west. When my father learned of this threat, he made the difficult decision to remain in Hagen at my uncle's home. The ensuing separation from my mother and sisters would last for years.

Meanwhile, after initially transferring from a POW camp in the United States to one in England, my brother Otto finally returned to Germany in May 1948, three years after the end of the war. On his arrival, he stayed with Anneliese and me for a couple of weeks in Wolfenbüttel, where I attempted to convince him to bring his longtime girlfriend to live in the western zone after their marriage. Instead, he chose to live with her in the eastern zone where she could remain close to her family. He later regretted their decision when they became permanently stuck there. Both episodes with my family members reflected the heartrending personal consequences of Germany's political division.

During my last year of college in Wolfenbüttel, Anneliese became pregnant. When we were out for a stroll one evening during her eighth month, she accidentally tripped and fell to the ground, landing on her belly. Afraid to let her walk home, I found a small child's wagon and carted her back to our apartment. Anneliese's fall left her with a large bruise on her stomach, but fortunately did not lead to any medical complications. In June 1949, she gave birth to a healthy baby boy, Harald.

The hardships that Anneliese and I shared together only seemed to reinforce the bond between us. Despite the challenges in our marriage, the late 1940s was a surprisingly contented time for us, simply because we were at last together after the many painful years of separation and uncertainty during the war.

CHAPTER 19

A NEW LIFE ABROAD

LEAVING OUR HOMELAND

After I graduated with my long-sought electrical engineering degree (*Diplom Ingeneiur-Fach*) in August 1949, I immediately accepted a position with H.F.C. Müller in Hamburg, a subsidiary of Phillips Electronics. My new job involved selling and servicing X-Ray machines and other medical equipment.

Based in Wolfenbüttel, I constantly traveled by train around a region stretching from the Harz Mountains to the North Sea, calling on dentists, doctors and hospitals. When one of the doctors asked to test our equipment by X-raying my hand, his examination revealed a metal splinter from a Russian shell lodged in one of my fingers. After removing the splinter, he bought our machine.

Though well-paid employment was very hard to come by in post-war Germany, I did not feel fulfilled by my work. It was not just a lack of any natural talent in sales; I simply drew no satisfaction from the job. My hope of finding a different position that involved active, hands-on work that utilized my engineering background was discouraged by the very limited opportunities available at that time. The subtle role that social status played in influencing hiring decisions also aggravated me. I wanted to be judged on my ability, not on whether I came from an aristocratic background.

Even more ominously, the Cold War had intensified in 1948 during a confrontation between the Western Allies and the Soviet Union over access to the western sector of Berlin. While the Western Allies responded to the Russian blockade with an airlift rather than with force, Cold War tensions and the threat of potential military hostilities in Europe persisted into the early 1950s. Listening to the news, the outbreak of war seemed more likely to me than a continuance of the fragile peace.

If a new conflict started, there was little doubt that the government would immediately call me back into service because of my military experience. Communist Russia was still a threat to Germany, but I felt that six years of soldiering, mostly in combat, had fulfilled any duty that I owed to my country. My first responsibility was now to take care of my wife and child.

In the early summer of 1951, the international situation and postwar economic problems seemed to offer little promise of a secure and prosperous future in Germany. I increasingly began to think that I could best protect and provide for my family elsewhere. After anguishing over Germany's condition and our family's financial circumstances, Anneliese and I finally reached the very difficult decision to emigrate from our homeland. Our plan was to live and work in another country for a decade or so, until our family's financial condition had improved, the German economy had fully recovered, and the threat of war had diminished.

Our first choice was to go to Argentina, where many other Germans had emigrated, but I was not able to speak Spanish. Although speaking French better than English at that time, I thought we would have the greatest opportunity to build the life that we wanted in the United States. Commonly viewed as a land of opportunity for immigrants, America was the natural choice. Disappointed to learn that the quota for German immigrants to the United States was already filled, Anneliese and I settled on going to Canada.

After deciding to emigrate to Canada, I continued to work out of Wolfenbüttel for Müller until I received my Canadian visa three months later. In August 1951 we sold our few pieces of furniture, raising just enough cash for me to purchase three ship tickets to Canada. Anneliese and Harald would temporarily remain behind with Anneliese's father in Hamburg, while I sought employment and a place for us to live.

My education and determination to carve out a better life for my family provided me with skills and motivation. Yet making a fresh start overseas would be a struggle given my lack of money, connections, and limited command of the language. A deep sense of uncertainty pervaded my thoughts as I prepared to set out alone.

The temporary separation from my wife and son in Germany would be difficult enough. Even more painful was the knowledge that we would be leaving behind our families and native land. Though it was not something that factored into our thinking at the time, I recognize now that our plan must have come as a great shock to my close-knit family, particularly my mother. Since almost my entire family resided behind the Iron Curtain, I could not even say goodbye to them in person. They only learned about our decision to leave Germany in a letter.

At the Hamburg train station, I bade farewell to my father-in-law, Anneliese, and my son. Everyone was crying as I boarded the railroad car to start my journey for the trip across France to the port of Calais. When the train reached Lüneburg half an hour later on its first stop, I met my father on the platform and embraced him in another difficult goodbye.

Heavy-hearted, I departed my loved ones, not knowing where I would build a new life for my family or when we would see each other again. Perhaps only six years of war could have hardened me to leave them and my homeland for an unknown future.

CANADA: August 1951–July 1956

During the train trip to the coast of France, I received my first impression of what to expect on the other side of the Atlantic. Conversing in English with an American couple sitting next to me, the question of what I would do if I developed a hole in my socks somehow came up. In response, I told them that I would probably have to mend it myself since I was alone.

Somewhat dismayed by my comment, the American woman informed me that they did not do that in the United States. If a pair of socks developed a hole, Americans would simply throw them away and buy a new pair. I thought that Americans must be rich to live so extravagantly.

Departing from Calais in mid-August, I soon discovered that an empty 1,500-ton freighter bobs like a cork on the ocean. Half seasick, my only hope was for a rapid crossing. However, a hurricane in the middle of the Atlantic forced our captain to sail back toward France until the storm passed. Ultimately, a voyage that should have taken eight days lasted two weeks.

Finally reaching the town of Mont-Joli at the mouth of the St. Lawrence River on Quebec's Gaspé Peninsula on August 27, I disembarked from the ship with two suitcases, a radio, and about ten dollars in my pocket. In order to earn an extra five dollars, I spent a day working on the dock loading pulpwood aboard the freighter for its return trip. Already missing Anneliese and Harald terribly, I would have embarked on the return voyage if it had been possible.

Using a train ticket provided by the Canadian government, I set out on the 350-mile trip down to Montreal. As an electrical engineer, the first thing that drew my attention was that the power and phone lines were strung between poles above ground, instead of being buried as in Europe. There would be many more such differences that I would encounter in the coming months.

After completing my processing as a Canadian immigrant in Montreal, I stored my suitcases in a locker and immediately began to hunt for a job in one of the local factories. With my limited funds I could not even afford to take buses or streetcars and was forced to walk for miles.

At the end of my first day, I was exhausted and my feet ached. Even my mind was fatigued from my immersion in a mixture of French and English. Despite my greater fluency in French, the heavily accented Québecois French made it almost as difficult for me to comprehend as English.

Returning to my room at the hostel that first night, I met the Swedish man with whom I would share a bed and instantly fell asleep. In the middle of the night, I came awake to a hand groping me from across the bed. In a shocked stupor, I stumbled to my feet. Already under strain, I was confronted with a bizarre situation that I had never before faced. In my groggy anger I wanted to punch the guy out, but that meant risking trouble with the police.

Uncertain what to do, I knew that I could not remain in the room.

Quickly packing my suitcases, I headed out into the street about three o'clock in the morning. Craving rest, it was the last place I wanted to be. Locating another place to stay after a long hunt through the neighborhood, I fell back asleep asking myself whether I had made an awful mistake in leaving Germany.

Despite my doubts, I renewed my search for work the following morning. While Canadian businesses acknowledged my years of practical experience working as an electrician, they did not recognize any German engineering degree. At the end of the week, I was unable to afford to search further and accepted a more menial job as an electrician at Sorel Industries, Ltd. Located in the Montreal suburb of Longueuil, it is one of the largest heavy equipment manufacturers in eastern Canada.

During the day I would disassemble, clean, and reassemble electrical motors. In the evening, I would return to my new hostel. A couple of weeks after finding a job, I was eating supper in a restaurant near my lodgings. To my amazement, a Canadian soldier sitting beside me picked up where my Swedish roommate had left off. Already very homesick, this episode further magnified my loneliness and unhappiness.

Meanwhile, back in Germany, Anneliese ran short of money but was too proud to ask for financial help. To avoid making such an embarrassing request, she went to a shop where she pawned some of our few remaining valuables. This gave her just enough cash to survive until her departure.

About three weeks after I started work, my prospects greatly improved when Sorel shifted me to much more interesting work as a draftsman. They needed a German-speaking engineer to assist them in exploiting captured schematics of a German design that would be used to build a four-barreled weapons system for the U.S. Navy. Now earning enough money to support myself adequately and rent a one-room apartment in the center of Montreal, I was ready to welcome Anneliese and Harald.

Following three long months of separation, they finally arrived in Canada on the ocean liner *Homeline* in October 1951, bringing an end to my isolation. With our finances rapidly improving, we quickly moved out of our cramped residence in the center of the city into a larger apartment across the St. Lawrence River in Longueuil, closer to my job. On October 9, 1952, our daughter Marion was born. Our family and happiness grew together.

Of course, there were also challenges that we experienced as we made our new lives. As a young German boy who spoke with an accent, Harald probably faced the hardest adjustment. Early on, he got into a couple of fistfights with another kid at school because of his limited English, but it was nothing too serious.

There were also advantages to life in Canada as Anneliese and I discovered when we found that a pound of the animal lard that we liked to use as a spread for bread and for cooking oil was priced at only 15 cents. While we had considered lard to be a luxury item back in Germany, we now enjoyed slathering it on everything we ate, at least until we learned how unhealthy it was.

In May 1953, Anneliese and I decided to leave Montreal in pursuit of better career opportunities in the city of Hamilton, Ontario, located 375 miles to the southwest. Almost immediately after our arrival, I obtained a job with a construction company.

The next day, however, I accepted an even better offer from The Steel Company of Canada, which operated the largest steel plant in the country. After working there as a draftsman for a couple of months, the company transferred me to the engineering department and placed me in charge of maintaining an electric arc furnace.

An arc furnace is a brick-lined container with a moveable roof. After loading scrap iron into the container and closing the roof, the operator extends three moving electrodes down through the roof of the container to create an electric arc that melts the scrap iron. Electric furnaces had previously been used to melt scrap steel into iron, but we utilized a recently developed technology that gave an arc furnace the capacity to produce high-quality steel from scrap steel.

While never explicitly requesting a raise, I regularly asked my employers for more responsibilities. As I proved myself, I continued to earn more responsibilities and a higher income. Meanwhile, the experience that I received working with the first arc electric furnace of its type in North America would prove invaluable to my career.

Anneliese and I were ambitious and our life continued to improve in Hamilton. We moved to progressively larger apartments three times and bought our first car. During this time, my English language ability also improved through daily practice.

In November 1954, Anneliese opened her own shop, "Kenilworth Florist," in the center of the city. She had my support to pursue this long-time dream of hers, though it meant further changes in our lives. Harold (formerly Harald) had already begun grade school, but we had to place Marion at a daycare center run by nuns while Anneliese was at work. On my lunch hour and in my spare time, meanwhile, I played delivery boy for the florist shop. Unfortunately, her business made little profit despite her hard work.

On Christmas Eve 1954, Anneliese was stuck in the shop preparing flower arrangements while I delivered them around town, preventing us from being with our children as usual. Listening to Christmas carols on my car's radio with the snow falling outside, tears ran down my cheeks as I despaired at the thought of Harold and Marion alone when I had enjoyed such wonderful Christmases as a child. It made me cherish that Christmas Eve even more when we finally were able to celebrate later that night.

In the end, Anneliese decided to close her shop before the following Christmas after giving the business venture her best effort.

ESCAPING EAST GERMANY

In the early 1950s my brother Hans was still living on the farm in Püggen with my mother, my sisters, and Aunt Hedwig, while Otto had married and was living and working on the farm belonging to his wife's family in nearby Hohengrieben.

The East German government had not yet attempted to seize our family's farm in Püggen outright, but continued to require ever-higher production quotas from my remaining family members after my father's decision to remain in the west. Although other farms were also unable to meet their quotas, the Communist authorities persistently prosecuted my family because of its known hostility to the regime.

Shortly before Christmas in 1951, Otto received an order to go down to the office of Püggen's mayor. Growing concerned when he failed to return after an hour and a half, my sister Marlene went down to check on him and learned that they were waiting for the arrival of

Communist authorities from the city of Salzwedel, about 10 miles away. When the officials appeared shortly afterward, they took Otto away in handcuffs.

In Salzwedel, a judge sentenced my brother to 15 months in prison because our family's farm had failed to meet its production quota, apparently unaware that my mother now held the title to the farm and that Otto himself was now living in Hohengrieben. The court also informed Otto that the farm would be confiscated as a result of both the failure to meet the quota as well as my father's illegal departure to the West in 1948.

When people in Püggen learned about Otto's prison sentence, they were so upset that they cornered the local police detachment in a basement in the village until his release was granted. The East German police soon rearrested Otto, but allowed him out of prison again in the middle of February 1952. He returned to Hohengrieben and had little further involvement with affairs on the farm in Püggen.

At this same time, the government went forward with its confiscation of my family's bank account and farm, placing it under the supervision of a government *Treuhändler* (trustee). In addition to claiming furniture from our home, the government also began confiscating horses from the farm to use elsewhere, and starting killing the farm's cattle for meat, even if a cow was pregnant.

Because my sister Christa was working at a photography shop in Salzwedel, my oldest sister Marlene had the primary responsibility of looking out for my mother and my sister Margarete. Now an employee of the state, Marlene earned hourly wages to work on our farm. Because it was now state property, my family was no longer able to take eggs, milk, or anything else from its production. Though she fed and took care of the remaining animals, all other operations on the farm ceased.

In March of 1953, Herr Schmerschneider, the same local Lutheran pastor who had warned that my father would be arrested if he returned to Püggen in 1948, passed along new information. This time, he alerted my mother and sisters that the Communists intended to take Marlene and Christa to a camp on the island of Rügen in the Baltic Sea to perform manual labor as punishment for my father's illegal departure six years earlier.

Under mounting pressure, my mother and sisters finally made the heartrending decision to leave our old family farm forever and escape to West Germany. It was more than leaving a house and property; it meant accepting the surrender of the family's legacy, land on which our ancestors had lived for centuries.

In preparation for their departure, my mother and sisters began collecting our personal items, clothing, bedcovers, and other belongings for shipment to my father in West Germany by mail, posting the parcels from different locations to avoid detection. While they were able to mail some of our valuables, they could not risk sending everything by that route.

Among the items not sent were some very valuable old coins that my parents had dug up from our farm's ornamental garden in the 1920s. Dating from the Thirty Years War of 1618 to 1648, these coins had likely been buried by the earlier residents before they fled into the surrounding woods to escape marauding soldiers.

When I was a student in Wolfenbüttel and my parents had no money, they gave me part of the collection to help me out. Though pawning part of the collection, I returned the remainder to my mother before I left for Canada. As she readied to leave for West Germany, my mother entrusted the entire collection for safekeeping with one of the few neighbors on whom she felt she could rely. Sadly, this neighbor betrayed that trust and sold our family's treasure.

The increasing use of barbed wire fencing, guard dogs, and minefields along the border had made an unauthorized crossing to the West almost impossible, but at this time there was still an escape route through the divided city of Berlin. Because anyone who tried to depart to the West without official permission faced arrest and imprisonment by the East German secret police, my mother and sisters kept their intentions secret from our neighbors and continued to behave normally until the day they departed.

Leaving everything behind except small suitcases, they began to sneak out of Püggen on Friday, April 3, 1953, just two days before Easter. Agreeing to meet in West Berlin, they split up to avoid drawing the attention of one of the many government informers.

While my mother crossed a field out of our village and caught the train in Beetzendorf, Margarete left from the stop nearest our farm in

Siedenlangenbeck, where she joined my mother on board the same train. Meanwhile, Christa remained in Salzwedel after work on Friday and Marlene stayed on the farm to feed the animals.

Telling the *Treuhändler* that she was leaving Püggen to attend a church confirmation of a relative, and would not be back until the beginning of the week, Marlene said goodbye to Aunt Hedwig. On the morning of Easter Sunday, she walked out the entrance of our farm for the last time with our dog barking behind her. After boarding the train at Siedenlangenbeck, Marlene met up with Christa in Salzwedel.

Upon reaching East Berlin, my mother and Margarete and my older sisters separately caught the subway train that still ran between the Communist-controlled eastern zone and the Allied-controlled western zone. Their joyful reunion at Spandau in West Berlin meant that they were safe and free, though they lacked the money to buy a ticket to West Germany.

Finally, about a month later, they purchased plane tickets to Hannover with funds that I sent them from Canada. When they arrived by train in Lüneburg from Hannover that May, my father was waiting on the platform to embrace them all for the first time in four and a half years.

Learning they had fled, the East German government immediately assumed total control of the property in Püggen. Soon afterward, it demolished all the buildings, except for the *Altenteil* where my grandparents had lived.

The fate of our home and farm was tragic, but this loss was far outweighed by the sense of euphoria that my mother and sisters felt as a result of their successful escape from Communist control. Though my family never expected to recover our farm following its seizure by the East German authorities, my three sisters eventually won a court battle to regain title to our property following German reunification in 1990.

My family was thrilled when the border dividing Germany suddenly disappeared during the wave of East European revolutions in 1989, but Otto was the happiest one of all. He and his family finally had a chance to live in a free society and travel for the first time in decades. Tragically for him, some members of our family had already passed away before the wall came down. As for most Germans, my

family found that the nation's defeat and division had lasting consequences that proved much greater than the direct impact of the war
itself.

THE UNITED STATES: July 1956–December 1982

By the mid-1950s, Anneliese and I had decided not to return to
Germany after growing increasingly comfortable with our new lives in
North America, but we still wanted to try to emigrate to the United
States as we had always planned to do.

At the American consulate on the Canadian side of Niagara Falls,
I applied for a visa that would permit me to bring my family to live in
the United States as legal aliens. Because of my background and work
experience, they issued us a visa to emigrate in less than three months.

Shortly after receiving permission in the summer of 1956, I
resigned my job and drove down alone to Cleveland, Ohio. Given my
experience, I had five different job offers from construction companies
and a steel manufacturer within a week.

Many of the positions interested me, but I ultimately accepted a
position as an electrical engineer with a large industrial construction
firm that offered to double my salary. We settled quickly into a quiet
family life, driving around northern Ohio for sightseeing on weekends.
About a year later, on October 22, 1957, our son Norman Ralph was
born. Afterward, Anneliese and I joked that our children could form
their own United Nations, representing Germany, Canada, and the
United States.

In late 1958, I left the job with my first American employer and
went to work for another Cleveland firm. At the age of 38, I became
the chief electrical engineer at Jones and Laughlin Steel Company.
Working with two 200-ton capacity electric arc furnaces, I now began
to develop an international reputation for my innovative expertise in
maximizing the efficiency of these furnaces in terms of the amount of
time and energy used relative to the quantity of steel produced. Today,
the industry uses this type of furnace to produce roughly 50 percent of
the steel made in the United States, but it was a cutting edge technology in the late 1950s.

During the ensuing decade, we took the children to visit our family in Germany about once a year. My parents doted on their grand-children, though my conservatively dressed mother sometimes thought that Marion wore outfits that were "too colorful." While sometimes missing our families and Germany, we never regretted our decision to build new lives in America.

As immigrants, Anneliese and I constantly sought to blend our German heritage with the American lifestyle. While we spoke German together, we usually tried to speak English with our children. Instilling German values like hard work and punctuality were particularly important to us and probably led Anneliese and I to be more strict than most American parents. To teach responsibility, we assigned all the children regular chores in the house and in the yard. The children knew that when I told them to be home by five o'clock, it meant five o'clock. They also learned to value our time together as a family.

Growing up in Püggen, Sundays had always been a day for fami-ly. Anneliese and I tried to make this a family time in Cleveland too. Following church in the morning, she and I took turns preparing something special, typically a traditional German meal. After a nap, we would pack the kids into the car for a Sunday drive into the coun-try or to a local park for a hike and rock-climbing. Some Sundays, we would drive up to Lake Erie for picnics.

Returning home, we would have *Abendbrot*, a light meal consist-ing of an open-face sandwich. Like most American families, our Sundays often finished with the family sitting around the television watching shows like Gunsmoke or The FBI. Perhaps our separation from our extended family back in Germany made the bonds among our immediate family tighter.

Twice a year, Cleveland held a festival celebrating German her-itage that offered traditional food, music, and dancing. Anneliese and I always loved dancing together, frequently reminiscing about our first meeting in the dance hall in Lüneburg.

About this time, I entered a local hospital after experiencing severe back problems resulting from the war. As I lay in traction to prevent movement, a man with a broken hip was placed on the room's other bed. Later that night, the other patient asked me for a smoke. When I told him I was unable to move, he tried to get out of bed to retrieve his cigarettes from the drawer in the table next to him. With his broken hip, he collapsed immediately on the floor, unable to move. I pushed the button for a nurse and they lifted him back into bed.

That drama would be repeated three times that night. As a daily smoker of cigarettes, cigars, or a pipe since the invasion of Russia in 1941, this pathetic exhibition seemed like a warning to me. If smoking was so addictive that it could cause that kind of insane behavior, I wanted nothing to do with it. Deciding never to smoke again, I quit for good.

In 1961, at the end of the five-year required waiting period, our family proudly attended a ceremony at which we became citizens of the United States, breaking the last legal connection with our Fatherland. Making up my mind that my family and I would be Americans, I dropped the German part of my identity almost completely. Even the legal spelling of our family's name was changed from Lübbecke to Lubbeck, though this was partly because I was tired of hearing my name mispronounced as "Lubbeckee," instead of the proper "Luebbeckeh."

On January 1, 1964, I went to work for the Union Carbide Corporation after leaving the Jones and Laughlin Steel Company. Rather quickly, I worked my way up to the position of Manager of Arc Furnace Technology in the division which made graphite electrodes for steel-making arc furnaces.

At Union Carbide, I also started to travel all over the country and the world, consulting with large and small steel companies and foundries about setting up new electric arc furnaces and optimizing their manufacturing process. Even though operating or monitoring an electric arc furnace was much safer than many of my earlier jobs, adjusting a furnace could still be dangerous.

As I was operating one of our client's large furnaces, I entered the control cubicle to adjust the manufacturing process. Inside the cramped control space, I had to maneuver my body among the uninsulated copper bars running down along the sides of the cubicle.

When my elbow accidentally touched one of these bars carrying 380 volts, the shock nearly knocked me unconscious leaving me barely able to remain on my feet. Though managing to avoid a fall against the side of the cubicle that could easily have electrocuted me, the experience reminded me that I could never allow myself to become complacent about the hazards of my work.

With a growing reputation as an expert in the field, there were increasing demands on my time. I joined half a dozen professional societies in my field and wrote several articles in industry magazines as well as a book on the arc melting process. Giving about 500 presentations on the technical process of melting steel in electric arc furnaces to groups ranging in size from 15 to 300 people, I learned over the years that it was critical to speak very deliberately when explaining complex aspects of my work.

While my work-related travel schedule disrupted our calm family life to some extent, I still managed to be home almost every weekend. On my trips to Europe, South America, and South Africa, Anneliese occasionally traveled with me for a vacation.

By 1968, Harold, my oldest son, was already in college at Purdue University studying electrical engineering, while Marion was in high school and Ralph was in middle school. At this time, we purchased eight acres of wooded land close to the town of Medina, outside Cleveland. Because our home in Seven Hills sold quickly and it was impossible to rent an apartment for just a few months, Anneliese proposed that we camp on our property during the summer of 1969 while our new home was under construction.

Every morning, I would bathe in an improvised shower, dress for work in our tent, and walk out of the woods to my car parked on the street in front of our property. It was not particularly comfortable, but it was an interesting six-month adventure. Finally, we moved into our new home, scenically set in the middle of the woods. We enjoyed our refuge from the hustle of city life.

Though I regularly attended a Lutheran Church before and after emigrating, as an engineer I had sometimes struggled with the lack of adequate scientific evidence to support what I read in the Bible. Only in the late 1960s did I really reach the point where my faith took, allowing me to embrace the Christian message and find an inner spiritual peace.

In 1974, this faith was tested when we received traumatic news. After Anneliese began experiencing pain, doctors diagnosed her with breast cancer. Over the course of the 14 years that followed, Anneliese endured numerous and frequent surgical operations as well as chemotherapy and radiation treatments. The cancer went into remission, but always returned.

Despite her constant suffering, she remained cheerful and refused to reveal any indication of her pain to others. Her profound faith in God gave her the fortitude and strength to live a full life, in spite of her illness. My faith helped me to support her through the grueling struggle while my love for her only deepened.

RETIREMENT: January 1983–Present

Although Anneliese and I had originally planned to buy our retirement home in the warmer climate of South Carolina, the stunning mountain vistas in North Carolina, plus the ubiquitous insects in South Carolina, convinced us to change our mind. At the end of April 1983, Anneliese and I moved into our new home on the side of Sunset Mountain in Asheville, North Carolina. Because of my accumulated vacation time, I continued to receive my regular salary from Union Carbide until the end of the year.

Immediately following my official retirement on January 1, 1984, I formed the William Lubbeck Company, Inc. acting as a consultant to the steel and foundry industry. Working part-time, I continued to visit some of the customers with whom I had developed a good relationship.

During the preceding years, Harold graduated from Purdue as an electrical engineer and began work with a power company in Akron, Ohio. Marion obtained an art degree from Oxford University in Oxford, Ohio, while Ralph earned an industrial engineering degree at Southern Illinois University.

They all married and had children who became an endless source of joy for Anneliese and me. After long years of battling cancer, Anneliese's health was declining, but she once more collected her strength for a journey back to Medina, Ohio in the late summer of 1988, determined not to miss the baptism of our youngest grandchild.

On December 2, 1988, the love of my life and my wife of 43 years passed away. Though we had known that the day would come, it was still a terrible loss for me and our family. Living with all of those loving memories is sometimes nearly unbearable and I miss her every day.

A wonderful wife and loving mother, I know her soul rests easy in Heaven, free of the physical torment of cancer. When God calls me home, I will be buried next to her in the cemetery in Wendisch-Evern, close to Lüneburg where we first met.

EPILOGUE

WHEN I TELL OTHER AMERICANS that I am from Germany, they often respond that they also have relatives who came from Germany. At least 50 million Americans claim a degree of German ancestry, making Germany, after Britain, perhaps the second largest country of origin for the United States.

At the same time, German-Americans are perhaps less visible than many other ethnic groups in the United States because they tend to integrate into the general population rather than concentrating together like other ethnic communities. While I remain proud of my German heritage and occasionally participate in various cultural activities, my ambition has been to become a full participant in mainstream American life.

Theodore Roosevelt perfectly expressed my own feelings about immigration in a written message he composed for a public gathering on January 3, 1919, three days before he died:

> In the first place, we should insist that if the immigrant who comes here in good faith becomes an American and assimilates himself to us, he shall be treated on an exact equality with everyone else, for it is an outrage to discriminate against any such man because of creed, or birthplace, or origin. But this is predicated upon the man's becoming in very fact an American and nothing but an American... There can be no divided allegiance here. Any man who says he is an American but something else also, isn't an American at all... we have room for but one [sole] loyalty, and that is to the American people.[1]

At the same time, I have not forgotten the values that I learned in my younger years in Germany: discipline, the need for education, and the importance of family. The United States gave me a chance to fulfill my potential and live a life in harmony with those values. Though planning to be buried next to Anneliese in Germany, I have also grown to feel completely American in my national identity.

The United States has been good to me and has allowed me to build a life I could only dream of when I left Germany with ten dollars in my pocket. My son Harold served as an officer in the U.S. Army. Tears come to my eyes when there's a funeral for an American soldier or a band plays the national anthem at the raising of the Stars and Stripes.

Despite the numerous books, movies and television documentaries about the Second World War, I never personally encountered any serious discrimination because of my German background, nor has anyone attempted to link me to the crimes of the Nazi regime. I was not a Nazi soldier; I was a German soldier fulfilling his duties as a citizen and a patriot.

Many histories of the war misrepresent this situation, but I believe a majority of Americans realize the difference. While it is true that Germans put Hitler and the Nazis in power, they did so only because the economic misery caused by the Great Depression made many Germans susceptible to Nazi propaganda. They did not obtain the largest share of the vote because of German support for their racial policies or their aggressive territorial designs.

Some interesting experiences have resulted from my unique background. June 6, 2004 was the sixtieth anniversary of the American D-Day landings in France. To honor a local American veteran and friend who had fought at Normandy, a group of us held a dinner celebration at a local Asheville restaurant. Having participated in a number of these types of activities over my five decades in the United States, it did not seem odd to me to honor someone who had fought against the army in which I served. I respected him as a fellow veteran serving my adopted country.

At the end of the meal, the waitress suddenly appeared at my side with cake and ice cream. Thinking that I was also a U.S. Army veteran, she said in a sincere tone, "Thank you for your service." The whole table erupted in laughter and I joined them.

There was an obvious irony to be accidentally honored as an American veteran. Yet I still feel a deep sense of pride in my own military service, even if it was for my old homeland in Germany rather than for my new home in America. Just as the two nations have made peace, I have made peace between the parts of my past.

Since the end of the war, I have not had contact with anyone in my old 58th Infantry Division, except my last regimental commander, Werner Ebeling, who became a general in the post-war *Bundeswehr* (West German Army). It was a choice of career that was not popular after the war.

In Germany today, few people want to serve in the armed forces, and military conscription is unpopular. In my youth, citizens treated soldiers with respect and you saw many uniformed troops out in public. Contemporary German soldiers lack this same respect and rarely wear their uniforms when they leave the barracks. In my opinion, today's Americans are more patriotic than most Germans, displaying a love and belief in their country resembling that found in Germany during the 1930s and 1940s.

Looking back, I believe the Second World War started with the harsh Treaty of Versailles ending the First World War. Yet I think the Allied powers made a similar mistake after the Second World War by dividing Germany and stripping its centuries-old eastern agricultural provinces of East Prussia, Pomerania, Silesia, and eastern Brandenburg.

While West and East Germany have been reunited, the tragic experience of the people expelled from these former German provinces has been largely overshadowed by Hitler's crimes. Literally millions of people lost their homes and land and became refugees. Compared to the difficulties my family experienced after the war, those Germans suffered a much worse fate. The costs and consequences of the war still reverberate to the present.

The history of the last 60 years has turned out much differently than I expected. West Germany experienced a rapid economic recovery soon after my wife and I emigrated, which I attribute to two factors. First, the German people showed great energy and determination to rebuild in the post-war ruins. Confronted with these conditions, business management and the trade unions worked cooperatively to rebuild industry. Second, the Marshall Plan helped provide the financial resources to reinforce this process. Though I have never regretted my decision to emigrate, I believe in retrospect that I could have succeeded there as well.

It was only with the end of the Second World War and the start of the Cold War that Germans began to think in terms of West and East, but the Western countries and Russia were always viewed very differently inside Germany. Before the war, Germans had felt excluded from the more developed group of Western states on the one hand, and culturally superior to the Soviet Union on the other.

Following the nation's defeat, most West Germans came to feel themselves full members of the Western community. Beyond sharing a common sense of the external threat from the USSR, West Germans also adopted a much more liberal culture, which made it more similar to other Western societies. Integration into the European Union has only reinforced Germany's sense of identity with the West. Perhaps this process of integration rather than isolation partly explains why Germans were more willing to accept the territorial losses inflicted on the nation after the Second World War than they were after the First World War.

With my personal experience of living under the Nazi dictatorship for twelve years and having had family living under the East German Communist dictatorship, I learned that dictatorial regimes can be much the same in practice, whatever their ideological differences. They will do whatever is necessary to maintain their hold on power. In this struggle to retain control over society, the media's influence is very powerful, especially when the government prevents the expression of alternative points of view.

The passage of time has left me with a much more questioning and cynical attitude toward authority. I have learned much about Hitler's regime of which I was unaware during the war. As I read about the concentration camps and other aspects of the Nazi dictatorship, my eyes were opened to the repressive and sinister nature of the regime.

In retrospect, it is clear that the Nazi propaganda against the Jews was highly effective in generating a climate of indifference toward their fate. At the time, I wondered if it was just when Jewish people lost their shops or were banned from a particular area, but I did not seriously concern myself with what was happening to them. Other than the anti-Jewish attacks on *Kristallnacht*, I was personally unaware of any other incidents of violent mistreatment.

Although I knew that the Nazis incarcerated political enemies of their regime, including Jews, I had no idea where they went or what happened to them. Some of these opponents emerged from confinement and I assumed that the others who had been arrested would also eventually be released. Of course, none of these matters was ever publicly discussed under the Nazi dictatorship.

If German citizens had come to widely learn about the mass murder of Jews and other ideologically targeted groups in the camps during the war, I believe it would have provoked a strong anti-Nazi reaction. Mass extermination was legally unconscionable as well as morally revolting to most Germans. It was a criminal atrocity perpetrated by racist fanatics.

When looking back at the suffering of the Soviet civilians during the conflict, I see it as part of the broader tragedy of the war. The starvation of the civilians in Leningrad during the siege was similar to the death of German civilians under Allied bombs. Our struggle was against the Communist regime, not the Russian people, just as the Allied fight was against the Nazis, not the German people. Yet war's victims are often the innocent and I mourn for them all.

Whatever our misgivings about the Nazis and their policies at the time, the soldiers I fought with shared an optimistic vision of Germany's post-war future. Instead, it turned out that we were simply the guinea pigs in Hitler's mad scheme to build an Aryan utopia in Europe.

When Americans look back at the war, it is important they understand why so many Germans were ready to fight and die. As I have tried to convey in this book, we risked our lives out of a sense of patriotic love for and duty to our country in a war that we then believed was unavoidable.

Although it is obvious to me now that the Nazi propagandists greatly manipulated the German public, we sincerely believed that the West was trying to maintain the unjust peace forced on Germany at Versailles, while the Communist government of the Soviet Union posed an imminent and mortal threat to Germany and European civilization. No German soldier I knew was fighting out of a devotion to the Nazi regime or in support of its racist policies, which we did not even begin to fully comprehend at that time.

The Nazi crimes happened long before most of today's Germans were born, but almost all Germans now willingly acknowledge and utterly abhor the evils of that period. It is my hope that my fellow Americans will likewise come to fully appreciate that Germany today is a far different place than the one that existed in 1945.

The war ended more than 60 years ago and I left Germany 55 years ago. Coming to America as immigrants from Germany, my wife and I were able to build a new life and become full citizens in its society. Our children are successful and have given us ten grandchildren and great-grandchilden who are completely American in their identity and outlook.

This is the legacy of a former German soldier who 60 years ago fought for a nation at war with the United States. My immigrant experience is in some ways unique, but it is really part of the collective story of the American people. Perhaps it is also in a small way similar to the experience of the German people, who have made a difficult journey to become full members of the Western community of nations since the end of the Second World War.

This book is left as my testament to my family and to my fellow citizens in hope of presenting a better understanding of the suffering experienced on all sides during war. Life is short, but for many it was far too brief.

May the future be guided by the Almighty to bring hope, love, understanding, and peace to this world.

ACKNOWLEDGMENTS

There are a number of people who assisted us in our endeavor to tell William Lubbeck's story.

We are indebted to Maury Hurt, who initially introduced us and encouraged us to write this work. His constant readiness to support the project in any way possible proved invaluable. We would also like to thank his family, who so graciously played host following our meetings in Asheville.

Back in Germany, Bill's sisters Marlene, Christa, and Margarete played an important role in helping to recollect a number of the events described in the book. In the United States, his children Harold, Marion, and Ralph also offered their encouragement and memories.

There are a number of others who assisted the project in a variety of ways. William and Mary Eleanor Hurt and Amy and Fred Trainer reviewed the text and offered us countless suggestions on wording and content. We also greatly appreciate Scott Jenkinson's timely aid in dealing with a variety of technical problems.

Professor Bill Forstchen at Montreat College provided us with helpful advice on writing and organizing a memoir. We are also grateful for the assistance of Professors Stephen Fritz at East Tennessee State University and Kurt Piehler at the University of Tennessee, who presented a number of useful ideas as we developed the book.

Finally, we would like to thank David Farnsworth and Steve Smith at Casemate Publishers who appreciated the importance of this story and guided it to publication.

William Lubbeck and David Hurt

APPENDICES

APPENDIX A
GERMAN INFANTRY REGIMENT IN WORLD WAR II
(Organization and Equipment)
1940

A) REGIMENTAL UNITS

1) Regimental commander, regimental staff, ordinance officer, communication officer, staff captain. Also staff platoon, including office personal, messengers, and drivers.
2) Regimental supply unit (*Tross*)
> Regimental medical officer (M.D.), two veterinarians, weapon repair platoon, kitchen, food supply units (*Tross*), food supply officer, paymaster, and luggage unit.
3) Communications platoon (*Nachrichten Zug*)
> Communications sergeant, four telegraph units (Range: 9.3 miles), and four telephone units (Range: 2.5 miles).
4) Cavalry platoon (*Reiterzug*)
> Three units, one wagon, one blacksmith, and one kitchen.
5) Engineering unit with six engineering platoons, six light machine guns, and three tool wagons.

B) THREE INFANTRY BATTALIONS

1) Each with battalion commander, adjutant, ordinance officer, battalion medical officer, veterinarian, and battalion staff.

2) First battalion:

Infantry companies 1, 2, and 3, each with twelve light machineguns and three 50-mm mortars; plus one machinegun company (Company 4) with twelve heavy machineguns and six 80-mm mortars, and a supply unit.

3) Second battalion:

Infantry companies 5, 6, and 7, plus one machinegun company (Company 8) (Armament the same as in first battalion).

4) Third battalion:

Infantry companies 9, 10, and 11 plus one machine company (Company 12) (Armament is the same as in first battalion).

C) ONE HEAVY WEAPONS COMPANY (Company 13)

1) One company commander, four weapons platoons, communication platoon, and supply units.

Armament:

Platoons 1, 2, and 3 with two 75-mm light howitzers each
(Range: 5,630 yards or 3.2 miles).
Platoon 4 with two 150-mm heavy howitzers
(Range: 5,140 yards or 2.9 miles).
In 1942, a platoon with three 105-mm mortars was added.

D) ONE ANTITANK COMPANY (Company 14)

1) One company commander and four weapon platoons.

Armament:

Each platoon with three 37-mm anti-tank guns, one light machinegun, and supply units.
In 1941, two 37-mm guns were replaced with two 50-mm guns.

E) Each Company had its own master sergeant, responsible for supply units, weapon repair sergeant, and field kitchen as well as medical person.

Sergeants usually command company platoons.

F) TOTAL REGIMENTAL ARMAMENT:

118   Light machineguns
  36   Heavy machineguns
  27   50-mm mortars
  18   80-mm mortars
   6   75-mm light howitzers (In 1942, three add'l 105-mm mortars)
   2   150-mm heavy howitzers
  12   37-mm anti-tank guns (In 1941, two 50-mm)

APPENDIX B
REFERENCE OF PLACE NAMES

This book uses the names of population centers and geographic locations as they were known at the time. Following is a list of how are known today.

Historic Name – Contemporary Usage

Dudergof – Mozhaiskii
Düna River – Daugava River
Dünaburg – Daugavpils
Elbing – Elblag
Fischhausen – Primorsk
Frisches Haff – Vistula Isthmus
Frische Nehrung – Vistula Isthmus
Gdingen – Gdynia
Gulf of Danzig – Gulf of Gdansk
Heiligenbeil – Mamonovo
Hela – Hel
Heyderkrug – Silute
Königsburg – Kaliningrad
Krasnogvardeisk — Gatcina
Kurisches Haff – Curonian Bay
Kurische Nehrung – Curonian Isthmus
Labiau – Polessk
Lake Peipus – Lake Chudskoye
Leningrad – St. Petersburg
Libau – Liepaja
Memel – Klaipeda
Oranienbaum – Lomonosov
Pillau – Baltiysk
Reval – Tallinn
Stutthof – Sztutowo
Tilsit – Sovetsk
Weichsel River Estuary – Vistula River Estuary

ENDNOTE

The 154th Infantry Regiment, in which I served from 1939 to 1945, suffered total casualties as follows: 300 officers of which 73 were killed; 2,241 non-commissioned officers of which 485 where killed; and 10,810 other enlisted personnel of which 1,824 were killed. Of its total of 13,351 casualties, 2,382 were killed, 10,021 were wounded, and 948 soldiers were listed as missing. Among the divisions in Army Group North, the 58th Infantry Division received the second highest number of decorations.[2]

REFERENCES

1. *Federal Textbook on Citizenship Training* (US Government Printing Office, 1931), Lesson 61.
2. Von Zydowitz, Kurt. *Die Geschichte der 58. Infanterie-Division 1939–1945* (Podzun: Kiel, 1952).